MAJESTY IN MISERY

1: DARK GETHSEMANE

MAJESTY IN MISERY

1: DARK GETHSEMANE

*Select Sermons on the
Passion of Christ from*
C. H. SPURGEON

THE BANNER OF TRUTH TRUST

THE BANNER OF TRUTH TRUST
3 Murrayfield Road, Edinburgh EH12 6EL, UK
P.O. Box 621, Carlisle, PA 17013, USA

*

© The Banner of Truth Trust 2005
ISBN 0 85151 904 0

*

Typeset in 11.5 /13 pt Sabon MT at the
Banner of Truth Trust, Edinburgh
Printed in the USA by
Versa Press, Inc.,
East Peoria, IL.

CONTENTS

G O TO DARK G ETHSEMANE,
Ye that feel the tempter's power;
Your Redeemer's conflict see;
Watch with Him one bitter hour;
Turn not from His griefs away;
Learn of Jesus Christ to pray.
James Montgomery, 1771–1854

The whole story of our Lord's passion is exceedingly rich in meaning. One is tempted to linger over every separate sentence of the narratives given by the evangelists. It were possible to preach several series of sermons upon the whole story, and there is not a single incident, though it may seem to be but accidental, which might not furnish a wealth of holy thought to the careful student.

. . . Oh how few minutes have I in which to speak of such a lesson, the matchless love of Jesus, that for your sakes and mine he would not merely suffer in body, but consented even to bear the horror of being accounted a sinner, and coming under the wrath of God because of our sins: though it cost him suffering unto death and sore amazement, yet sooner than that we shall perish, the Lord smarted as our surety. Can we not cheerfully endure persecution for his sake? Can we not labour earnestly for him? Are we so ungenerous that his cause shall know a lack while we have the means of helping it? Are we so base that his work shall flag while we have strength to carry it on? I charge you by Gethsemane, my brethren, if you have a part and lot in the passion of your Saviour, love him much who loved you so immeasurably, and spend and be spent for him.

C. H. SPURGEON, 1834–92

I

THE CRISIS OF THIS WORLD [1]

Now is the judgment of this world: now shall the
prince of this world be cast out. And I, if I be lifted up
from the earth, will draw all men unto me. This he
said, signifying what death he should die.
JOHN 12:31–33

OUR LORD PASSED through his passion in a kind of rehearsal
before it came. He saw those Greeks, who came to Philip, and
whom Andrew and Philip brought to him, and his heart was
flushed with joy. This was to be the result of his death, that the
Gentiles would be gathered to him. That thought reminded him
of his approaching decease. It was very near; only a few days would
elapse, and then he would die upon the cross. In anticipation of
Calvary, his soul was full of trouble; not that he feared death, but
his death was to be a very peculiar one. He was to die the just for
the unjust; he was to bear our sins in his own body on the tree;
and his pure and holy soul shrank from contact with sin. To stand
in the sinner's place, to bear his Father's wrath, this bewildered
him. He was very faint of heart, and he cried, 'What shall I say?
Father, save me from this hour: but for this cause came I unto this
hour. Father, glorify thy name.' Without any wicked weakness, he
proved how truly human he was; without any sinful repining at
his Father's will, he saw how terrible that will was, and he
shuddered at what it included. This was a kind of rehearsal for
Gethsemane; it was a sipping of that cup whereof he was to drink
until his sweat was, as it were, great drops of blood falling down

[1] Sermon No. 2,338. Preached at the Metropolitan Tabernacle on Sunday evening,
6 October 1889.

to the ground, while his whole soul poured out the agonized petition, 'O my Father, if it be possible, let this cup pass from me: nevertheless not as I will, but as thou wilt.'

When our Lord Jesus was in this great distress of mind, in anticipation of the terrible sufferings he was about to endure, his Father spoke to him; and when you are in your direst distress, God will speak to you. If you are his child, when the weakness of your flesh seems ready to prevail over your spirit, you, too, shall have a reassuring voice out of the excellent glory even as your Master had. He seemed to recover himself at once, and bracing himself up, he indulged his heart again with a vision of the glorious result of his death. Then he uttered the happy words on which we are to meditate tonight, in which he summed up the consequences of his death in these three points: 'Now is the judgment of this world: now shall the prince of this world be cast out. And I, if I be lifted up from the earth, will draw all men unto me.'

Let us, first, *consider the threefold result of Christ's death:* and when we have done that, let us *think about Christ's death as it is described in our text.*

1. THE THREEFOLD RESULT OF CHRIST'S DEATH

There is, first, *the judgment of the world:* 'Now is the judgment of this world.'

If you like, you may read it 'crisis', for that is the Greek word used here: 'Now is the crisis of this world.' The world is sick, it grows worse: and the physician says that its malady has come to a climax, it is a case of kill or cure. There was a crisis in the world's disease, and that crisis was when Christ died; his death was the turning point, the hinge of the world's history. There have been many hinges in history; every nation has a hinge in its history: the cross of Christ was the hinge of the world's history; it had reached the turning point. I thank God that the death of Christ was the future death of sin. When he died, the archenemy received his death-stroke. That death was the bruising of Christ's heel; but in that death he bruised the old serpent's head. Now there is hope for the world; its crisis is passed. Now will the gods of the heathen fall; now will the dark ignorance of men yield to the Light of the world. After this crisis, there shall come a new heaven and a new earth wherein dwelleth righteousness for Christ's first coming is a pledge of his second coming, wherein he will exterminate sin, and make the wilderness and the solitary place to blossom as the rose. Thus we may render our Saviour's words, 'Now is the crisis of this world', the turning point, the hinge, on which all its history hangs. Still, I greatly prefer to keep to our old version, which is a translation, whereas mine is only a borrowing of the original word 'crisis'.

'Now is the judgment of this world.' This means that, when Christ died, the world that lieth in the wicked one, the ungodly world, was judged in this sense; first, it was convicted of being guiltiest of the guilty. I daresay you have heard people rise pretty phrases about the dignity of human nature, and so on. They are lying phrases; for human nature is as bad as it can be. If you want the proof of that assertion, behold how God himself came here among men, incarnate virtue robed in love! Did men love him? Did they fall down before him, and do him homage? The homage of the world was, 'Crucify him! Crucify him!' The world hates virtue; it cannot bear perfection; it might endure benevolence, but absolute purity and righteousness it cannot. Its native instincts are wrong; it is not towards the light that men are going, their backs are to the sun, they are journeying into the thick darkness.

And, next, the world was convicted of the stupendous crime of murdering the Son of God. I will not call it regicide, but deicide; and this is the crime of crimes. Truly was the world guilty of all that prophets ever charged it with, and much more. When wicked men slew the Prince of life, the Holy One and the Just, then was it proven that the world is at heart atheistic, that it hates God, and would put God himself to death if he were within its grasp. Thus did men put the Incarnate God to death when he submitted himself to their power. You need not talk about the virtues of the world; it slew the Christ, and that is enough to condemn it. We want no other proof of its guilt; you cannot bring evidence more complete and overwhelming than this, they slew the Lord of life and glory, they said, 'This is the heir; come, let us kill him, and the inheritance shall be ours.'

Christ's death was the judgment of this world, next, by sentencing the world; for if Christ, who was perfectly innocent, must die when he stood in the sinner's place, what think you, O guilty men, will not you also die? If the Well-beloved of heaven, bearing nothing but imputed guilt, sins not his own, must nevertheless be smitten of God and afflicted, and a voice must be heard, 'Awake, O sword, against my shepherd, and against the man that is my fellow, saith the LORD of hosts,' if he must die on yonder cruel tree, if he must cry, 'My God, my God, why hast thou forsaken me?' then, be sure of this, there is wrath treasured up against the day of wrath, and no soul of man that doeth evil shall go unpunished. Is there not a God who is the Judge of all the earth, and who must do right? If it be right to smite the Innocent, who assumed the place of the guilty, it must surely be right that the truly guilty should die the death. 'The soul that sinneth, it shall die.' So there was not only the conviction, but also the sentence of the world, when Jesus died.

And more than that, there is the final ending of the trial when the world rejects Christ. As long as you are here, my hearers, and Christ is preached to you, there is hope for you; but in that day when you reject Christ finally, and will have none of him, when you cry, 'Away with him, away with him! We will not be washed in his blood, we will not be clothed in his righteousness'; in that day you seal your doom, and there remains no hope for you. There is one window in heaven, and through it streams the light of life; but if that be closed, no other will ever be opened. 'There is none other name under heaven given among men, whereby we must be saved.' If you have for the last time put Christ away, if you have altogether done with him, you have ended your probation, you have finished your trial, you have put out your last candle, you are for ever doomed. When Christ is so rejected as actually to be made away with as he was upon the cross, then is the judgment of this world.

I wish that I had time to pause here to press these points upon you who belong to the world. There are but two parties, the world and the church of God. If you are not of the church of God, you belong to the world; and the world is judged by the death of Christ. If you are not a Christian, you are a member of that great corporation called the world. Men sometimes speak of a Christian world and an un-Christian world, a religious world and an irreligious world, a sporting world, a laughing world, a thieving world, a trading world; but all that is really of the world is outside the bounds of the church of God. He that believeth in Christ has escaped from the world.

'They are not of the world, even as I am not of the world', said Christ concerning his disciples; but to the unbelieving Jews he said, 'Ye are from beneath; I am from above: ye are of this world; I am not of this world.'

Thus, you see that, as the first result of the death of Christ, the world is judged, the world is convicted, the world is sentenced for its rejection of Christ. A Christ-rejecting world is a doomed world; may none of you belong to that world!

The second result of Christ's death is *the casting out of Satan:* 'Now shall the prince of this world be cast out.'

He who holds sway over it shall now lose his throne. The prince of this world is Satan, the archenemy of God and man; but he is not always to reign as the prince of the power of the air, the chief of the rulers of the darkness of this world. He is to be cast out of his present dominions.

By the death of Christ, Satan's accusations against believers are answered. One of the practices in which he most delights is that of accusing the people of God; and, alas! he has plenty of cause for his charges; but whenever he accuses us, our one answer is, 'Jesus died.' He says, 'These people have sinned'; and we reply, 'True; but Jesus died for them'; and the cross of Christ stops the mouth of the accuser. Even a feeble saint, looking up to his crucified and risen Saviour, can boldly sing —

> I may my fierce accuser face,
> And tell him thou hast died.

Next, Christ's cross spoils Satan of his universal monarchy. He could once lord it over the whole world, and he does very much of that even now; but there is a people over whom he cannot sway his evil sceptre, there is a race which has broken loose from him. They are free, and they defy him to enslave them again. They care not for his threats, they are not to be won by his blandishments; and though he worries and tempts them, yet he cannot destroy them. He can boast no longer of universal dominion. There is a seed of the woman that has revolted from him, for Jesus, by his death, hath redeemed them out of the hand of the enemy, and they are free.

I heard a story of an old black woman, who was waiting upon a lady visiting friends in the South, some time after the American Civil War. The lady said to the black servant, 'You may very well wait upon a Northerner with great attention, for it is through us that you are free.' 'Free, missy, free?' exclaimed the black servant woman; 'I's a slave. I was born a slave.' 'Oh, but you are free! Do you not know that there has been an Act passed by which you are all free?' 'Yes, I did hear something about dat; and I said to old massa, "I hear dat we is all free." He says, "Stuff and nonsense", so I's bin stoppin' here workin' for him. Is it true, missy, that we is all free?' 'Oh, yes!' she answered, 'you are all free, every slave is free now.' 'Then,' said the woman, 'I don't bin serve old massa any longer; I bid him "Good-bye."'

And so it is when Christ sets us free; we do not serve the old massa Satan any longer, we bid him 'Goodbye.' When we are set free from the dominion of the devil, by the emancipating redemption of our Lord and Saviour Jesus Christ, Satan's tyrannical power is crippled. He still has great influence, and he does his worst to injure the kingdom of Christ by persecution, by false doctrine, and by a thousand other methods; but Christ has broken his right arm, he cannot work as once he did; and more and more, as the fruit of the Redeemer's passion, will Satan's power be curtailed until, at last, he shall be utterly cast out, and the triumphant shout shall be heard, 'Hallelujah, for the Lord God omnipotent reigneth!' Let us never imagine that the devil is going to conquer in the great battle between right and wrong. God's Word tells us plainly enough what his end is to be: 'And the devil that deceived them was cast into the lake of fire and brimstone, where the beast and the false prophet are, and shall be tormented day and night for ever and ever.'

Now, if any of you suffer through Satan tempting you to despair, if he comes to some of you, and entices you to commit a sin which you hate, and against which you strive with all the might God gives you, if, by a mysterious force that you cannot comprehend, he seems to make you do otherwise than you would, take courage,

6

and stand up against him, for when Jesus died, he said that, by his death, the prince of darkness was cast out, and so he is. Sin shall not have dominion over you, nor shall Satan either. Only be you bold in resisting him, claim your liberty as a child of God, and fight under the command of Christ, for the cross is the conquering banner for all who would overthrow the power of Satan.

> By all hell's host withstood;
> We all hell's host o'erthrow;
> And conquering them, through Jesu's blood
> We still to conquer go.

The third result of Christ's death is *the central attraction of his cross:* 'I, if I be lifted up from the earth, will draw all men unto me.'

Christ on the cross has become the great magnet attracting men to himself. What did he mean by this saying? Did he not mean that his sphere of influence would be widened? 'While I am here,' said he, 'I draw a few men to me; these fishermen have become my disciples, these Greeks have come to see me; but when I am lifted up upon the cross, I shall draw all men unto me, men of all sorts, men out of all nations, multitudes of men, not only of this one age, but of all ages, till the world shall end. I shall become the centre of a wider circle, a circle wide as the world. I shall draw all men unto me.'

But why is it that Christ does draw men to himself? I answer that it is because, by dying on the cross, he gave a new and brighter display of his love. Men came to Christ because of his love while he walked the earth alive; little children especially did so; but after he had died that shameful death, how could they help coming to him? 'Scarcely for a righteous man will one die: yet peradventure for a good man some would even dare to die. But God commendeth his love toward us, in that, while we were yet sinners, Christ died for us.' 'Herein is love.' And to all the ages the masterpiece of love is the dying Christ praying for his enemies, 'Father, forgive them; for they know not what they do.' Christ on the cross draws sinners to himself, Christ crucified attracts through the infinite love to men which is displayed in that death.

A part of the attraction lies in the wonderful blessings which come to us through Christ's death. We were drawn to him because we received pardon through his wounds, we came to him because we found eternal life through his death upon the tree. Jesus bore the sin of his people, he died in our stead; and by so doing he put away all our iniquities, blotted them out, cast them into the depths of the sea. Only as he was lifted up upon the cross could that be said to be the case; but when he was crucified, he finished transgression, made an end of sin, and brought in everlasting righteousness. Beloved, this is a great attraction to perishing sinners; it is a drawing of love to which they must yield. When Jesus thus attracts us, we run to him, because pardon and eternal life are to be found through his uplifting on the cross. I would that some here might be drawn to Christ at this moment by the mighty magnet of his death. Remember how the poet sings of the attraction of the cross —

> So great, so vast a sacrifice
> May well my hope revive:
> If God's own Son thus bleeds and dies,
> The sinner sure may live.
>
> Oh, that these cords of love divine
> Might draw me, Lord, to thee!
> Thou hast my heart, it shall be thine,
> Thine it shall ever be!

The death of Christ attracted to him multitudes of the sons of men because it expanded the hearts of his people. While he was alive and with them, they never burned with such enthusiasm as after he had died. One of the first effects of his death was the outpouring of the Spirit of God upon them, infusing them with new life, a holy fervour, and a sacred enthusiasm, which made them go unto the utmost ends of the earth, publishing among the Gentiles full redemption through his precious blood. Christ, when he was lifted up, made his followers disseminate themselves throughout all populations of the globe till their line went forth to the ends of the earth; and, like the sun o'er every clime, so did the gospel of Jesus Christ enlighten every nation under heaven. 'I, if I be lifted up from the earth, will draw all men unto me.' Christ is the centre of mankind. He is the Shiloh, and unto him shall the gathering of the people be. They shall come away from the abominations of Rome; they shall come away from the crescent of the false prophet; they shall come away from the idols of the dark places of the earth; they shall come away from infidelity and philosophy; and shall come crowding to his dear feet as they feel the marvellous magnetism of his atoning death.

These three things, then, resulted from the death of Christ, the wicked world was judged, the power of Satan was broken, and Christ was made the central attraction of sinners to himself; and that attracting power is working now. Oh, that these three wonders might be wrought in our midst tonight, according to our measure!

2. THE DEATH OF CHRIST AS DESCRIBED IN OUR TEXT

How much the Holy Spirit desires that we should read the Scriptures intelligently! He had recorded these words of the Lord Jesus, 'I, if I be lifted up from the earth, will draw all men unto me.' If that had been all, we might have asked – Does that lifting up from the earth mean Christ's death? Does it mean his ascension, his going up from the earth till the cloud received him? Or does it mean our preaching of Christ, when we lift him up before men, as Moses lifted up the serpent in the wilderness? So, to avoid all question, the Holy Spirit added the thirty-third verse, 'This he said, *signifying what death he should die.*' If there is anything that the Spirit wishes us to be specially clear about, it is all expressions that have to do with our Lord's death. Let us thank him for that comment inserted here, lest we should make any mistake upon so vital a subject.

Now looking at the words, I want you to notice that *Christ went to his death with a clear view of what it was to be.* There is many a man who has rushed into the battle, and died without any idea of what a gunshot wound would be, or what the piercing of a lance would be; but our Lord, as it were, took stock of his death, and looked it calmly in the face. He does not speak of it as barely death, but he describes the manner of it: 'I, if I be lifted up from the earth.' In his own mind, he had gone through the nailing to the wood, and he had come to the uplifting of that wood into the air, and the fixing of its socket in the ground, and in spirit he felt himself already hanging there, lifted up from the earth. Just think of this wondrous fact, as Isaac Watts puts it —

> This was compassion like a God,
>   That when the Saviour knew
> The price of pardon was his blood,
>   He pity ne'er withdrew.

Knowing that his death was to be by crucifixion, he did not turn from it; he set his face like a flint to endure all that 'the cross' meant. He fully knew what it meant; but you and I do not. There are depths in his sufferings that must be unknown to us, but he knew them all; yet, with love that was strong as death, he went through it all for your redemption, O believer! Then, love him in return, with a resolute, determined consecration of thy whole being, yield thyself up to him, not spasmodically, but of love aforethought, to be wholly his. Somebody said to me, the other day, that all religion nowadays either suffered from paralysis or convulsions. I do not want you to have either of those complaints, though I like the convulsions better than the paralysis. Let us not have convulsed religion, but let us have strongly fixed principles, knowing what we have to do, and why we do it, and then, like the Saviour, let us go forward, expecting difficulty, expecting loss, expecting ridicule, but willingly and wilfully facing it all for his dear sake, as he, on his part, endured even the cross for our sake.

Notice, next, that though our Saviour knew the bitterness of his death, *he read its issues in another light.* 'I, if I be lifted up' – do you catch the thought? He does not merely mean lifted up on the cross, he means another kind of uplifting, he means being exalted. When he was lifted up upon the cross, men thought it degradation; but he looked into his death as one looks into an opal, till he sees wondrous rainbows and flames of fire in the precious stone. So Jesus looked into his passion till he saw his glory. Down in the crimson depths of that blood-cup, he saw that he was really being lifted up when men thought that he was being cast down. That crown of thorns was a more wondrous diadem than monarch ever wore. His cross was his throne. With his outspread hands, he ruled the nations; and with his feet fixed there, he trampled on the enemies of men. O glorious Christ, when I have had a vision of thy cross, I have seen it at first like a common gibbet, and thou wast hanging on it like a felon; but, as I have looked, I have seen it begin to rise, and tower aloft till it has reached the highest heaven, and by its mighty power lifted up myriads to the throne of God. I have seen its arms extend and expand until they have embraced all the earth. I have seen the foot of it go down deep as our helpless miseries are; and what a vision I have had of thy magnificence, O thou crucified One! As Jesus looked forward to his death, he saw more than we can even now see in it, and he perceived that it was his glory to be lifted up on the cross of Calvary.

Further, *he beheld in it the supply of our great need*. 'I, if I be lifted up from the earth, will draw'. He saw that we were far away, and could not of ourselves come nigh; so he said, 'If I am lifted up, I will draw them.' He saw that we would not wish to come, that we should be so hard-hearted and stiff-necked that we would not come if we were called. 'But,' said he, 'I from the cross will draw them. As a magnet draws the steel, I will attract them.' Oh, think of the cross of Christ in that light! Some have thought that, if we preach the gospel, we shall always have a congregation. I am not sure of that; but if the gospel does not attract a congregation, I do not know what will. But Christ does not say, 'I, if I be lifted up, will draw all men to little Bethel, or to Salem.' He says, 'I will draw all men unto me', that is, to himself; and we only come to Christ because Christ comes to us. No man ever comes to Christ unless Christ draws him, and the only magnet that Christ ever uses is himself. I do believe that we slander Christ when we think that we are to draw the people by something else but the preaching of Christ crucified. We know that the greatest crowd in London has been held together these thirty years by nothing but the preaching of Christ crucified. Where is our music? Where is our oratory? Where is anything of attractive architecture, or beauty of ritual? 'A bare service', they call it. Yes, but Christ makes up for all deficiencies. Preach Christ, and men will be drawn to him, for so the text says, 'I, if I be lifted up from the earth, will draw all men unto me.' They are held back by Satan; but the cross will draw them. They are held back by despair; but the cross will attract them. They are held back by want of desire; but the cross will breed desire. They are held back by love of sin; but the cross will make them hate the sin that crucified the Saviour. 'I will draw them. All sorts of men I will draw unto myself', says the crucified Christ. Thus he supplies our great need.

Observe, too, that *Jesus knew that he would live to exercise that attraction.* He says, 'I, if I be lifted up from the earth' – what then? 'Shall I be dead? No; I will draw all men unto me.' He lives. Going to death, he expects to live, he glories in his life, he tells of what he means to do after he is risen from the dead. O glorious Christ, to look beyond thy death, and find comfort in thy risen life! Cannot you, my brothers, my sisters, sometimes look beyond the grave, and find comfort in what you will do in heaven? Oh, will we not in heaven glorify our Lord? In the anticipation of what we will then do in honour of our precious Saviour, let us now take up arms against our present trouble, borrowing our weapons from the armoury of the future after our earthly life is over.

Jesus saw, too (and here I must finish), that *the day would come when he would be surrounded by a mighty company.* Can you not see him? He is lifted up upon the cross, and he begins to draw; and men come to him, a few at Jerusalem – nay, did I say 'a few'? Three thousand in one day! The Crucified has pierced their hearts, the Crucified has begotten faith in them, the Crucified has drawn thousands to himself. He is preached in Damascus, he is preached at Antioch, he is preached at Corinth, he is preached at Rome, and everywhere he draws sinners to himself, and great companies come to him. By-and-by, he is preached in far-off Britain; some pioneer evangelist finds a place in these islands where he can preach to the uncivilized the gospel of Christ, and Jesus draws them to himself. He draws men till, all over Rome's vast empire, Christ crucified is drawing them, from Caesar's palace and from Caesar's prison; from the slave at the mill to the senator who rules the city, Christ is drawing them. The kings who wear their crowns by permission of the Roman power, some of them bow before King Jesus; he is drawing them. The people on the isles of the sea, and on every coast, he is drawing them. And today he is still drawing them. From the sunny islands of the southern sea, from the far north of Greenland, from Africa, from China, from everywhere, he draws them more and more; and here, in this our favoured island, he has drawn myriads to himself; but the day shall come when that drawing power will begin to operate yet more freely. They shall run to him; they shall fly to him with swift wings, as doves fly to their cots; they shall come to him as on a sudden, till the church shall cry in astonishment, 'Who hath begotten me these? These, where had they been?' As the drops of the morning dew are seen, glittering like diamonds on every hedge, and on every blade of grass, when once the sun is up, so shall Christ's converts be, like Abraham's promised seed, 'so many as the stars of the sky in multitude, and as the sand which is by the sea shore innumerable.' Christ's people shall be willing in the day of his power; and the great attraction by which they will be drawn to him will be his death on the cross. Oh, that he would draw many to himself tonight! Let this be our prayer to him —

> Dear Saviour, draw reluctant hearts,
> To thee let sinners fly,
> And take the bliss thy love imparts,
> And drink, and never die.

> Amen.

2

LOVE STRONGER THAN DEATH[1]

'When Jesus knew that his hour was come that
he should depart out of this world unto the Father,
having loved his own which were in the world,
he loved them unto the end.'
JOHN 13:1.

THIS IS A KIND OF PREFACE to the story of the foot-washing, and a very wonderful preface it is, when coupled with the third and fourth verses, upon which I commented. 'Jesus knowing that the Father had given all things into his hands, and that he was come from God, and went to God; he riseth from supper, and laid aside his garments; and took a towel, and girded himself.' This is the frame of the picture that is here presented to us. To what shall I compare it? It is like unto a gate of the golden city; each gate is one several pearl, and surely this verse is a jewel of inestimable price. The foot-washing picture is set within this precious frame.

This memorable and symbolical act took place at the end of our Lord's sojourn here below. The passion was the end of his life, and we may consider that the passion was about to begin. That same night he would go to Gethsemane, and in less than twenty-four hours, the dear hands that washed the disciples' feet would be nailed to the accursed wood, and he who spoke so tenderly to his little band of followers would be in his death agonies.

It is an important thing to know how a man feels when he comes to the real crisis of his life. He has cultivated a great variety of

[1] Sermon No. 2,377. Preached at the Metropolitan Tabernacle on Thursday evening, 5 July 1888.

feelings during his career; but what has been his ruling passion? You will see it now. It has passed into a proverb that, 'The ruling passion is strong in death'; and there is great truth in the saying. In the light of the man's departure, we shall see what power really ruled him. It was precisely so with our divine Master. He had almost reached the end of his earthly life; he had come to a season of awful agony; he was about to endure the great and terrible death of the cross, by which he was to purchase eternal redemption for all his people. What will be uppermost in his mind now? What will he think of his disciples now that he has so many other things to think of, now that the thought of his approaching death comes over him, now that the agony and bloody sweat of Gethsemane are so near? What will Jesus think of his disciples at such a time as this, and under such circumstances as these? Our text is the answer to that question: 'When Jesus knew that his hour was come, that he should depart out of this world unto the Father, having loved his own which were in the world, he loved them unto the end.' His love was burning as brightly at the Paschal supper as ever it burned before. Ay, and it seemed as if, in that wondrous prayer that is recorded in the seventeenth chapter of John, and in the wonderful discourse which accompanied it, the love of Jesus had never flamed out so clearly before! Then were the great beacon fires lit, and the fierce winds that blew around the Saviour fanned them to their full force of flame. Now can you say of Jesus, 'Behold how he loved his disciples!' for even at the end of his life he still loved those whom he had loved aforetime.

With that thought in your minds, will you follow me while I take the text to pieces, and dwell upon almost every word of it?

I. First, then, concerning our blessed Master, let us consider WITH WHOM HE ASSOCIATED, and of whom this verse now speaks. They are called, 'his own'. It is a brief description, but it is wonderfully full: 'Having loved his own which were in the world, he loved them unto the end.'

'His own'. There was a circle – sometimes a wide circle – round the Saviour, made up of publicans and sinners, and he had a measure of love to all of them, a benevolent desire to bless them; but there was an inner circle, containing the twelve apostles and some godly women, who had joined themselves unto him. These were 'his own'. To them he often expounded the hidden meaning of a parable which he left unexplained to the crowd. To them he often brought many a dainty dish which was specially reserved for their table, and not intended for the multitude. Bread and fish would do for the crowd; but Jesus had choicer fare for 'his own'. They were a special people; many knew them, many despised them, but Jesus loved them, and this was the main thing which made them 'his own'.

You know how they came to be 'his own'? *He chose them or ever the earth was.* A man may surely choose his own wife, and Christ chose his own spouse, he chose his own church; and while the Scripture stands, that doctrine can never be eradicated from it. Before the day-star knew its place, or planets ran their rounds, Christ had made his choice; and, having made it, he stood to it. He chose them for his love; and he loved them for his choice.

Having loved them, and chosen them, *he espoused them unto himself.* 'They shall be mine', said he; 'I will be married to them, I will be bone of their bone, and flesh of their flesh.' Consequently, in the fullness of time, he came here, made one with our humanity, that he might be seen to be a true husband to 'his own' – 'his own' by choice, 'his own' by espousal.

They were 'his own' also, for *his Father gave them to him.* The Father committed them into his hands. 'Thine they were', said Jesus, 'and thou gavest them me.' The Father loved the Son, and committed all things into his hand; but he made a special committal of his own chosen people. He gave them to him, and entered with him into surety engagements on their behalf, that as they were his sheep, committed to his charge, he would deliver them up, and not one of them should be torn by the wolf, or die of the frost or the heat, but that all should pass again under the rod of him that counts them. That great Shepherd of the sheep will take care of the whole flock that was entrusted to his care; he will not lose one of his sheep or lambs. At the last, Jesus will say, 'Here am I, Father, and the children that thou hast given me; of all that thou gavest me I have lost none.' Thus, they are 'his own' by his own choice, 'his own' by espousal, and 'his own' by his Father's gift.

But these whom he called 'his own' were soon to be his *by a wondrous purchase*. He looked upon their redemption as being already accomplished, for in his prayer he said to his Father, 'I have finished the work which thou gavest me to do.' Beloved friends, have you ever thought how dearly we are Christ's by his redemption of us? 'Ye are not your own; ye are bought with a price.' Have you ever realized the price that was paid for you? I sometimes think that, if I could have been there, I would have said, 'O thou great and glorious Lord, I beseech thee not to pay such a price for me; it is too great a sacrifice that thou shouldest be made sin for me, that I might be made the righteousness of God in thee!' But he would do it. He loved us better than he loved himself. He would do it; and he has paid the purchase price for us, and we are his; and we will not run back from the glad confession. Well may he call us 'his own' when it cost him so much to redeem us.

But we have become 'his own' *by his conquest of us*. He had called his disciples by his grace; he had drawn each one of them by cords of love, and they had run after him: and it is just so with you and me. You remember when he drew you; do you not? Can you ever forget when, at last, you yielded to the power of those bands of love, those cords of a man? Often since then have you sung —

> Oh, happy day, that fix'd my choice
> On thee, my Saviour, and my God;
> Well may this glowing heart rejoice,
> And tell its raptures all abroad!
>
> 'Tis done! the great transaction's done;
> I am my Lord's, and he is mine:
> He drew me, and I followed on,
> Charm'd to confess the voice divine.

Beloved, you are 'his own' now because *you have yielded yourselves to him*. You delight to think that you are his. There is no greater joy to you than to feel that you belong to Christ. The fact that you are truly Christ's is the fountain of innumerable pleasures and blessings to your heart. Jesus calls us 'his own' – his own sheep, his own disciples, his own friends, his own brethren, the members of his body. What a title for us to wear, 'His own'! I have heard of some who have felt it an honour to be called, 'The Devil's Own'. I trust that you have escaped from such a title as that; and now you are Christ's own. How many regiments have felt pleasure in being called the King's Own, the Queen's Own, the Prince's Own! Oh, but we are HIS OWN! He owns us; he calls us 'his own'. Thus he distinguishes us from the rest of mankind, and sets us apart unto himself. 'My name shall be named on them', says he. They are 'his own'. Surely, this is the highest honour that can be put upon us even in the last great day. 'They shall be mine, saith the Lord of hosts, in that day when I make up my jewels.'

Now I trust we can say that we desire to serve Christ in our vocation. I feel happy to be amongst the favoured few whose vocation it is to serve Christ, those who are permitted to spend all their time, and all their strength, in that dear service. We are 'his own'; but so are you 'his own' if you believe in him, you also are Christ's own, up in a garret; Christ's own, at the washtub; Christ's own, in the fields at the plough; Christ's own, making the hay. I am not wandering from my subject when I say this, for Christ has 'his own' among all these classes. 'His own' were fishermen, 'his own' cast the net into the Sea of Galilee, 'his own' drew it to shore, 'his own' were the poor of this world. His own, his very own, his choicest and his best friends and followers, were just such. They were unlearned and ignorant men, yet they were 'his own'. So the apostle saith, 'God hath chosen the foolish things of the world to confound the wise; and God hath chosen the weak things of the world to confound the things which are mighty; and base things of the world, and things which are despised, hath God chosen, yea, and things which are not, to bring to nought things that are: that no flesh should glory in his presence.' Oh, the wondrous sovereignty of divine love! I trust that there are some here tonight whom Christ calls 'his own' although they do not yet know that it is so. Bought with his blood, and they are not aware of it? Chosen before the foundation of the world, and yet they have not discovered it? May the Lord reveal to you his everlasting love, and help you to make your calling and election sure from this time forth!

I have said as much as time will permit me to say about our Lord's dear associates, the disciples, whom he calls 'his own'.

II. Now, in the second place, you have a full description of HOW JESUS HAD FELT TOWARDS THEM up to that moment: 'Having loved his own'.

How much can be done with one stroke of a pen! I have sometimes marvelled to see how much a great artist can do by a single touch; his work has seemed unfinished, but he has come with a brush, and just thrown in a few strokes, and the canvas that was dead has seemed to live before you. Now, John is a great master of the art of word-painting, and he gives you the whole history of Christ's dealings with his disciples in these few words, 'Having loved his own'.

For, remember, *that is how he began with them.* They were poor and inconsiderable; but he loved them, and he showed his love to them by calling them to be his disciples. That love wrought upon their hearts, and made them obedient to his call. He began by loving them. David says, 'Thou hast loved my soul out of the pit.' I do not know a more beautiful description of conversion and salvation. The love of God loves us up out of the pit, and loves us to Christ. Thus Christ loved his people from the beginning, and proved his love by drawing them to himself, and the cords he used to draw them were the bands of his love.

Having begun by loving them, *he went on teaching them*; but all his teaching was love, for they were such dull scholars, quick to forget, yet slow to remember, that he had to keep on loving them, or he would have been tired of trying to train them. 'Have I been so long time with you, and yet hast thou not known me, Philip?' There is a mass of love in that question. So was it when he was dealing with Thomas; in his tenderness he submitted without question to the doubting disciple's test. He said to him, 'Reach hither thy finger, and behold my hands; and reach hither thy hand, and thrust it into my side: and be not faithless, but believing.' All his teaching was uttered with lips of love, and all his instruction consisted of lessons of love.

The Lord kept on loving his disciples, *although their natures were wonderfully imperfect*, all of them. There was not one among them who had what one would call an all-round nature, unless it was John, and even he was nasty in temper, and would have called down fire from heaven upon certain Samaritans. Yet the Master kept on loving them. He had made up his mind to love them, and he never ceased to love them as long as he was with them, and he has gone on loving them ever since. At the time when he was about to depart out of the world unto the Father, they still needed to have their feet washed, and he loved them enough to render even that lowly service for them. All the infirmities, the imperfections, the carnality, the dullness, and the slowness of their nature, which he saw much more clearly than they saw it, did not make him cease to love them: 'Having loved his own which were in the world, he loved them unto the end.'

Strangest of all, when he opened his eyes, and looked into the future, and saw that *they would soon be cowardly and faithless*, he loved them all the same. He said, 'All ye shall be offended because of me this night', and so it came to pass, for 'they all forsook him, and fled.' He told Peter that he would deny him thrice; and so it was, yet it was true all the while, 'Having loved his own which were in the world, he loved them unto the end.' That sums it all up. There was never a touch of hate, there was never any anger, there was never any weariness, there was never any lukewarmness in Jesus towards his disciples; but it was always just this, 'Having loved his own which were in the world, he loved them unto the end.' That is the love of Christ to his chosen, and that is the love of Christ to me. I do not think that those gentlemen who have written a *Life of Christ* could write this part of it. This is a portion of the life of Christ that wants not so much to be written as to be known in the heart, and in the soul.

How have you found Christ, my brother? If you have known him, what has been his conduct towards you? You answer, 'Love'. As for me, I never knew, I never heard of such a lover as he is; I never dreamed that he could be such as he has been to me. Oh, how I must have vexed and grieved his gracious heart, and caused him pain; but never, never, never once have I had anything from him but love! 'Having loved his own'. That expression sums up the whole of Christ's conduct towards his chosen people. It is like a miniature painting; it has every feature of his character. There it is, all of it. You may apply a microscope, and look as long as you like, but you will find that it is all there. 'Having loved his own'.

So then, you have seen your Lord associated with his disciples up to this point, and you have learned that he has manifested nothing else towards them but love.

III. But now, thirdly, WHAT A CHANGE WAS COMING OVER HIM! 'Jesus knew that his hour was come that he should depart out of this world unto the Father.'

Dear friends, it was a wonderful change that was coming over him, for, in the first place, though it is so tenderly described here, yet *he knew that he had to die*. You do not wish me, I am sure, to tell you of all the surroundings of the cross, of all the bitterness and woe that culminated in that cup of mingled wormwood and gall. Your heart can never fail to remember the wounds he endured when suffering for you. Well, now, if you and I had to bear all that Christ had to suffer, it would engross our thoughts, we should not be able to think of anything else but that; but it did not engross our Lord's thoughts. He still thought of 'his own'. He loved 'his own' unto the end. He went on with that same calm, solid, resolute love which he had shown towards them aforetime. He set his face like a flint to go up to Jerusalem; but there was no flint in his heart, it had all gone into his face. He had undertaken the work of his people's redemption, and he must go through with it. Death itself could not change his love. You know the love of which Solomon sings at the end of the Canticles: 'Many waters cannot quench love, neither can the floods drown it'; and he says, 'Love is strong as death.' Truly, in our Lord's case, love was stronger than that death of deaths which he deigned to die that he might make us live. Now is his great 'hour' of trial; but he is true to 'his own' even in this dread hour. He is about to die; but he still loves 'his own'.

Dear brethren, that is not all. Jesus was about to depart out of this world, *to go away from his disciples*. After a while, he would see them no more with his bodily eyes; neither would they hear his voice leading them and teaching them. It may be true that 'Absence makes the heart grow fonder', but, alas, we have met with many instances in which mortal men have quite forgotten those whom they professed to love when once the sea has rolled between them. Many hearts are dependent upon eyesight. It is a pity that it should be so; but it was not so with Christ. All the distance between earth and heaven was soon to intervene between our Lord and his disciples; but yet he loved them, and he loves them still. No distance makes any difference between Jesus and 'his own': 'Having loved his own which were in the world, he loved them unto the end.'

Yet, remember, that the Saviour was about to undergo a very wonderful change in another respect, *he was going unto the Father*. Have any of us the slightest idea of what he is now with the Father? I will not attempt to describe the supernal splendours of his throne, the glories which his redeemed delight to lay at his feet, the songs which angels and cherubim and seraphim continually present before him; but this verse we love, and we can truly sing,

> Now though he reigns exalted high,
>   His love is still as great;
> Well he remembers Calvary,
>   Nor lets his saints forget.

I cannot describe these wonderful changes of our Lord, from life to death, from death to resurrection, from resurrection to ascension, from ascension to the glories of his Father's throne. Would all these changes make any alteration in him? No, none of them. 'Having loved his own which were in the world, he loved them unto the end.'

I shall try to speak of that presently, that will be my last point; but before we come to that theme, we must see what would be the condition of 'his own'. I have shown you what would be Christ's condition, and the change that would take place in him.

IV. Now, fourthly, WHAT WOULD BE THEIR CONDITION?

Why, they would remain where they were: 'His own which were in the world'. To me, there seems to be a great abyss of meaning in that expression, 'in the world'. Some of you know more about what this means than others of us do. The church of God in London is nothing but a camp in the midst of heathendom. The sooner we believe that terrible truth the better, because it is really so; and the church of God in the world is nothing but a travelling tent in the midst of a world that lieth in the wicked one. We are 'in the world'. Now, some of you know what it is to be 'in the world'. When you get home tonight, there will be little but oaths and cursing. Some of God's dear people, whom he loves with all his heart, are still in the world, seeing that which vexes them as much as Lot was vexed by the filthy conversation of the men of Sodom. 'In the world!' Now, those whom Christ was about to leave in the world would be left in the midst of all the abounding wickedness, and idolatry, and blasphemy, in about as ungodly an age as man could live in; yet he left them 'in the world'.

Being in the world, you see, they began to be *persecuted*. They were stoned; they were shut up in prison; they were dragged into the amphitheatre to be torn of lions; but 'he loved them unto the end'. You know how that blessed eighth chapter of the Epistle to the Romans concludes. 'Who shall separate us from the love of Christ? shall tribulation, or distress, or persecution, or famine, or nakedness, or peril, or sword? As it is written, For thy sake we are killed all the day long; we are accounted as sheep for the slaughter. Nay, in all these things we are more than conquerors through him that loved us. For I am persuaded, that neither death, nor life, nor angels, nor principalities, nor powers, nor things present, nor things to come, nor height, nor depth, nor any other creature, shall be able to separate us from the love of God, which is in Christ Jesus our Lord.'

In addition to being persecuted, they were liable to be severely *tempted*. All kinds of bribes were put in their way, and all sorts of pleasures and lusts were presented to them; they were men of like passions with ourselves, so those temptations were very real to them. They were 'in the world', and Jesus was gone to heaven. They were 'in the world' also in *affliction*.

Ah, dear friends, we find that we, too, are, in this sense, 'in the world'. However closely we live to God, we have pains of body, and we have to grieve as we see our dear relatives suffering. We have losses and crosses because we are 'in the world'. God's curse still rests upon the earth: 'Thorns also and thistles shall it bring forth to thee.' You may do what you like with it, but you cannot make it stop bringing forth thorns and thistles. They will continue to spring up as surely as the dust will return to the dust from whence it was taken.

In the world, of course, they were in *great labour*, for they were left in the world to seek to convert it, or, at least, to call out the redeemed of Christ from among man by preaching the gospel to every creature. And, being 'in the world', they were surrounded by much weakness, weakness of body and weakness of mind, always needing to call to their Lord for help. He was up there upon the throne, and they were down in the dungeon. He was up there, clothed with all power, and they were down here in all weakness.

V. NOW, HOW WILL JESUS BEHAVE TOWARDS THEM? That is our last question. We began with it, and we will finish with it. Well, here is the answer. 'Having loved his own which were in the world, he loved them unto the end'; and we may rest sure that he always will love them, and that he will never change from the tenderness of his heart towards them. 'He loved them unto the end.' What does that sentence mean?

I think it means, first, that *he loved them right on*. The Hebrew, 'His mercy endureth for ever', might be rendered, 'His mercy endureth to the end.' That is, to the end which has no end, for there never will be an end to his mercy; and his love is continual, everlasting love, it will never come to an end. Christ himself, in his passion, may be said to have come to an end, and he loved his disciples until his death; but it means that he loves them without any end, for ever and ever. Having loved them while he was in the world with them, he loves them right straight on, and always will love them when time shall be no more.

I am sure, dear friends, you believe in the everlasting love of God towards his people. If any of you do not, you are robbing your-selves of one of the greatest comforts that are to be found in the Scriptures. If the Lord can change, where are we? Everything has gone when his everlasting love is gone. I delight to believe that the mountains shall depart, and the hills be removed; but his kindness shall not depart from us, neither shall the covenant of his peace be removed; it standeth fast for ever and ever.

But the sentence may be rendered, '*He loved them to perfection.*' 'Having loved his own which were in the world, he loved them to perfection.' He could not love them any better; that was impossible. He could not love them more wisely; that would be out of the question. He could not love them more intensely; that is not supposable, Whatever the perfection of love may be, that Jesus Christ bestows upon his people. There is no such love in all the world as the love of Christ to his people; and if you were to gather up all the loves that ever were, of men and women, of mothers and children, of friends and friends, and heap up all these loves, the love of Jesus is of superior quality to them all, for none of those loves are absolutely perfect, but Jesus Christ loves to perfection.

Those of you who have the Revised Version will find in the margin the following words, *'to the uttermost'*. 'Having loved his own which were in the world, he loved them to the uttermost', to that which is uttermost, farthest, and most distant; or, if I turn the word in another way, 'He loved them utterly', unutterably, in such a way that you cannot tell, or conceive, or describe, or imagine, how much he loved his people. He loved his people to the utmost stretch of love. So is it, there is no love like his, and, as I said just now, all the loves in the world, compressed into one, would not equal it. 'Having loved his own which were in the world, he loved them to the uttermost.'

Now, it does seem to me that this truth ought to tempt some poor soul to wish to enjoy Christ's love. 'Oh!' says one, 'if I did but get that love, I should never lose it. He would love me to the uttermost. Oh, if I could but creep in among his people!' The way to discover Christ's love to thee is that thou shouldest begin by trusting him; and surely he will help thee to do this. He is so true, so good, so able to save unto the uttermost, that if thou wilt come and trust him, trust him wholly, trust him now, trust him just as thou art, then he will save thee to the uttermost, and show his love to thee to the uttermost. I have been preaching what I trust will comfort God's people; but I wish that some poor soul would come to Christ through it. I believe that is the right way to preach the gospel. Have you not noticed, in the story of the Prodigal Son, that the father said, 'Bring forth the best robe, and put it on him; and put a ring on his hand, and shoes on his feet and so on, but he did not go on to say, 'Feed him'. Do you notice what he said? It was, 'Let us eat, and be merry.' 'Well, but I thought he was thinking about his son.' Yes, and he says, 'Let us eat.' So, dear brothers and sisters in Christ, let us eat, and then sinners will begin to feel their mouths watering, and they also will want to eat, and to have a share of the feast. This is the only way to make them eat; you can bring a horse to the water, but you cannot make him drink; but you are very likely to do so if you set another horse a-drinking. So, if you and I enjoy the sweetness of the love of Christ, there may be some in the gallery, and some downstairs who will say, 'We wish that we know it, too', and they will be wanting it; that is the way to make them eat. I pray the Lord, by his Spirit, to lead them to put their trust in this loving Saviour, and each one to say,

> Jesu, lover of my soul,
> Let me to thy bosom fly.

He will let you fly to his bosom; therefore,

> Come, and welcome; sinner, come.

3

'AFTER TWO DAYS IS
THE PASSOVER' [1]

'Ye know that after two days is . . . the passover,
and the Son of man is betrayed be crucified.'
MATTHEW 26:2

ONE LIKES TO KNOW how a great commander feels before a
battle. What is his state of mind, and how does he look forward
to tomorrow's struggle? While yet the balances are trembling, how
does he act? How does he bear himself? One likes to know the
condition of heart of one's fellow in the prospect of a great trial.
There is a serious operation to be performed; how is the sufferer
supported in the prospect of the surgeon's knife and of the danger
that will attend it? Or, perhaps, death itself is rapidly approaching;
in what condition of heart is our departing friend? How does he
anticipate the great change? I take it that it is sometimes much
harder to look upon a battle than to fight one – more difficult to
foresee an ill than it is to bear it; and, perhaps, the foresight even
of death is much more trying than death itself ever proves to be to
a Christian man. Can we be confident before the battle begins?
Can we be calm before the clouds burst in the time of storm? Can
we rest in God before the iron gate is opened, and we pass through
it into the unknown world? These are questions well worth asking.

I thought that it would be very profitable to us if we tried to
look at our Master in this condition – the great Captain of our
salvation before the battle – the great Sacrifice led to the altar
where his blood is about to be shed. How does he behave himself?

[1] Sermon No. 2,522. Preached at the Metropolitan Tabernacle on Sunday evening,
1 November 1885.

May there not be something specially instructive in this last word of his, when he seems, as it were, to take off the robes of the teacher and prophet, and to put on his priestly garments? May there not be something for us to learn from the state of his mind and spirit, and from his language, just before his passion? It is a small window, but a great deal of light may come through it. The Master said to his disciples, 'Ye know that after two days is the passover, and the Son of man is betrayed to be crucified.'

I. The first thing I would say upon these words to you, beloved in Christ Jesus, is ADMIRE YOUR SAVIOUR. Hear him speak, and regard him in holy contemplation, on purpose that admiration of him may be greatly excited.

Admire *his calmness*. There is no token of any disturbance of mind, there are no evidences of dismay, there is not even a quiver of fear, nor the least degree of anxiety about him. He speaks not boastfully; else we should suspect that he was not brave. He speaks very solemnly, for it was a terrible ordeal that lay before him, look at it as he might; but still, with what true peace of mind, in what tones of quiet serenity, does he say to his little band of followers, 'Ye know that after two days is the passover, and the Son of man is betrayed to be crucified.'

This calmness is very wonderful, because there was so much that was bitter and cruel about his approaching death: 'The Son of man is betrayed.' The Saviour felt that betrayal most keenly; it was a very bitter part of the deadly potion which he had to drink. 'He that eateth bread with me hath lifted up his heel against me', was a venomous drop that went right into his soul. David, in his great sorrow, had to say, 'For it was not an enemy that reproached me; then I could have borne it: neither was it he that hated me that did magnify himself against me; then I would have hid myself from him; but it was thou, a man mine equal, my guide, and mine acquaintance. We took sweet counsel together, and walked into the house of God in company.' And it was a very, very, very bitter thing to Christ to be betrayed by Judas; yet he talks of it calmly, and speaks of it when it was not absolutely necessary, one would think, to mention that incidental circumstance. He might have said, 'In two days I shall be crucified'; but he did say, 'In two days the Son of man is betrayed to be crucified.'

Do not forget, also, the extraordinary bitterness that is concentrated in that word 'crucified'. Somehow, we have got used to the cross, and the glory which surrounds our Lord has taken away from our minds much of the shame which is and should ever be associated with the gibbet. The cross was the hangman's gibbet of those days, it implied all the shame that the gallows could imply with us today, and more, for a freeman may be hanged, but crucifixion was a death reserved for slaves. Nor was it merely the shame of crucifixion, but it was the great pain of it. It was an exquisitely cruel death, in which the body was tormented for a considerable length of time to the very highest degree, and the nails passing through the flesh just where the nerves are most plentiful, and tearing and rending through those parts of the body by the weight which had to be sustained on hands and feet, caused torture of a kind which I will not attempt to describe. Beside that, remember, veiled beneath the words 'to be crucified' lay our Saviour's inward and spiritual crucifixion, for his Father's forsaking of him was the essence, the extreme gall, of the bitterness that he endured. It meant that he had to die upon the accursed tree, deserted even by his Father; yet he talked of it, truly with all solemnity, but yet without the slightest trace of trembling. 'Ye know', said he to his disciples, 'that in two days is the passover, and the Son of man is betrayed to be crucified.' Admire, then, the calm, brave heart of your divine Lord, conscious – far more conscious than you and I can be – of what was meant by being betrayed and being crucified, cognizant of every pang that should ever come upon him – the bloody sweat, the scourge, the thorn-crown, the fevered thirst, the tongue cleaving to the roof of his mouth, and all the dust of death that would surround and choke him; yet he speaks of it as though it were no more an unusual event than the passover itself: 'Ye know that after two days is the passover, and the Son of man is betrayed to be crucified.'

I want you to admire, next, your Saviour's *strong resolve*, his resolute purpose to go through all this suffering that he might effect our redemption. If he had willed it, he might have paused, he might have gone back, he might have given up the enterprise.

You know how the flesh, in sight of all that pain and grief, cried, 'If it be possible, let this cup pass from me'; but here we see, before the passion came, that strong and firm and brave resolve which, when the passion did come, would not, could not, and did not flinch or hesitate, much less turn back. He could sweat great drops of blood, but he could not give up the work he came to do. He could bow his head to death, but he could not, and would not, cease to love his people whom he loved so much as to end his life for their sakes upon the accursed tree. Here are no regrets, and no faltering. Our Lord speaks as you and I would speak of something about which our mind is quite made up, concerning which there is no room for argument or debate: 'Ye know that after two days is the passover, and the Son of man is betrayed to be crucified.' If he had said, 'After two years', I could understand something of his purpose concerning an event that was so distant; but within two days to be betrayed, within forty-eight hours to be betrayed for crucifixion, and yet to talk of it so, O my Lord, truly thy love for us is strong as death, thy jealousy o'ercomes even the grave itself!

Admire him, then, dear friends; let your inmost heart adore and love him. But I want you to notice also *how absorbed he was in his approaching betrayal and death*; that truth comes out in the words of our text: 'Ye know that after two days is the passover, and the Son of man is betrayed to be crucified.' Ah, dear Lord, thou didst speak the truth! They did know it, and yet thou didst speak to them with loving partiality, for they did not really know it. They did not as yet understand that their Master must die, and that he would rise again from the dead. He had often repeated to them the assurance that it would be so; but, somehow, they had not truly believed it, realized it, grasped it. Ah, but he had! He had; and, you know, it is the way of men who have realized a great truth to talk to others as if it was as real to them as to themselves. You remember how the spouse asks the watchmen of the city, 'Saw ye him whom my soul loveth?' She does not tell them any name, but she talks of her Beloved as if there were no other 'him' in all the world; and the Lord here so well knew, and was so wholly absorbed in the great work before him, that he said to these forgetful, these ignorant disciples, 'Ye know that after two days is the passover, and the Son of man is betrayed to be crucified.' Why, they had only a little while before walked with him through the streets of Jerusalem! The people had strewn the road with their garments and with branches of palm trees; scarcely had the sound of their hosannas died away out of the disciples' ears, yet Jesus says to them, 'Ye know that after two days is the passover, and the Son of man is betrayed to be crucified; you have not forgotten that, have you?' Ah, but they had! They were still dreaming of an earthly sovereignty, and he was dreaming of nothing, but sternly, solemnly setting his face like a flint to go to prison and to death for their redemption, and for yours, and for mine, sacredly resolved to go through with it, and even 'straitened' till his baptism of blood should be accomplished, and he should be immersed in unknown deeps of grief and suffering. Having all his thought taken up with that subject, our Lord therefore talked to his disciples as if they were taken up with it, too. This is the language of One who is altogether absorbed with this gigantic enterprise which he has made to be the very summit of his ambition, though he knows that it will involve him in shame and death. Admire him, brothers and sisters, that he should be so taken up with the passion of winning souls as to forget everything else, and have this only upon his mind, and upon his lips: 'After two days is the passover, and the Son of man is betrayed to be crucified.'

I cannot help adding one other thing in which I admire the Saviour; and that is, *how wise he was to tell his disciples this!* You see, all he cared for was their good. He was not mentioning his suffering that he might ask for their sympathy. There is no trace of his crying, like Job, 'Have pity upon me, have pity upon me, O ye my friends; for the hand of God hath touched me.' No, our Lord told his disciples this for their sakes; first, that they might not be surprised when it came to pass, as though some strange thing had happened unto them – that, when he was betrayed and crucified, it might not be quite so dire a blighting of all their hopes since he had prepared them for it beforehand. And, moreover, it was intended to strengthen them when they should come into the trial, so that they should say, 'It is all just as he told us it would be; how true he is! He told us about this sorrow beforehand; and, therefore, if he spake the truth then, we will believe that all the rest that he said is also true. And did he not say that he would rise again from the dead? Then, depend upon it, he will do so. He died when he said he would die, and he will rise again when he said he would rise again.' This saying of our Lord was well and wisely uttered, that the crucifixion should not come upon them as a thing unknown to him; but that, when they were in the midst of the trial, they should remember that he told them all about it, and so they would be comforted.

I ask you, then, dear friends, to think with reverent affection of this calm speech of your divine Master, this resolved and determined utterance, this all-absorbing thought of his concerning the purchase of his people by his blood, and this generous wisdom of his in making it all known beforehand to those who were round about him, and who truly loved him. I do not like to turn from that thought until you have in your own heart felt this intense admiration of your Lord.

II. But, secondly, I want to take your thoughts a little way – not from the text – but from that particular line of meditation, and now to ask you to CONSIDER YOUR SACRIFICE.

The Master says, 'Ye know that after two days is the Passover, and the Son of man is betrayed to be crucified.' I cannot help reading it like this – 'Ye know that after two days is THE PASSOVER. All the other passovers have been passovers only in name, passovers in type, passovers in emblem, passovers foreshadowing the passover; but after two days is the real passover, and the Son of man is betrayed to be crucified.' At any rate, I want you to notice how true it is that our Lord Jesus Christ is our Passover: 'Christ our Passover is sacrificed for us.' What the paschal lamb was to Israel in Egypt, that the Lord Jesus Christ is to us. Let us think of that for a few minutes. Put the passover and the cross together, for indeed they are one.

And, first, *here is a lamb*. Was there another man who ever lived who was so worthy to be called a lamb, as was Jesus Christ? I have never heard or read of any character that so fully realizes what must be meant by 'the Lamb of God'. Other men have been like lambs, but there is a touch of the tiger about us all at times. There was none about him; he was the Lamb of all lambs – the Lamb of God, the most lamb-like of all men who ever lived or died, for there was no trace of anything about him that was contrary to tenderness, and love, and gentleness. There were other qualities, of course, but none that were contrary to these; there were some that were as necessary to a complete character as even gentleness was, and he failed in nothing; but, still, if you only view him from that one side of his gentleness, there was none so worthy to be called a lamb as he.

The lamb of the passover, however, *had to be perfect*; it must be without spot or blemish. And where can you find the like of Jesus for spotlessness and perfection in every respect?. There is nothing in him redundant, there is nothing in him deficient; the character of the Christ is absolutely perfect, insomuch that his very enemies, who have denied his deity, have been charmed with his humanity; and those who have even tried to undermine his teaching, have, nevertheless, reverently bowed before his example. He is the Lamb of God 'without blemish and without spot'.

The paschal lamb also *had to be slain*. You know how Christ was slain; there is no need to dwell upon the sufferings and death of our Well-beloved. The lamb *had to be roasted with fire*. That was the method by which it was prepared; and, truly, Christ our Passover was roasted with fire. Through what fiery sufferings, through what consuming griefs, did he pass! There was nought about him that was sodden at all with water; but every bit of him was roasted with the fire of human hatred, and also with the divine and righteous ire of the thrice-holy God.

You remember, too, that in the paschal lamb *not a bone was to be broken*. Our Lord stood in imminent jeopardy of having his bones broken, for with iron bars the Roman soldiers went to break the legs of the three crucified persons, that they might die the more quickly; but John tells us, 'When they came to Jesus, and saw that he was dead already, they brake not his legs: but one of the soldiers with a spear pierced his side, and forthwith came there out blood and water. And he that saw it bare record, and his record is true: and he knoweth that he saith true, that ye might believe. For these things were done, that the scripture should be fulfilled, a bone of him shall not be broken. And again another scripture saith, they shall look on him whom they pierced.' In all this is Christ our true Paschal Lamb.

But you know, dear friends, that the chief point about the paschal lamb lay in *the sprinkling of the blood*. The blood of the lamb was caught in a basin; and then, the father of the family took a bunch of hyssop, dipped it in the blood, and struck the lintel and the two side posts of the house, outside the door; then, when the destroying angel flew through the land of Egypt to smite the firstborn of men and of cattle, from the firstborn of Pharaoh that was on the throne to the firstborn of one that was in the dungeon, he passed by every house that was sprinkled with the blood; and these are the Lord's memorable words concerning that ordinance, 'When I see the blood, I will pass over you.' God's sight of the blood was the reason for his passing over his people, and not smiting them. And you know, beloved, that the reason why God does not smite you on account of sin is that he sees the sprinkled blood of Jesus under which you are sheltering. That blood is sprinkled upon you; and as God sees it, he knows that expiation has been made, the substitutionary sacrifice has been slain, and he passes you by. Thus is Christ, the true Passover, accepted in your stead, and you are saved through him.

Remember, too, that the paschal lamb *furnished food for a supper*. It was both a security and a feast for the people. The whole family stood round the table that night, and ate of the roasted lamb. With bitter herbs did they eat it, as if to remind them of the bitterness of their bondage in Egypt; with their loins girt, and with their walking staves in their hands, as men who were about to quit their homes, and go on a long journey never to return – thus they stood and ate the paschal lamb. They all ate it, and they ate it all; for not a relic of it must be left until the morning. If there was too much for one family, then others must come in to share it; and if any was left, it must be destroyed by fire. Is not this, dear friends, just what Christ is to us – our spiritual meat, the food of our souls? We receive a whole Christ, and feed upon a whole Christ – often with bitter herbs of repentance and humiliation; but still we feed on him, and we all eat of the same spiritual meat, even as we are all sprinkled with the one precious blood, if indeed we be the true Israel of God.

O beloved, let us bless our Lord for the true Passover! It was a night to be remembered when Israel came out of Egypt; but it is a night to be remembered even more when you and I, by the sprinkling of the blood of Jesus, are once for all passed over by the angel of avenging justice, and we live when others die – a night to be remembered when our eager lips begin to feed on him whose flesh is meat indeed, and we eat and live for ever. Is not that the teaching of this text? Did not the Saviour mean this when he said, 'Ye know that after two days is the passover, and the Son of man is betrayed to be crucified'? These two things are bracketed together; as in mathematics, there is a sort of mark of 'equals' put between them to signify that the one is equal to the other – the feast of the passover, and the fact that the Son of man is betrayed to be crucified.

III. Now I turn to a third point, and I think I shall have your earnest attention upon that, because there is something in it which very deeply interests all of us who belong to Christ. I have already asked you to admire your Saviour, and to consider your sacrifice; now, dear friends, ADORE YOUR LORD.

I ask you to adore your Lord, first, for *his foresight*. 'After two days the Son of man is betrayed to be crucified.' We cannot prophesy concerning the future. The man who can tell me what will happen in two days must be something more than man. As to many events, it is as difficult to foresee two minutes as to foresee two centuries, unless there be some causes operating which must produce certain effects. In our Lord's case, the influences seemed all to point away from betrayal and crucifixion. He was extremely popular; to all appearance he was beloved by the mass of the people; and even the scribes and Pharisees, who sought his death, were thoroughly afraid of him; yet, with that clear foresight of the eye which shines in no head but that which is divine, Jesus says, 'After two days the Son of man is betrayed.' He sees it all as if it had already happened; he does not say, 'shall be', but he so fully sees it, he is such a true Seer, that he says, 'The Son of man is betrayed to be crucified.'

Now, beloved, if he thus foresaw his own betrayal and death, let us adore him, for *he can foresee our trials and death*. He knows all that is going to happen to us; he knows what will happen to me within two days. I bless him that I do not; I would far rather that the eyes which see into the future should be in his head than in mine, they are safer there. But, brother, if within two days, or two months, or two years, you are to pass through some bitter agony, some scourging and buffeting, which looks very improbable now, you may not see that it may be so, but there is One who sees it. The sheep's best eyes are in the shepherd's head, the sheep will do well enough if he can see what is just before him, especially if he can see his shepherd; that is all he wants to see. But the shepherd can see into the cold winter, the shepherd can see into the wild wood where lurks the wolf, the shepherd can see everything. And I want you, dear friends, to adore your Lord because, if in his humiliation he foresaw his betrayal and death, from the vantage ground of his glory he can now see your griefs and your woes that are yet in reserve; and it ought to be enough for you that he knows all about you. He knows what your difficulty will be, and he will pray for you that your faith fail not. Adore your Lord, then, for his foresight.

I want you next to adore him for *his wonderful providence*. There was a providence which surrounded the Christ of God at that time; it was according to the divine purpose and will that he should die at the passover, and at that particular passover, and that he should die by being betrayed, and by being crucified. Without entering into the question of the responsibility and free will of men, I am sure that the providence of their Lord and Master wrought this all out. I wonder that they did not take up stones to stone him; but they could not, for he must be crucified. I wonder that they did not hire an assassin, for there were plenty in those days who would have stabbed him for a shilling. But no; he must be crucified. I marvel that they had not slain him long ago, for they did take up stones again and again to stone him; but his hour was not then come. There was a providence working all the while, and shaping his end as it shapes ours. He was immortal till his work was done. But when the two days of which he spake should be over, he must die. With cruel and wicked hands, and of their own voluntary and evil will, they crucified and slew the Christ; yet it was all according to 'the determinate counsel and foreknowledge of God'. I never yet pretended to explain how free agency and absolute predesti-nation can both be true; but I am sure that they are both true, both written in Scripture, and both facts. To reconcile them, is no business of mine or yours; but to admire how they are reconciled in fact, is a business of yours and mine, and therefore let us do so now.

I want you, next, to admire your Lord by recognizing his *extraordinary correctness as a prophet.* Let me read on beyond our text: 'Ye know that after two days is the feast of the passover, and the Son of man is betrayed to be crucified. Then assembled together the chief priests, and the scribes, and the elders of the people, into the palace of the high priest, who was called Caiaphas, and consulted that they might take Jesus by subtlety, and kill him. But they said, not on the feast day' – mark that – 'not on the feast day, lest there be an uproar among the people.' Now, note this. It must be on the feast day, and it shall be on the feast day; yet they said, 'not on the feast day'. But what does it matter what they say? Do you not observe how they were checkmated all round, how their purpose was like the whistling wind, and the eternal purpose stood firm in every particular? They said, 'We will take him by subtlety, and kill him'; but they did not, they took him by force. They said, 'We will kill him'; but they did not, for he died by the hands of the Romans. They meant to slay him privately, but they could not, for he must be hung up before high noon in the midst of the people. And, above all, they said, 'Not on the feast day. Not on the feast day.' I think I hear old Caiaphas there, with all his wisdom and all his cunning, saying, 'Not on the feast day', and Annas and all the priests join in the chorus, 'Not on the feast day. Postpone it a little till the million have departed, the vulgar throng who, perhaps, would make a riot in his favour.' There they stood with their broad-bordered garments and their phylacteries, and they were of opinion that what Caiaphas had proposed, and Annas had seconded, should be carried unanimously: 'Not on the feast day.' But Christ had said, 'After two days is the feast day, and the Son of man is betrayed to be crucified.' We do not know how it all came to be hurried on against their deliberate will; but Judas ran to them in hot haste, and said, 'What will ye give me?' and they were so eager for Christ's death that they overleaped themselves. 'We will give you thirty pieces of silver', said they; and they weighed them out to him, little thinking how quick he would be about his accursed business. Soon he comes back, and says, 'He is in the garden; you can easily take him there while he is in prayer with a few of his disciples; I will conduct you thither'; and ere long the deed of darkness is done. These crafty, cruel men had said, 'not on the feast day'; but it was on the feast day, as Jesus had foretold that it would be.

Now, beloved, when our Lord tells us anything, let us always believe it. Whatever may appear to be against his statements, let us make nothing of it all. A man in Jerusalem at that time might have said, 'The Christ cannot be put to death unless these scribes and elders of the people agree to it; and you can see that they have resolved not to have it on the feast day. He will not be crucified on the passover, the whole type will break down, and it will be shown that he is not what he professed to be.' Ah, but they may say, 'Not on the feast day', till they are hoarse; but he has said, 'After two days is the feast day, and the Son of man is betrayed to be crucified'; and so it came to pass.

Our Lord has said that he will come again; yet men ask, 'Where is the promise of his coming?' Brothers, be you sure that he will come. He has always kept his word, and he will come, as he said. Ah, but they say that he will not come to punish the ungodly who have defied him; but he will! The Son of man shall sit upon the throne of his glory, and before him shall be gathered all nations; he shall separate them the one from the other as a shepherd divideth the sheep from the goats, and he will say to those on his left hand, 'Depart, ye cursed', as surely as he will say to those on his right hand, 'Come, ye blessed'. Every jot and tittle that has ever fallen from the lips of Christ is sure to come to pass, for you know that he said, 'Heaven and earth shall pass away, but my words shall not pass away.' Rest you upon the eternal purpose of God, and the faithful promise of Christ, which shall never fail; for not one of Christ's words shall fall to the ground unfulfilled. Let us adore him, then, as our true Prophet. 'Very God of very God', 'the faithful and true Witness', 'the Prince of the kings of the earth', we do adore thee this very hour!

IV. Now, fourthly, and lastly, dear friends, I want you to IMITATE YOUR EXEMPLAR.

I will not detain you more than a minute or two upon this point; but I want you, as far as your Lord is imitable, to imitate him in the spirit of this verse. I have told you that there was no boasting in him, but that there was a deep calm and a firm resolve even in the immediate prospect of a cruel and shameful death; and I think that you should imitate your Lord in this respect. Suppose that, in two days, there shall come a 'post' from the New Jerusalem to tell you that the silver cord is about to be loosed, and the golden bowl to be broken, and that your spirit must return to God who gave it. In such a case, it behoves you, dear follower of Christ, to receive that message with as much calmness as Christ delivered his own death-warrant, though it had to be spoken in such language as this: 'Ye know that after two days is the feast of the passover, and the Son of man is betrayed to be crucified.' It will not run like that with you; but it may be that in two days tuberculosis will end in haemorrhage, or that old age will bring down the frail tent of your mortality, or that the disease which is now upon you will drag you to the grave. Well, if it be so in two days – ah, if it were so in two hours, or two minutes! – it is for the child of God to say, 'Thy will be done', just as the Master did. Happy was that woman who said, 'Every morning, before I come downstairs, I dip my foot in the river of death, and I shall not be afraid to plunge into it for the last time.' They who die daily, as we all should, are always ready to die. I like Bengel's notion concerning death. He says, 'I do not think that a Christian should make any fuss about dying. When I am in company, and somebody comes to the door, and says, "Mr Bengel is wanted", I let the company go on with their talk, and I just slip out, and I am gone. Perhaps, after a little while, they say, "Mr Bengel is gone." Yes, that is all; and that is how I would like to die, for God to knock at my door, and for me to be gone, without making any ado about it.'

> Strangers into life we come,
> And dying is but going home.

I do not think that there ought to be any jerk on the metals when we arrive at the heavenly terminus; we just run straight on into the shed where the engine stops – nay, into the glory, where we

39

shall rest for ever and ever. I think I have heard of a captain, who was so skilled that, when he had arranged all the steering gear, he had not to alter a point for thousands of miles; and when he came to the harbour, he had so guided the vessel that he sailed straight in. If you get the Lord Jesus Christ on board the vessel of your life, you will find that he is such a skilful Steersman that you will never have to alter your course. He will so set your ship's head that, between here and heaven, there will be nothing to do but to go right on; and then, all of a sudden, you will hear a voice saying, 'Furl sail! Let go the anchor!' You will hear a little rattle of the chain, and the vessel will be still for ever in that port which is truly called, the Fair Havens.

That is how it should be, and I am going to finish by saying that I believe that is how it will be. If I say to you that it ought to be so, you will perhaps say to me, 'Ah, sir, but I am often subject to bondage through fear of death!' Yes, but you will not be when you come to die. O poor Little-faith, you want to have strength now to die with! But God knows that you are not going to die for some time yet; so what would you do with dying grace if he were to give it to you now? Where would you pack it up, and lay it by? It will be quite time to get dying grace when you come to die. Have I not seen some fidgety old folk who have been really a trouble to other people through their getting so worried and anxious? But all of a sudden there has come upon them such a beautiful quiet. It has been said, 'Oh, grandma is so different! Something is going to happen, we feel sure.' One day, she had not anything to trouble her. Everybody could see that she was seriously unwell; but the dear old eyes sparkled with unusual brightness, and there was an almost unearthly smile upon her face, and she said at night, 'I don't feel quite as well as usual; I think, tomorrow morning, I shall lie a little later.' And she did; so they went up to her. She said that she had had a blessed night; she did not know whether she had slept, but she had seen in the night such a wondrous sight, though she could not describe what it was like. They all gathered round the bed, for they perceived that something very mysterious had happened to her; and she blessed them all, and said, 'Good-bye; meet me in heaven'; and she was gone. And they have said to me afterwards, 'Our dear old grandma used always to be afraid of dying; but it did not come to much when she really came to die, did it?' I have often seen it so; it is no strange story that I am telling you now. A Christian man has been so unwise as to be always fearing that he would play the fool when he came to die; and yet, when it has come to the time of night, the dear child of God, who had long been in the dark, has received his candle; his Lord has given him his bedroom candle, and he has gone upstairs, and by its light he has passed away into the land where they need no candle, neither light of the sun, but the Lord God giveth them light. I believe that many of us will die just like that; I believe that you will, my dear sister. I believe that you will, my dear brother. As your days, your strength shall be; and as your last day is, so shall your strength be. And I should not wonder if, one of these days, you or I will be heard saying, 'Now, dear friends, the doctor has told me that I cannot live long. I asked him how long, and he said, "Perhaps, a week", and I was a little disappointed that I had to wait so long.' I should not wonder if those around us should hear us say, 'Well, it is only two days according to their reckoning, and perhaps it will not be two days. I think that I shall go next Sunday morning, just when the bells are ringing the people into the house of prayer on earth. Just then, I shall hear heaven's bells ringing, and I shall say, "Good-bye", and be where I have often longed to be, where my treasure is, where my Best-beloved is.' So may it be with you all, for Christ's sake! Amen.

4

THE BLOOD SHED FOR MANY [1]

'For this is my blood of the new testament, which
is shed for many for the remission of sins.'
MATTHEW 26:28

THE LORD JESUS CHRIST was then alive, sitting at the table,
and yet, pointing to the cup filled with red wine, he said, 'This is
my blood, which is shed for many.' This proves that he could not
have intended that the wine was literally his blood. Surely it is no
longer necessary to refute the gross and carnal dogma of tran-
substantiation, which is obviously absurd. There sat the living Lord
at the supper, with his blood in his veins, and therefore the wine
could not literally be his blood. Value the symbol, but to confound
it with the thing symbolized would draw into the idolatrous
worship of a piece of bread.

Our Lord spoke of his blood as shed when as yet the nails had
not pierced his hands and feet, and the spear had not broached
his side. Is not this to be accounted for by the fact that our Lord
was so taken up with the thought of our redemption by his death
that he speaks of that as done which he was so resolved to do?
Enjoying loving communion with his chosen disciples, he spake
freely; his heart did not study accuracy so much as feeling; and so,
in speech as in feeling, he antedated his great work of atonement,
and spoke of it as done. To set forth the future intent of the blessed
ordinance of the Lord's Supper he must of necessity treat his death
as an accomplished fact; and his complete absorption in his work

---

[1] Sermon No. 1,971. Preached at the Metropolitan Tabernacle on Sunday
morning, 3 July 1887.

made it easy and natural for him to do so. He ignores moods and tenses; 'his work is before him.'

By the use of such language, our Lord also shows us the abiding presence of the great sacrifice as a power and an influence. He is the 'Lamb slain from the foundation of the world', and therefore he speaks of his blood as shed. In a few hours it would be literally poured forth; but long ages before, the Lord God had regarded it as done. In full confidence in the great Surety that he would never draw back from the perfect fulfilment of his engagements, the Father saved multitudes in virtue of the future sin-offering. He communed with myriads of saints on the strength of the purification which would in the fullness of time be presented by the great High Priest. Could not the Father trust his Son? He did so; and by this act set us a great example of faith. God himself is in very deed the Father of the faithful, seeing that he himself reposed the utmost confidence in Jesus, and because of what he would yet do in the pouring out of his soul unto death, he 'opened the kingdom of heaven to all believers.' What, my soul! canst thou not trust the sacrifice now that it has been presented? If the foresight of it was enough for God, is not the consummation of it enough for thee? 'Behold the Lamb of God', who even before he died was described as taking away the sin of the world. If this was so before he went to Calvary, how surely is it so now that he has said in verity and truth, 'It is finished'!

Dear friends, I am going to preach to you again upon the cornerstone of the gospel. How many times will this make, I wonder? The doctrine of Christ crucified is always with me. As the Roman sentinel in Pompeii stood to his post even when the city was destroyed, so do I stand to the truth of the atonement though the church is being buried beneath the boiling mud-showers of modern heresy. Everything else can wait, but this one truth must be proclaimed with a voice of thunder. Others may preach as they will, but as for this pulpit, it shall always resound with the substitution of Christ. 'God forbid that I should glory save in the cross of our Lord Jesus Christ.' Some may continually preach Christ as an example, and others may perpetually discourse upon his coming to glory: we also preach both of these, but mainly we preach Christ *crucified*, to the Jews a stumbling-block, and to the Greeks foolishness; but to them that are saved Christ the power of God, and the wisdom of God.

You have before you a cup, filled with wine, which Jesus has just blessed, and presented to his disciples. As you look into its rosy depths, hear him speak of the cup as his blood; for thus he would teach us a solemn lesson.

I. Note, first, THE IMPORTANCE OF THE PRECIOUS BLOOD OF CHRIST. The vital importance of the great truth of the death of Christ as a vicarious sacrifice, is set before us in this cup, which is the memorial of his blood shed for many.

Blood represents suffering; but it goes further, and suggests suffering unto death. 'The blood is the life thereof', and when blood is too copiously shed death is suggested. Remember that in the sacred supper you have the bread as a separate emblem of the body, and then the wine as a separate symbol of the blood: thus you have a clear picture of death, since the blood is separated from the flesh. 'As often as ye eat this bread, and drink this cup, ye do show the Lord's death.' Both acts are essential.

Upon the death of Christ you are invited to fix your attention, and upon that only. In the suffering of our Lord unto death we see the boundless stretch of his love. 'Greater love hath no man than this, that he lay down his life for his friends.' Jesus could not be more loving to us than to yield himself unto death, even the death of the cross. O my Lord, in thy bloody sweat, and in the piercing of thy hands, and feet, and side, I see the highest proof of thy love! Here I see that Jesus 'loved me, and gave himself for me.' Beloved, I beg you to consider often and lovingly the sufferings of your Redeemer, unto the pouring out of his heart's blood. Go with him to Gethsemane, and thence to the house of Caiaphas and Annas, and then to Pilate's hall and Herod's place of mockery! Behold your Lord beneath the cruel scourges, and in the hands of the executioners upon the hill of shame. Forget not one of the sorrows which were mingled in the bitter cup of his crucifixion – its pain, its mockery, its shame. It was a death reserved for slaves and felons. To make its deep abysses absolutely bottomless, he was forsaken even of his God. Let the darkness of 'Eloi, Eloi, lama sabachthani', bear down upon your spirit till, as you sink in awe, you also rise in love. He loved you better than he loved himself! The cup means love, even to the shedding of his blood for you.

It means something more. We have called our Lord, in our hymn, 'Giver of life for life', and that is what this cup means. He gave up his life that we might live. He stood in our place and stead in the day of Jehovah's wrath, receiving into his bosom the fiery sword which was unsheathed for our destruction. The pouring out of his blood has made our peace with God. Jehovah made the soul of his only-begotten an offering for sin, that the guilty might be cleared. 'He hath made him to be sin for us, who knew no sin; that we might be made the righteousness of God in him.' That is what the wine in the cup means: it means the death of Jesus in our stead. It means the blood poured out from the heart of the incarnate God, that we might have fellowship with God, the sin which divided us being expiated by his death.

Our blessed Saviour would have us hold his death in great reverence: it is to be *our chief memory*. Both the emblems of the Lord's Supper set forth the Saviour's death. This peculiarly Christian ordinance teaches nothing if it does not teach this. Christ's death for men is the great doctrine of the church. We profess ourselves partakers of the merit of his death when we come to this table; our Lord's death is then remembered, shown, declared, testified, and trusted in. Evidently the Lord Jesus means us to treat the fact of his death as a truth to be made pre-eminently prominent: he would not have instituted an ordinance specially to remind us of the shedding of his blood, if he had not regarded it as the forefront of his whole earthly career. The other ordinance of our holy faith also sets forth our Lord's death. Are we not 'Buried with him by baptism into death?' Is not baptism an emblem of his being immersed beneath the waves of sorrow and death? Baptism shows us that participation in Christ's suffering by which we begin to live; the Lord's Supper shows us that participation in Christ's suffering by which that life is sustained. Both institutions point to his death.

Besides, beloved, we know from Holy Scripture that this doctrine of the death of Christ is the very core of Christianity. Leave out the cross, and you have killed the religion of Jesus. Atonement by the blood of Jesus is not an arm of Christian truth; it is the heart of it. Even as the Lord said of the animal, 'The blood is the life thereof', so is it true of the gospel – the sacrificial death of Jesus is the vital point of our profession. I know nothing of Christianity without the blood of Christ. No teaching is healthy which throws the cross into the background. The other day, when I was enquiring about the welfare of a certain congregation, my informant told me that there had been few additions to the church, although the minister was a man of ability and industry. Furthermore, he let me see the reason for failure, for he added, 'I have attended there for several years, and during all that time I do not remember hearing a sermon upon the sacrifice of Christ. The atonement is not denied, but it is left out.' If this be so, what is to become of our churches? If the light of the atonement is put under a bushel, the darkness will be dense. In omitting the cross you have cut the Achilles tendon of the church: it cannot move, nor even stand, when this is gone. Holy work falls to the ground: it faints and dies when the blood of Jesus is taken away. The cross must be put in the front more than ever by the faithful, because so many are unfaithful. Let us endeavour to make amends for the dishonour done to our divine Master by those who deny or dishonour his vicarious sacrifice: let us abide steadfast in this faith while others waver, and preach Christ crucified if all else forbear. Grace, mercy, and peace be to all who exalt Christ crucified!

This remembrance of the death of Christ must be *a constant remembrance*. The Lord's Supper was meant to be a frequent feast of fellowship. It is a grievous mistake of the church when the communion is held but once in the year, or once in a quarter of a year; and I cannot remember any Scripture which justifies once in the month. I should not feel satisfied without breaking bread on every Lord's-day. It has come to me even oftener than once a week; for it has been my delight to break bread with many a little company of Christian friends. Whenever this Supper is celebrated, we declare that 'Christ died for our sins according to the Scriptures.' We cannot think of that death too often. Never was man blamed in heaven for preaching Christ too much; nay, not even on earth to the sons of God was the cross ever too much spoken of. Outsiders may say, 'This man harps only upon one string.' Do you wonder? The carnal mind is enmity against God, and it specially shows its hatred by railing at the cross. Saintly ones find here, in the perpetual monotony of the cross, a greater variety than in all other doctrines put together. Preach you Christ, and Christ, and Christ, and Christ, and nothing else but Christ, and opened ears shall find in your ministry a wondrous harmony of linked sweetnesses, a charming perfectness of all manner of delicious voices. All good things lie within the compass of the cross; its outstretched arms overshadow the whole world of thought; from the east even unto the west it sheds a hallowed influence; meanwhile, its foot is planted deep in the eternal mysteries, and its top pierces all earth-born clouds, and rises to the throne of the Most High. Christ is lifted up upon the cross, that he may draw all men unto him; and if we desire to draw them, this must be our magnet.

Beloved, the precious blood of Christ should be had by us *in vivid remembrance*. There is something to me most homely about that cup filled with the fruit of the vine. The bread of the Supper is the bread of our common meal, and the wine is the usual attendant of feasts. That same pure blood of the grape which is set on our sacramental table I drink with my friend. Look at those ruby, ruddy drops, suggesting your Lord's own blood. I had not dared to invent the symbol, nor might any man of mortal mould have ventured on such a thing, lest he should seem to bring that august death down to our lowly level; but in infinite condescension Jesus himself chooses the symbol, and while by its materialism he sets forth the reality of the sacrifice, by its commonness he shows how freely we may partake thereof. He would not have us know him after the flesh, and forget the spiritual nature of his griefs; but yet he would have us know that he was in a real body when he bled, and that he died a real death, and became most truly fit for burial and therefore he symbolizes his blood, not by some airy fancy, or mystic sign, but by common wine in the cup. Thus would he reach us by our eye and by our taste, using two gates of our nature which lead up to the castle of the heart, but are not often the King's roadway thereto. O blessed Master, dost thou arrange to teach us so forcibly? Then let us be impressed with the reality of the lesson, and never treat thy passion as a thing of sentiment, nor make it a myth, nor view it as a dream of poetry. Thou shalt be in death most real to us, even as is that cup whereof we drink.

The dear memorials of our Lord's blood-shedding are intended for *a personal remembrance*. There is no Lord's Supper except as the wine touches the lip, and is received into the communicant's own self. All must partake. He says, 'Drink ye all of it.' You cannot take the Lord's Supper by deputy or representative; you must each of you approach the table, and personally eat and drink. Beloved, we *must* come into personal contact with the death of Christ. This is essential. We must each one say, 'He loved me, and gave himself for me.' In his blood you must be personally washed; by his blood you must be personally reconciled to God; through his blood you must personally have access to God; and by his blood you must personally overcome the enemy of your souls. As the Israelite's own door must be smeared with the blood of the Paschal lamb, so must you individually partake of the true Sacrifice, and know each one for himself the power of his redemption.

As it is personal, it is a charming fact that it is *a happy remembrance*. Our remembrance of Christ is chastened with repentance, but it is also perfumed with faith. The Lord's Supper is no funeral meal, but a festival; most fitly do we begin it with the giving of thanks, and close it with a hymn. It is by many called the 'Eucharist', or the giving of thanks: it is not a fast, but a feast. My happiest moments are spent with the King at his table, when his banner over me is love, the death of Christ is a well-spring of solemn joy. Before our great Sacrifice died, the best token of his death was the blood of bulls and of goats. See how the victims writhe in death! The sacrificial knife does terrible work at the foot of the altar; it is hard to stand by, and see the creatures bleed. After our Lord's death was over, the blood of animals was not the type, but the blood of the grape. That which was terrible in prospect is joyous in remembrance. That which was blood in the shedding is wine in the receiving. It came from him with a wound, but it comes to us with a blessing. His blood is our song in the house of our pilgrimage, and it shall add the best music to our heavenly harmonies as we sing before the throne: 'Unto him that hath loved us, and washed us from our sins in his own blood; to him be glory for ever and ever.' If our Lord Jesus has made the memory of his love to be more sweet than wine, let us never turn from it as though it had become a distasteful theme. Let us find our choicest pleasures at the cross.

Once more, our Saviour meant us to maintain the doctrine of his death, and the shedding of his blood for the remission of sins, even to the end of time, for he made it to be of *perpetual remembrance*. We drink this cup 'until he come'. If the Lord Jesus had foreseen with approbation the changes in religious thought which would be brought about by growing 'culture', he would surely have arranged a change of symbols to suit the change of doctrines. Would he not have warned us that, towards the end of the nineteenth century, men would become so 'enlightened' that the faith of Christendom must of necessity take a new departure, and therefore he had appointed a change of sacramental memorials? But he has not warned us of the coming of those eminently great and wise men who have changed all things, and abolished the old-fashioned truths for which martyrs died. Brethren, I do not believe in the wisdom of these men, and their changes I abhor; but had there been any ground for such changes, the Lord's Supper would not have been made of perpetual obligation. The perpetuity of ordinances indicates a perpetuity of doctrine. But hear the moderns talk – 'The Apostles, the Fathers, the Puritans, they were excellent men, no doubt, but then, you see, they lived before the uprise of those wonderful scientific men who have enlightened us so much.' Let me repeat what I have said. If we had come to a new point as to believing, should we not have come to a new point as to the ordinances in which those beliefs are embodied? I think so. The evident intent of Christ in giving us settled ordinances, and especially in settling this one which so clearly commemorates his blood-shedding, was that we might know that the truth of his sacrifice is for ever fixed and settled, and must unchangeably remain the essence of his gospel. Neither nineteen centuries, nor nineteen thousand centuries, can make the slightest difference in this truth, nor in the relative proportion of this truth to other truths, so long as this dispensation lasts. Until he comes a second time without a sin-offering unto salvation, the grand work of his first coming must be kept first and foremost in all our teaching, trusting, and testifying. As in the southern hemisphere the cross is the mariner's guide, so, under all skies, is the death of our Redeemer the polestar of our hope upon the sea of life. In life and in death we will glory in the cross of Christ, and never be ashamed of it, be we where we may.

II. Secondly, note well THE CONNECTION OF THE BLOOD OF CHRIST WITH THE COVENANT. Read the text again: 'This is my blood of the new testament.' The translation would be better, 'This is my blood of the covenant.'

What is this covenant? The covenant is that which I read to you just now in Jeremiah 31:33: 'This shall be the covenant that I will make with the house of Israel; After those days, saith the Lord, I will put my law in their inward parts, and write it in their hearts; and will be their God, and they shall be my people.' See also Jeremiah 32:40: 'And I will make an everlasting covenant with them, that I will not turn away from them, to do them good; but I will put my fear in their hearts; that they shall not depart from me.' Turn also to Ezekiel 11:19: 'I will put a new spirit within you; and I will take the stony heart out of their flesh, and will give them an heart of flesh.' Look in the same prophecy at 36:26: 'A new heart also will I give you, and a new spirit will I put within you: and I will take away the stony heart out of your flesh, and I will give you an heart of flesh.' What a Magna Charta is this! The old covenant saith, 'Keep the law and live.' The new covenant is, 'Thou shalt live, and I will lead thee to keep my law, for I will write it on thine heart.' Happy men who know their standing under this covenant! What has the blood of Jesus Christ to do with this covenant? It has everything to do with it, for the covenant could never have been made apart from the blood of Jesus. Atonement was taken for granted in the establishment of the covenant. No one else could have stood as our representative, to fulfil our side of the covenant, except the Lord Jesus Christ; and even he could only have performed that covenant by shedding his blood. In that cup you see the emblem of the blood which made the covenant possible.

Moreover, the blood of Jesus makes the covenant sure. His death has fulfilled man's side of the covenant, and God's part standeth sure. The stipulation of the covenant is fulfilled in Christ, and now the tenor of it is pure promise. Note how the 'shalls' and 'wills' follow each other in quick succession. An arrangement of absolute grace on God's part towards the undeserving sons of men is now in full action through the sacrifice of Christ.

This covenant of grace, when rightly understood, exerts a blessed influence over the minds of men conscious of sin. The chaplain of a jail, a dear friend of mine, once told me of a surprising case of conversion in which a knowledge of the covenant of grace was the chief instrument of the Holy Spirit. My friend had under his charge a man most cunning and brutal. He was singularly repulsive, even in comparison with other convicts. He had been renowned for his daring, and for the utter absence of all feeling when committing acts of violence. I think he had been called 'the king of the garrotters'. The chaplain had spoken to him several times, but had not succeeded even in getting an answer. The man was sullenly set against all instruction. At last he expressed a desire for a certain book, but as it was not in the library the chaplain pointed to the Bible, which was placed in his cell, and said, 'Did you ever read *that* Book?' He gave no answer, but looked at the good man as if he would kill him. The question was kindly repeated, with the assurance that he would find it well worth reading. 'Sir,' said the convict, 'you would not ask me such a question if you knew who I was. What have I to do with a Book of that sort?' He was told that his character was well known to the chaplain, and that for this very reason he recommended the Bible as a Book which would suit his case. 'It would do me no good', he cried, 'I am past all feeling.' Doubling up his fist he struck the iron door of the cell, and said, 'My heart is as hard as that iron; there is nothing in any book that will ever touch me.' 'Well,' said the chaplain, 'you want a new heart. Did you ever read of the covenant of grace?' To which the man answered sullenly by enquiring what he meant by such talk. His friend replied, 'Listen to these words – "A new heart also will I give you, and a new spirit will I put within you."' The words struck the man with amazement, as well they might; he asked to have the passage found for him in the Bible. He read the words again and again; and when the chaplain came back to him next day, the wild beast was tamed. 'Oh, sir,' he said, 'I never dreamed of such a promise! I never believed it possible that God would speak in such a way as that to men. If he gives me a new heart it will be a miracle of mercy; and yet I think', he said, 'he is going to work that miracle upon me, for the very hope of a new nature is beginning, to touch me as I never was touched before.' That man became gentle in manner, obedient to authority, and childlike in spirit. Though my friend has nothing left of the sanguine hopes he once entertained of converted criminals, he yet believes that in this case no observer could have questioned the thorough nature of the work, and yet the only means was the doctrine of the covenant. My rebellious heart is not affected by the fact that God commands me to do this or that; but when he declares free and full forgiveness, and goes on to promise love and favour, and renewal of nature, I feel broken down. How can I rebel against One who does such wonders in me, and designs such great things for me?

> Dissolved by his goodness, I fall to the ground
> And weep to the praise of the mercy I've found.

How dear and precious this makes the blood of Christ, since it is the blood of the everlasting covenant! Coming under this blessed covenant, we henceforth adore the fullness of that grace which, at the cost of the most precious of all lives, has made this arrangement for unworthy men. You will perhaps say to me, 'Why did our translators use the word "testament" in our Authorized Version?' They were hardly so wise as usual in this instance, for "covenant' is the better word of the two to set forth the original; but yet the idea of a testament is there also. The original may signify either or both. The word 'settlement', which has dropped out of use nowadays, was often employed by our Calvinistic forefathers when they spoke of the everlasting arrangement of grace. The word settlement might take in both covenant and testament – there is a covenant of grace, but the covenant stipulation being fulfilled by our Lord Jesus, the arrangement becomes virtually a testament, through which, by the will of God, countless blessings are secured to the heirs of salvation. The blood of Jesus is the seal of the covenant, and transforms its blessings into bequests of love, entailed upon believers. The settlement or arrangement, by which God can be just and yet the justifier of the ungodly, and can deal with believers, not on terms of law, but on terms of pure grace, is established by the sacrifice of our Lord. O my brethren, as God's covenanted ones, drink ye of the cup with joy, and renew your pledge with the Lord your God!

III. A third point comes up in the text very manifestly: THE BLOOD HAS AN INTIMATE CONNECTION WITH REMISSION. The text says, 'This is my blood of the new covenant, which is shed for many for the remission of sins.' Jesus suffering, bleeding, dying, has procured for sinners the forgiveness of their sins.

Of what sins? Of all sins of every sort and kind, however heinous, aggravated, and multiplied. The blood of the covenant takes every sin away, be it what it may; there was never a sin believingly confessed and taken to Christ that ever baffled his power to cleanse it. This fountain has never been tried in vain. Murderers, thieves, liars, adulterers, and what not, have come to Jesus by penitence and faith, and through the merit of his sacrifice their sins have been put away.

Of what nature is the remission? It is pardon, freely given, acting immediately, and abiding for ever, so that there is no fear of the guilt ever being again laid to the charge of the forgiven one. Through the precious blood our sins are blotted out, cast into the depths of the sea, and removed as far from us as the east is from the west. Our sins cease to be, they are made an end of; they cannot be found against us any more for ever. Yes, hear it, hear it, O wide earth! Let the glad news startle thy darkest dens of infamy, there is absolute remission of sins! The precious blood of Christ cleanseth from all sin: yes, turns the scarlet into a whiteness which exceeds that of the newly-fallen snow – a whiteness which never can be tarnished. Washed by Jesus, the blackest of sinners shall appear before the judgment-seat of the all-seeing Judge without spot.

How is it the blood of Jesus effects this? The secret lies in the vicarious or substitutionary character of our Lord's suffering and death. Because he stood in our place the justice of God is vindicated, and the threatening of the law is fulfilled. It is now just for God to pardon sin. Christ's bearing the penalty of human sin instead of men has made the moral government of God perfect in justice, has laid a basis for peace of conscience, and has rendered sin immeasurably hateful, though its punishment does not fall upon the believer. This is the great secret, this is the heavenly news, the gospel of salvation, that through the blood of Jesus sin is justly put away. Oh, how my very soul loves this truth! Therefore do I speak it in unmistakable terms.

And for what end is this remission of sins secured? My brethren, if there were no other end for the remission of sins but its own self, it would be a noble purpose, and it would be worth preaching every day of our lives; but it does not end here. We mistake if we think that the pardon of sins is God's ultimatum. No, no; it is but a beginning, a means to a further purpose. He forgives our sins with the design of curing our sinfulness. We are pardoned that we may become holy. God forgives the sin that he may purify the sinner. If he had not aimed at thy holiness, there had not been so imperative a necessity for an atonement; but to impress thee with the guilt of sin, to make thee feel the evil which sin hath wrought, to let thee know thine obligation to divine love, the Lord has not forgiven thee without a sacrifice.

Ah, what a sacrifice! He aims at the death of thy sinfulness, that thou mayest henceforth love him, and serve him, and crucify the lusts which crucified thy Lord. The Lord aims at working in thee the likeness of his dear Son. Jesus hath saved thee by his self-sacrificing obedience to justice, that thou mayest yield thy whole soul to God, and be willing to die for the upholding of the kingdom of love and truth. The death of Christ for thee pledges thee to be dead to sin, that by his resurrection from the dead thou mayest rise into newness of life, and so become like thy Lord. Pardon by blood aims at this. Dost thou catch the thought? If thou believest in the Lord Jesus Christ, God's intent is to make thee like the Firstborn among many brethren, and to work in thee everything that is comely and of good report. Even this is not all: he hath a further design to bring thee into everlasting fellowship with himself. He is sanctifying thee, that thou mayest behold his face, and that thou mayest be fit to be a comrade of his only-begotten Son throughout eternity. Thou art to be the choice and dear companion of the Lord of love. He has a throne for thee, a mansion and a crown for thee, and an immortality of such inconceivable glory and blessedness that, if thou didst but form even a distant conception of it, no golden apple of earth would turn thee aside from pursuing the prize of thy high calling. Oh, to be for ever with the Lord! For ever to behold his face!

I fail to reach the height of this great argument! See, my brethren, to what the blood of your Lord destines you. O my soul, bless God for that one cup, which reminds thee of the great sacrifice, and prophesies to thee thy glory at the right hand of God for ever!

IV. I cannot forget to notice, in closing, THE CONNECTION OF THE BLOOD WITH MEN. We are told in the text that this blood is shed *'for many* for the remission of sins'. In that large word 'many' let us exceedingly rejoice. Christ's blood was not shed for the handful of apostles alone. There were but eleven of them who really partook of the blood symbolized by the cup. The Saviour does not say, 'This is my blood which is shed for you, the favoured eleven'; but 'shed for many'. Jesus did not die for the clergy alone. I recollect in Martin Luther's life that he saw, in one of the Romish churches, a picture of the Pope, and the cardinals, and bishops, and priests, and monks, and friars, all on board a ship. They were all safe, every one of them. As for the laity, poor wretches, they were struggling in the sea, and many of them drowning. Only those were saved to whom the good men in the ship were so kind as to hand out a rope or a plank. That is not our Lord's teaching: his blood is shed 'for many', and not for the few. He is not the Christ of a caste, or a class, but the Christ of all conditions of men. His blood is shed for many sinners, that their sins may be remitted. Those in the upper room were all Jews, but the Lord Jesus Christ said to them, 'This blood is shed for *many*', to let them see that he did not die alone for the seed of Abraham, but for all races of men that dwell upon the face of the earth. 'Shed for many'. His eye, I doubt not, glanced at these far-off islands, and at the vast lands beyond the western sea. He thought of Africa, and India, and the land of China. A multitude that no man can number gladdened the far-seeing and foreseeing eye of the Redeemer. He spoke with joyful emphasis when he said, 'shed for many for the remission of sins.' Believe in the immeasurable results of redemption. Whenever we are making arrangements for the preaching of this precious blood, let us make them on a large scale. The mansion of love should be built for a large family. Let us not sing –

> We are a garden walled around
> Pray keep the walls most tight and sound.

Let us expect to see large numbers brought within the sacred enclosure. We must yet break forth on the right hand and on the left. The masses must be compelled to come in. This blood is shed for many. A group of half-a-dozen converts makes us very glad, and so it should; but oh, to have half-a-dozen thousand at once! Why not? This blood is shed 'for many'. Let us cast the great net into the sea. You young men, preach the gospel in the streets of this crowded city, for it is meant for many! You who go from door to door, do not think you can be too hopeful, since your Saviour's blood is shed for many, and Christ's 'many' is a very great many. It is shed for all who ever shall believe in him – shed for thee, sinner, if thou wilt now trust him. Only confess thy sin, and trust Christ, and be assured that Jesus died in thy place and stead. It is shed for many so that no man or woman born shall ever trust Christ in vain, or find the atonement insufficient for him. Oh, for a large-hearted faith, so that by holy effort we may lengthen our cords, and strengthen our stakes, expecting to see the household of our Lord become exceeding numerous! He shall see of the travail of his soul, and shall be satisfied; by his righteousness shall he justify many, for he shall bear their iniquities. Dwell on that word 'many', and let it nerve you for far-reaching labours.

V. Now note THE CONNECTION OF THE BLOOD WITH OURSELVES. Dear hearer, are you among the many? Why are you not? May his grace bring you to trust in him, and you may not doubt that you are among the many. 'Ah,' say you, 'that is what I am listening for! How can I partake in the effect of this sacrifice?' Seest thou that wine-cup which I set before thee just now? How art thou to enjoy that wine which fills the cup? Its ruddy drops, how are they to be thine? The matter is very simple. I think I see thee take the chalice in thine hand, and raise it to thy mouth. Thou drinkest, and the deed is done. This is no mystery. Bread and wine are ours by eating and drinking. Christ is ours by our receiving him. The merit of his precious blood becomes ours by that simple child-like faith which accepts Jesus to be our all. We say, 'Here it is; I believe in it; I take it; I accept it as my own.' It is yours. No man can take from you that which you have eaten and drunk. Christ is yours for ever if you receive him into your heart.

If you have any question as to whether you have drunk, I will tell you how to solve it – *drink again!* If you have been eating, and you have really forgotten whether you have eaten or not – such things do occur to busy men, who eat but little; if, I say, you would be sure that you have eaten, *eat again!* If thou wilt be assured that thou hast believed in Jesus, believe again! Whenever thou hast any doubt about whether Christ is thine, take him over again. I like to begin again. Often I find the best way of going forward is to go back to my first faith in Jesus and as a sinner renew my confidence in my Saviour. 'Oh,' says the devil, 'thou art a preacher of the gospel, but thou dost not know it thyself.' At one time I used to argue with the accuser; but he is not worth it, and it is by no means profitable to one's own heart. We cannot convert or convince the devil; it is better to refer him to our Lord. When he tells me I am not a saint, I answer, 'Well, what am I, then?' 'A sinner', says he. 'Well, so are you!' 'Ah!' saith he, 'You will be lost.' 'No,' say I, 'that is why I shall not be lost, since Jesus Christ came into the world to save sinners, and I therefore trust in him to save me.' This is what Martin Luther calls cutting the devil's head off with his own sword, and it is the best course you can follow.

You say, 'If I take Christ to myself as a man takes a cup and drink the contents, am I saved?' Yes, thou art. 'How am I to know it?' Know it because God says so. 'He that believeth in him hath everlasting life.' If I did not feel a pulse of that life (as I did not at first), I nevertheless would believe that I had it, simply on the strength of the divine assurance. Since my conversion I have felt the pulsings of a life more strong and forcible than the life of the most vigorous youth that ever ran without weariness; but there are times when it is not so. Just now I feel the heavenly life joyously leaping within me, but when I do not feel it, I fall back on this: God has said 'He that believeth in him hath everlasting life.' God's words against all my feelings! I may get into a fainting fit, and my circumstances may operate upon my heart, as this hot weather operates upon my body, and make me feel dull and sleepy, but this cannot make the word of God of none effect. I go back to the Book, and believe the bare word of the Lord, 'He that believeth in him *hath* everlasting life.' That is enough for me. I believe, and therefore I live. Our inward experience is fine corroborative evidence, but God's testimony is the best foundation our confidence can have.

I recollect a story told of William Dawson, whom our Wesleyan friends used to call Billy Dawson, one of the best preachers that ever entered a pulpit. He once gave out as his text, 'Through this man is preached unto you the forgiveness of sins.' When he had given out his text he dropped down to the bottom of the pulpit, so that nothing could be seen of him, only there was a voice heard saying, 'Not the man in the pulpit, he is out of sight, but the Man in the Book. The Man described in the Book is the Man through whom is preached unto you the forgiveness of sins.' I put myself and you, and everybody else out of sight, and I preach to you the remission of sins through Jesus only. I would sing with the children, 'Nothing but the blood of Jesus.' Shut your eyes to all things but the cross. Jesus died, and rose again, and went to heaven, and all your hope must go with him! Come, my hearer, take Jesus by a distinct act of faith this morning! May God the Holy Ghost constrain thee to do so, and then thou mayest go on thy way rejoicing! So be it in the name of Jesus.

5

SORROW AT THE CROSS TURNED INTO JOY[1]

'Verily, verily, I say unto you, That ye shall weep and lament,
but the world shall rejoice: and ye shall be sorrowful, but your
sorrow shall be turned into joy. A woman when she is in travail
hath sorrow, because her hour is come: but as soon as she is
delivered of the child, she remembereth no more the anguish,
for joy that a man is born into the world. And ye now therefore have sorrow: but I will see you again, and your heart shall
rejoice, and your joy no man taketh from you.'

JOHN 16:20–22

WE WERE SINGING JUST NOW a hymn in which the first verse
started a difficult question:

> 'It is finish'd'; shall we raise
> Songs of sorrow, or of praise?
> Mourn to see the Saviour die,
> Or proclaim his victory?

The case is very well argued in the second and third verses:

> If of Calvary we tell,
> How can songs of triumph swell?
> If of man redeem'd from woe,
> How shall notes of mourning flow?
>
> Ours the guilt which pierced his side,
> Ours the sin for which he died;

---

[1] Sermon No. 1,442. Preached at the Metropolitan Tabernacle on Sunday
morning, 3 November 1878.

> But the blood which flow'd that day
> Wash'd our sin and guilt away.

The conclusion at which we arrived in the concluding verse seems to me to be the right one:

> Lamb of God! Thy death hath given
> Pardon, peace, and hope of heaven:
> 'It is finish'd'; let us raise
> Songs of thankfulness and praise!

The chief thought connected with the Redeemer's death should be that of grateful praise. That our Lord Jesus Christ died upon the cross is a very natural cause for sorrow, and well may they who pierced him, and we are all among the number, look unto him and mourn for their sin, and be in bitterness for him as one that is in bitterness for his firstborn. Before we know that we are pardoned our grief may well be exceeding heavy, for till sin is put away we stand guilty of the Saviour's blood. While our souls are only conscious of our guilty share in the Redeemer's blood, we may well stand aghast at the sight of the accursed tree, but the case is altered when by faith we discern the glorious fruit of our Lord's sufferings, and know that on the cross he saved us and triumphed in the deed. The feeling of sorrow at the sight of the crucified Saviour is one to be cultivated up to a certain point, especially if we take care to avoid mere sentiment and turn our grief into repentance: then it is 'godly sorrow', which worketh after a godly sort, and it is likely to create in us an intense horror of sin, and a strong determination to purge ourselves from all fellowship with the works of darkness. We do not therefore condemn those who frequently preach upon the sufferings of our Lord, with the view of exciting emotions of grief in the hearts of their hearers, for such emotions have a softening and sanctifying influence if attended by faith, and directed by sound wisdom.

There is, however, a middle path in everything, and this needs to be followed, for we believe that such preaching may be carried too far. It is most remarkable and instructive that the apostles do not appear in their sermons or epistles to have spoken of the death of our Lord with any kind of regret. The gospels mention their distress during the actual occurrence of the crucifixion, but after the resurrection, and especially after Pentecost, we hear of no such grief. I can scarcely find a passage from which I could preach a sermon upon sorrow on account of the death of Jesus, if I confine myself to the sayings and writings of the apostles; on the contrary, there are many expressions which treat of the crucifixion in the spirit of exulting joy. Remember the well-known exclamation of Paul – 'God forbid that I should glory save in the cross of our Lord Jesus Christ.' He had, no doubt, as vivid an idea of the agonies of our Lord as any of us have ever attained, and yet, instead of saying, 'God forbid that I should cease to weep at the sight of my crucified Master', he declares that he glories in his cross. The death of Jesus was to him a thing to rejoice in, and even to glory in; he kept no black fasts to commemorate the world's redemption. Note well the exalted key in which he speaks of our Lord's death in the epistle to the Colossians: 'Blotting out the handwriting of ordinances that was against us, which was contrary to us, and took it out of the way, nailing it to his cross; and having spoiled principalities and powers, he made a show of them openly, triumphing over them in it.' When you turn to John's epistles, where most of all pathos and tenderness would naturally abound, you hear no weeping and wailing, but he speaks of the cleansing blood, which is the very centre of the great sacrifice, in a calm, quiet, happy manner, which is far removed from bursting grief and flowing tears. He says, 'If we walk in the light, as he is in the light, we have fellowship one with another, and the blood of Jesus Christ his Son cleanseth us from all sin.' This allusion to the blood of atonement rather suggests joy and peace than woe and agony. 'This is he', saith John, 'that came by water and blood, even Jesus Christ; not by water only, but by water and blood'; and it is evidently to him a theme of congratulation and delight rather than a cause for sorrow that Jesus did come by blood as well as by water. So Peter, also, when he mentions the death of his Lord and Master, speaks of 'the precious blood of Christ', but not in words of sadness, and he describes our Lord's bearing our sins in his own body on the tree, but not in the language of lament. He says of those who suffered for the gospel, 'Rejoice, inasmuch as ye are partakers in Christ's sufferings.' Now, if he finds joy in those sufferings of ours which are in fellowship with the sufferings of Christ, much more I gather did he find ground for rejoicing in the sufferings of Christ himself. I do not believe that the 'three hours' agony', the darkened church, the altar in mourning, the tolling of a bell, and all the other mock funereal rites of superstition derive even the least encouragement from the spirit and language of the apostles. Those practical charades in which the crucifixion is mimicked in many churches on Good Friday are more worthy of the heathen women weeping for Thammuz, or of Baal's priests crying and cutting themselves with knives, than of a Christian assembly who know that the Lord is not here, for he is risen. Let us mourn by all means, for Jesus died; but by no means let us make mourning the prominent thought in connection with his death, if we have obtained thereby the pardon of our sins.

The language of our text allowed and yet forbade sorrow; it gave permission to weep, but only for a little while, and then it forbade all further weeping by the promise to turn the sorrow into joy. 'Ye shall weep and lament', that is, his disciples, while he was dying, and dead and buried, would be sorely distressed. 'And ye shall be sorrowful, but your sorrow shall be turned into joy'; their grief would end when they saw him risen from the dead; and so it did, for we read, 'Then were the disciples glad when they saw the Lord.' The sight of the cross to their unbelief was sadness, and sadness only, but now to the eye of faith it is the gladdest sight that ever the human eye can rest upon; the cross is as the light of the morning, which ends the long and dreary darkness which covered the nations. Oh, wounds of Jesus, ye are as stars, breaking the night of man's despair. Oh, spear, thou hast opened the fountain of healing for mortal woe. Oh, crown of thorns, thou art a constellation of promises. Eyes that were red with weeping sparkle with hope at the sight of thee, O bleeding Lord. As for thy tortured body, O Emmanuel, the blood which dropped therefrom cried from the ground, and proclaimed peace, pardon, and paradise to all believers. Though laid in the grave by thy weeping friends, thy body, O divine Saviour, is no longer in Joseph's tomb, for thou art risen from the dead, and we find in the songs of resurrection and ascension an abundant solace for the griefs of thy death. Like a woman to whom a son is born, we forget the travail for the joy of the glorious birth which the church and the world may now gaze upon with the utmost delight as they behold in Jesus 'the firstborn from the dead'.

The subject for this morning, then, you will readily guess is, how far we should sorrow for the death of Jesus, and how much further we are permitted to rejoice therein. The first point will be, *the death of our Lord was and still is a theme for sorrow*; but secondly, *that sorrow is transmuted into joy*. When we have meditated upon these two points we shall for a little space notice *a general principle which underlies all holy sorrow* as well as this particular form of it.

I. First, then, THE DEATH OF OUR LORD WAS AND IS A THEME FOR SORROW. I make a point of saying it was so, because during the three days of the Saviour's burial there was more cause for distress than there can be now that he is risen. To the disciples first of all the death of Jesus was *the loss of his personal presence*. It was a great delight to that little family to have the Lord always among them as their father and their teacher, and it was a great grief to think that they should no more hear his loving voice, or catch the smile of his benignant countenance. It brought untold comforts to them to be able to go to him with all their questions, to fly to him in every moment of difficulty, to resort to him in every hour of sorrow. Happy, happy disciples to have such a Master always in their midst, communing with them in love, guiding them by his perfect example, animating them by his glorious presence, relieving all their wants and guarding them from all ills. Do you wonder that their hearts were heavy at the prospect of his going away from them? They felt that they would be sheep without a shepherd: orphan children bereft of their best friend and helper. Do you wonder, I say, that they wept and lamented when the Rock of their confidence, the delight of their eyes, the hope of their souls, was taken from them? What would you think if your best earthly friend was hurried away from you by a shameful death? They sorrowed not only because of their own personal loss by his removal, but because he himself was very dear to them. They could not bear that he should be gone in whom their hearts centred all their affection. Their sorrow showed that their hearts were loyal to their Beloved, and would never receive another occupant to sit upon the throne of their affections. They wept and they lamented because their bosom's Lord was gone and his seat was empty. They could not endure the absence of their best Beloved. As pines the dove for its mate, so mourned they for him whom their soul loved. Whom had they in heaven if Jesus were gone? Certainly there was none upon earth that they could desire beside him. They were widowed, and they wept and refused to be comforted. Nothing could compensate them for Jesus' absence, for he was their all in all. For his sake they had left all and followed him, and now they cannot bear that they should lose him, and so lose more than all. You who have been bereaved of those whom you have dearly loved, and deeply revered, will be able to guess what kind of sorrow filled the hearts of the disciples when their Beloved said that he was about to go from them, and that they would not see him for awhile. This mourning was natural; and it is natural that we also should feel some regret that our Lord is away from us now, as to his bodily presence, though I trust we have by this time learned to see the expediency of his absence, and are so satisfied with it that we patiently wait, and quietly hope until his next appearing.

It added greatly to the disciples' sorrow that *the world would be rejoicing because their Lord was gone.* 'The world shall rejoice.' His eager enemies would hasten him off to Pilate's judgment-seat, and triumph when they forced an unwilling sentence from that time-serving ruler. They would rejoice when they saw him bearing his cross along the way of dolours. They would stand around the cross and mock him with their cruel gazes and with their ribald speeches, and when he was dead they would say, 'This deceiver can speak no more; we have triumphed over him who set our pretensions at nought, and exposed us before the people.' They thought that they had quenched the light which had proved painful to their darkened eyes, and therefore they were glad, and by their gladness swelled the torrent of the disciples' sorrow. Brethren, you know when you are in pain or in sorrow yourselves, how very bitter is the coarse laugh of an adversary who exults over your misery and extracts mirth from your tears. This made the disciples smart at their Lord's death. Why should the wicked rejoice over him? Why should the scornful Pharisee and priest insult over his dead body? This rubbed salt into the wounds of the downcast disciples, and infused a double gall and wormwood into the cup which was bitter enough already. You do not wonder, therefore, that they wept and lamented when their Lord was put to death by wicked hands. Magdalene weeping at the sepulchre acted as her gracious nature prompted her, and she was a fair sample of all the rest.

They had this also to make them sorrowful, that *his death was for a time the disappointment of all their hopes.* They at first had fondly looked for a kingdom – a temporal kingdom, such as their brother Jews expected. Even when our Lord had moderated their expectations and enlightened their views, so that they did not quite so much look for an actual temporal sovereignty, yet still that thought that 'this was he that would have restored the kingdom to Israel' lingered with them. If any of them were so enlightened as to believe in a spiritual kingdom, as perhaps some of them were in a measure, yet by Jesus' death it must have seemed that all their hopes were shattered. Without a leader, how could they succeed? How could a kingdom be set up when the King himself was slain? He who has been by cowardly hands betrayed, how can he reign? He that was to be the King has been spat upon and mocked, and nailed up like a felon to the gibbet of wood – where is his dominion? He is cut off out of the land of the living, who will now serve him? Clay cold his body lies in Joseph's tomb, and a seal is set upon the stone which shuts up the sepulchre; is there not an end of holy hopes, a final close to all holy ambitions? How can they be happy who have seen an end of their fairest life-dream? Poor followers of the dead monarch, how can they have hope for his cause and crown? Doubtless in their unbelief they sorrowed deeply because their hope seemed blasted and their faith o'erturned. They knew so little of the meaning of the present, and guessed so little of what the future would be, that sorrow filled their hearts, and they were ready to perish.

You must remember that added to this was *the sight which many of them had of their beloved Master in his agonies.* Who would not grieve to see him hurried away at dead of night from holy retirement to be falsely accused? Might not angels wish to weep in sympathy with him? Who can forbear to sorrow when Jesus stands insulted by menials, reviled by abjects, forsaken by his friends, blasphemed by his foes. It was enough to make a man's heart break to see the Lamb of God so roughly handled. Who can endure to see the innocent Saviour nailed up there in the midst of a scornful crew? Who could endure to see his pangs as they were mirrored in his countenance, or to hear his sorrows as they expressed themselves in his painful cries of 'I thirst', and in the still sharper agonising exclamation, 'My God, my God, why hast thou forsaken me?' It is little marvel that it was said of the Virgin that the sword pierced through her heart, for surely there was never sorrow like unto Jesus' sorrow, nor grief which could be likened unto his grief. His heavy woes must have pierced through the heart of all right-minded men who beheld his unexampled miseries; and especially must all personal lovers of Christ have felt ready to die themselves when they saw him thus put to death. Oh deeps of sorrow which my Lord has suffered, shall there be no deeps to answer to you? When all God's waves and billows go over thee, O Jesus, shall not we be plunged into sorrow also? Yes, verily, we will drink of thy cup and be baptized with thy baptism. We will now sit down before thy cross and watch with thee one hour, while love and grief conjointly occupy our souls.

Now, even at the recollection of what our Lord endured, every Christian feels sympathy with him. You cannot read the four stories of the Evangelists, and weave them into one by imagination and affection, without feeling that the minor key befits your voice at such a time, if you at all attempt to sing. There must be, it is natural that there should be, sorrow because Christ has died.

One of the sharpest points about our sorrow at Jesus' death is this – that *we were the cause of it*. We virtually crucified the Lord, seeing it was because we were sinners that he must needs be made a sacrifice. Had none of us gone astray like lost sheep, then our wanderings would not have been gathered up and laid upon the shepherd's head. The sword which pierced his heart through and through was forged by our offences: the vengeance was due for sins which we had committed, and justice exacted its rights at his hands. What loving disciple will refuse to sorrow when he sees that he himself has put his Lord to death?

Now, putting all these things together, I think I see abundant reason why the disciples should be sorrowful, and why they should even express their sorrow by weeping and lamenting. They sorrowed as those do who attend a funeral: for weeping and lamenting abound at eastern funerals. Orientals are much more demonstrative than we are, and therefore at the deaths of relatives they make a far greater show of grief by loud cries and flowing tears. The disciples are represented as using the same forcible expressions to set forth their woe – 'Ye shall weep and lament', a woe worthy of the buried One whom they mourned. 'Ye shall weep and lament': there was a double vent for a double sorrow, eyes wept and voices lamented. Christ's death was a true funeral to his followers, and caused a crushing sorrow as much as if they had each one been bereft of all his house. Who marvels that it was so?

'Sorrow hath filled your hearts', says Christ: they had no room to think of anything else but his death. Their heart was full to bursting with grief because he was taken from them, and that grief was so sharp as to be likened to one of the keenest pangs which nature is capable of bearing, the pangs of a travailing woman, pangs which seem as if they must bring death with them, and compared with which death itself might be a relief. The sharpness of their anguish in the hour of their trial was all that they could bear, more would have destroyed them. All this they felt, and it is no wonder if we feel in degree as they did when we take a retrospect of what the Saviour endured on our behalf. So far we are bound to concede that the death of our Lord worketh sorrow: but there is a moderation even in the most justifiable mourning, and we are not to indulge excessive grief even at the foot of the cross, lest it degenerate into folly.

II. Now, secondly, the truth taught expressly in the text is that THIS SORROW IS CHANGED INTO JOY. 'Your sorrow shall be turned into joy.' Not exchanged for joy, but actually transmuted, so that the grief becomes joy, the cause of sorrow becomes the source of rejoicing.

Begin with what I said was a very sharp point of this sorrow, and you will see at once how it is turned into joy. That Jesus Christ died for our sins is a sharp sorrow: we lament that our crimes became the nails and our unbelief the spear: and yet, my brethren, *this is the greatest joy of all*. If each one of us can say, 'He loved me, and gave himself for me', we are truly happy. If you know by personal faith that Jesus took your sin and suffered for it on the tree, so that now your debt is paid and your transgression is blotted out for ever by his precious blood, you do not want half-a-dozen words from me to indicate that this, which was the centre of your grief, is also the essence of your joy. What were it to us if he had saved all the rest of mankind if he had not redeemed us unto God by his blood? We might have been glad from sheer humanity that others should be benefited, but what would have been our deep regret to be ourselves excluded from the grace. Blessed be the Saviour's name, we are not excepted: in proportion as we repentantly upbraid ourselves for Jesus' death in that same measure may we believingly exult in the fact that his sacrifice has for ever put away our sins, and therefore being justified by faith we have peace with God through our Lord Jesus Christ. Because God hath condemned sin in the flesh of Jesus Christ, therefore he will no more condemn us; but we are henceforth free, that the righteousness of the law may be fulfilled in us who walk not after the flesh but after the Spirit. Heartily do we lament our sin, but we do not lament that Christ has put it away nor lament the death by which he put it away; rather do our hearts rejoice in all his atoning agonies, and glory at every mention of that death by which he has reconciled us unto God. 'Tis a sad thought that we committed the sin which burdened our Lord, but it is a joy to think that he has taken on himself our personal sin and carried it right away.

The next point of joy is that *Jesus Christ has now suffered all that was required of him*. That he should suffer was cause for grief, but that he has now suffered all is equal cause for joy. When a champion returns from the wars bearing the scars of conflict by which he gained his honours, does anyone lament over his campaigns? When he left the castle his wife hung about his neck and mourned that her lord must go to the wars, to bleed and perhaps to die; but when he returns with sounding trumpet and banner held aloft, bringing his trophies with him, honoured and exalted by reason of his victories in many lands, do his dearest friends regret his toils and sufferings? Do they keep fasts correspondent to the days in which he was covered with the sweat and dust of battle? Do they toll a bell on the anniversary of his conflict?

Do they weep over the scars which are still upon him? Do they not glory in them as honourable memorials of his valour? They reckon that the marks the hero bears in his flesh are the noblest insignia of his glory, and the best tokens of his prowess. So let us not grieve today that Jesus' hands were pierced; behold they are now 'as gold rings set with the beryl'. Let us not lament that his feet were nailed to the tree, for his legs are now as 'pillars of marble set upon sockets of fine gold'. The face more marred than that of any man is now the more lovely for its marring, and he himself, despite his agonies, is now endowed with a beauty, which even the ravished spouse in the song could only describe as 'altogether lovely'. The mighty love which enabled him to endure his mighty passion has impressed upon him charms altogether inconceivable in their sweetness. Let us not mourn, then, for the agony is all over now, and he is none the worse for having endured it. There is no cross for him now, except in the sense that the cross honours and glorifies him; there remains for him no cruel spear nor crown of thorns now, except that from these he derives a revenue of honour and titles ever new, which exult him higher and yet higher in the love of his saints. Glory be unto God, Christ has not left a pang un-suffered of all his substitutionary sorrows; of our dread ransom price he has paid the utmost farthing. The atoning griefs have all been endured, the cup of wrath is drunk quite dry, and because of this we, with all the hosts above, will rejoice for ever and ever.

We are glad, not only that the hour of travail is over, but that *our Lord has survived his pains*. He died a real death, but now he lives a real life, he did lie in the tomb, and it was no fiction that the breath had departed from him: it is equally no fiction that our Redeemer liveth. The Lord is risen indeed. He hath survived the death struggle and the agony, and he lives unhurt: he has come out of the furnace without so much as the smell of fire upon him. He is not injured in any faculty; whether human or divine. He is not robbed of any glory, but his name is now surrounded with brighter lustre than ever. He has lost no dominion, he claims superior rights and rules over a new empire. He is a gainer by his losses, he has risen by his descent. All along the line he is victorious at every point. Never yet was there a victory won but what it was in some respects a loss as well as a gain, but our Lord's triumph is unmingled glory – to himself a gain as well as to us who share in it. Shall we not then rejoice? What, would ye sit and weep by a mother as she exultingly shows her new-born child? Would you call together a company of mourners to lament and to bewail when the heir is born into the household? This were to mock the mother's gladness. And so today shall we use dreary music and sing dolorous hymns when the Lord is risen, and is not only unhurt, unharmed, and unconquered, but is far more glorified and exalted than before his death? He hath gone into the glory because all his work is done, shall not your sorrow be turned into joy in the most emphatic sense?

And there is this to add to it, that *the grand end which his death was meant to accomplish is all attained*. What was that end? I may divide it into three parts.

It was *the putting away of sin by the sacrifice of himself*, and that is complete. He hath finished transgression, he hath made an end of sin; he hath taken the whole load of the sin of his elect and hurled it into the bottomless abyss; if it be searched for it shall not be found, yea, it shall not be, saith the Lord. He hath put away our sin as far from us as the east is from the west, and he has risen again to prove that all for whom he died are justified in him.

A second purpose was *the salvation of his chosen*, and that salvation is secured. When he died and rose again the salvation of all that were in him was placed beyond all hazard. He hath redeemed us unto God by his blood by an effectual redemption. None shall be enslaved who were by him redeemed; none shall be left in sin or cast into hell whose names are graven on the palms of his hands. He has gone into glory, carrying their names upon his heart, and he stands pleading there for them, and therefore he is able to save them to the uttermost. 'I will', saith he, 'that they whom thou hast given me be with me where I am, that they may behold my glory', and that effectual plea secures their being with him and like him when the end shall be.

The grand object, however, of his death was *the glory of God*, and truly God is glorified in the death of his Son, beyond anything that was known before or since; for here the very heart of God is laid open to the inspection of all believing eyes – his justice and his love, his stern severity which will not pass by sin without atonement, and his boundless love that gives his best self, his darling from his bosom, that he may bleed and die in our stead:

> Here depths of wisdom shine,
> Which angels cannot trace
> The highest rank of cherubim
> Still lost in wonder gaze.

Yes, O Christ of God, 'It is finished.' Thou hast done all thou didst intend to do, the whole of thy design is achieved, not one purpose hath failed, nor even one part of it fallen through, and therefore shall we not rejoice? The child is born; shall we not be glad? The travail would have been a subject for great grief had the mother died, or had the child perished in the birth: but now that all is over, and all is well, why should we remember any more the anguish? Jesus lives, and his great salvation makes glad the sons of men. Wherefore should we tune the mournful string and mourn sore like doves? No! Ring out the clarion, for the battle is fought and the victory is won for ever. Victory, *Victory*, VICTORY! His own right hand and his holy arm hath gotten him the victory! Though the champion died in the conflict, yet in his death he slew death and destroyed him that had the power of death, that is, the devil. Our glorious Champion has risen from his fall, for he could not be holden by the bands of death. He hath smitten his enemies, but, as for himself, he hath come up from the grave, he hath risen as from the heart of the sea. Let us exult like Israel at the Red Sea when Pharaoh was overthrown! With timbrel and dance let the daughters of Israel go forth to sing unto the Lord, for he hath triumphed gloriously, and utterly destroyed all our adversaries.

We have not yet completed this work of changing sorrow into joy till we notice that *now the greatest possible blessings accrue to us, because he was made a curse for us.* Through his death come pardon, reconciliation, access, acceptance: his blood 'speaketh better things than that of Abel', and invokes all heaven's blessings upon our heads.

But Jesus is not dead. He is risen, and that resurrection brings justification, and the safeguard of his perpetual plea in heaven. It brings us his representative presence in glory, and the making all things ready for us in the many mansions: it brings us a share in that 'all power which is given unto him in heaven and in earth', in the strength of which he bids us go and teach all nations, baptizing them into his sacred name. Beloved, Pentecost comes to us because Jesus went away from us; the gifts of the Holy Spirit – illuminating, comforting, quickening the power to proclaim the word, and the might which attends that word – all have come to us because he is no longer with us, but through the regions of the dead has passed to reach his crown.

And now today we have this great joy again that because he died there is a kingdom set up in the world, a kingdom which never can be moved, a kingdom whose power lies in weakness, and yet it is irresistible: a kingdom whose glory lies in suffering, and yet it cannot be crushed: a kingdom of love, a kingdom of unselfishness, a kingdom of kindness, truth, purity, holiness, and happiness. Jesus wears the imperial purple of a kingdom in which God loves men and men love God: having proved himself the prince of self-sacrificing love he is justly exalted to the throne amid the acclamations of all his saints. His kingdom, shapeless as it looks to carnal eyes, like a stone cut out of a mountain without hands, will, nevertheless, break all the kingdoms of this world to shivers in due time, and fill the whole earth.

His kingdom will grow and extend till from a handful of corn upon the top of the mountains its fruit shall so increase that it shall shake like Lebanon; a kingdom which shall comprehend all ranks and conditions of men, men of all colours, of all lands and nations, encircling all even as the ocean surrounds many lands. The unsuffering kingdom of the suffering shepherd, inaugurated by his death, established by his resurrection, extended by the Pentecostal descent of the Holy Ghost, and secured by the eternal covenant, is hastening on. Every winged hour brings it nearer to its perfect manifestation. Yes, the kingdom comes: the kingdom whose foundation was laid in the blood of its King at Calvary. Happy are they who are helping it on, for when the Lord shall be revealed they also shall be manifested with him. The Chief among ten thousand and the ten thousand who were with him shall stand side by side in the day of victory, even as they stood side by side in the hour of strife. Then, indeed, our sorrow shall be turned into joy.

There we must leave the subject, only noticing this one fact, that that joy is right hearty joy. 'Your hearts shall rejoice', said the Saviour ours is no superficial mirth, but heart-deep bliss. That joy is also abiding joy. 'Your joy no man taketh from you.' No, nor devil either. Nor time nor eternity can rob us of it. At the foot of the cross there wells up a flashing, sparkling fountain of joy, which never can be dried up, but must flow on for ever; in summer and in winter shall it be, and none shall be able to keep us back from the living flood, but we shall drink to the full for ever and ever.

III. And, now, my last point is to be THE GENERAL PRINCIPLE INVOLVED IN THIS ONE PARTICULAR INSTANCE.

The general principle is this, *that in connection with Christ you must expect to have sorrow.* 'You shall weep and lament, but the world shall rejoice.' But whatever sorrow you feel in connection with Jesus there is this consolation – *the pangs are all birth-pangs, they are all the necessary preliminaries of an ever-increasing, abounding joy.* Brethren, since you have come to know Christ you have felt a smarter grief on account of sin. Let it continue with you, for it is working holiness in you, and holiness is happiness. You have felt of late a keener sensibility on account of the sins of those around you: do not wish to be deprived of it. It will be the means of your loving them more, praying more for them, and seeking more their good, and you will be the better qualified to do them real service and to lead them to your Lord. Perhaps you have had to bear a little persecution, hard words, and the cold shoulder. Do not fret, for all this is needful to make you have fellowship with Christ's sufferings that you may know more of him and may become more like him. You sometimes see the cause of Christ as it were dead, and you are grieved about it, as well you may be. The enemy triumphs, false doctrine is advanced, Jesus seems to be crucified afresh, or hidden away in the grave, forgotten, as a dead man out of mind. It is well that you should feel this, but in that very feeling there should be the full persuasion that the truth of Christ cannot long be buried, but waits to rise again with power. Never did the gospel lie in the grave more than its three days. Never did a lion roar upon it but what it turned and rent the enemy, and found honey in its carcase in after days. Whenever truth seems to be repulsed, she does but draw back to take a more wondrous leap forward. As when the tide ebbs out very far, we expect it again to return in the fullness of its strength, so is it with the church. If we see a small fall in the tide we know that it will not rise very far, but when we see the stream sinking right away, and leaving the riverbed almost dry, we expect to see it roll in at flood tide till the banks overflow. Always look for the triumph of Christianity when others tell you it is defeated; expect to find in the very quarter where it is covered with most obloquy and shame, that there it will win its most glorious laurels. The truth's superlative victories follow upon its worst defeats. Have faith in God. You tell me you have that; then, saith your Master, 'Ye believe in God, believe also in me.' Believe in Christ, trust in him, rest in him, fight for him, labour for him, suffer for him, for he must conquer. Even now doth he sit as King upon the hill of Zion, and soon the heathen shall become his inheritance, and the uttermost parts of the earth shall be his possession. Your sorrow shall be turned into joy in all these cases.

Whenever your sorrow is the result of your belonging to Christ always congratulate yourself upon it, since as the spring begetteth the summer so doth sorrow in connection with Christ bring forth to us joy in the Lord. By-and-by will come your last sorrow: unless the Lord should suddenly appear you will die. But be content to die. Look forward to it without the slightest alarm. Death is the gate of endless joy, and shall we dread to enter there? No, Jesus being with you, meet death joyfully, for to die is to burst the bonds of this death which everywhere surrounds us, and to enter into the true life of liberty and bliss. Even to the end sorrow shall be to you the birth-pang of your joy. Carry that thought with you and be always glad.

With one remark I finish. I will not dwell upon it, but leave it to abide in the memories of those whom it concerns. I present it to the minds of all those who are not believers in Christ. Did you notice that the Lord said, 'Ye shall weep and lament, but the world shall rejoice: ye shall be sorrowful, but your sorrow shall be turned into joy.' Now, what is implied there to complete the sentence? Why, that the world's joy shall be turned into sorrow. Even so shall it be. There is not a pleasure which the ungodly man enjoys when he is indulging in sin but what will curdle into grief and be his sorrow for ever. Depend upon it that the wine of transgression will sour into the griping vinegar of remorse, which shall dissolve the rebel's soul. The sparks which now delight you shall kindle the flames of your eternal misery. Every sin, though sweet when it is like a green fig, is bitterness itself when it cometh to its ripeness. Woe unto you that laugh now, for you shall mourn and weep. Woe unto you that now rejoice in sin, for ye shall gnash your teeth, and weep and wail because of that very Christ whom now you reject. All things will soon be turned upside down. Blessed are ye that mourn now, for ye shall be comforted, but woe unto you that are full this day, for ye shall hunger. The sun will soon be set for you that rejoice in sin. Sadness like a thick cloud is now descending to surround you eternally in its horrid gloom. Out of that cloud shall leap the flashes of eternal justice, and forth from it shall peal the thunder-claps of righteous condemnation. 'Upon the wicked he shall rain snares, fire and brimstone, and an horrible tempest: this shall be the portion of their cup.' The Lord deliver you from such a doom by leading you now to yield to Jesus, and to believe in his name. May he grant this prayer for Jesus' sake. Amen.

6

ALONE, YET *NOT* ALONE [1]

'Jesus answered them, Do ye now believe? Behold, the
hour cometh, yea, is now come, that ye shall be scattered,
every man to his own, and shall leave me alone: and yet I
am not alone, because the Father is with me.'
JOHN 16:31, 32

OUR LORD LOOKS FOR FAITH as the result of his teaching;
and I think that I hear him say, at the end of every service, 'Do ye
now believe? You have listened; you have made remarks upon the
speaker; do ye now believe? You have been made to feel, you have
brushed the tear away; but do ye now believe? For anything short
of believing leaves you short of salvation.'

I would like to put the question of my text to every hearer in this
great house tonight. You have listened now to years of sermons;
'Do ye now believe?' You are getting grey now, the gospel is very
familiar to your ear; you have heard it preached for many, many
years; but 'do ye now believe?' This is the crucial point. According
to your answer, truthfully given to this question, you may decide
as to your condition before God, 'Do ye now believe?'

Christ loves faith wherever he sees it; it is to him a precious thing.
To you that believe, he is precious, he is an honour; and upon him
you who believe confer all the honour it is possible for you to
confer. Your trust adorns him with jewels, your confidence in him
puts the crown on his head. But our Lord is very discriminating;
he distinguishes between faith and presumption, and between faith
and our idea of faith. These disciples said now that they were sure:

[1] Sermon No. 2,271. Preached at the Metropolitan Tabernacle on Sunday evening,
2 March 1890.

'Now are we sure that thou knowest all things, and needest not that any man should ask thee.' 'Yes! Yes!' the Saviour seemed to say, 'That is your measure of your own faith; but I do not measure it in the same way that you do.' If there be any here who say, 'As to the matter of faith, I need no caution, I scarcely need admonition, I believe, oh! you cannot tell how firmly.' No, my dear friend, and perhaps you cannot tell how weakly you believe! At any rate, do not mistake your belief in your own faith for faith in Christ; for belief in your own faith may be only self-conceit; but faith in Christ gives glory to God, and brings salvation to the believer.

To take the disciples down a notch, the Saviour reminds them that, whatever faith they had, they were a long while coming to it. 'Do ye now believe? Three years have I been teaching you; three years have I wrought miracles in your midst; three years have you seen me, and you might in me have seen the Father, but after all this time have you at last come to a little faith?' Oh! friends, we have never any reason to boast of our faith; for we have been very long coming to it. We do trust Christ now; I hope that many of us can sincerely say that we lean all our weight on him. We believe in God, we believe also in his Son, Jesus Christ; but it took months to drive us out of our self-confidence; it took years to lift us out of despair; it has taken all this time for the Lord, in the power of his own Spirit, to work out what little faith we have.

Then our Lord reminded them of another thing more humbling still, that as their faith was long in coming, it might be very quick in going. 'Do ye now believe?' saith he. 'Behold, the hour cometh, yea, is now come, that ye shall be scattered, every man to his own, and shall leave me alone.' O beloved, a little trouble arises, an unforeseen difficulty occurs, and where is your faith? A little persecution, the idle banter of an unbeliever, the sarcasm of an agnostic, and where is your faith? Is it not so with many, that while in good company, they can almost brag of their faith; but if the company is changed, they certainly have no faith to brag of? The men who were so glib of tongue are quiet now; and though, before, they wore their helmets bedight with plumes, they would hide them away, and hide their heads, too, if they could. They are ashamed of him, now, in whom, once, they gloried. O friends, let him that glorieth, glory only in the Lord. Let the believer never vaunt his believing, lest he be reminded how long he was in coming to it, and how soon he may be parted from it.

Our Lord's disciples did not very readily take this caution. I do not suppose any of them took it; certainly Peter did not, and the rest of them were very much like him. When Peter said to Jesus, 'Though all men shall be offended because of thee, yet will I never be offended'; and 'Though I should die with thee, yet will I not deny thee'; we read, 'Likewise also said all the disciples.' We may say tonight, 'There is no man among us who will ever be a traitor to Christ; there is no woman here who will ever grow cold of heart.' That is our self-flattery. What others have done, however base and mean, we too are capable of doing. If we think we are not, it is our pride, and our pride alone that makes us think so. Our Saviour, therefore, to call the particular attention of his disciples to their danger, said, not merely 'the hour cometh', but, 'Behold, the hour cometh.' He puts in a 'Behold!' an '*Ecce!*' As the old writers used to put a hand in the margin, or an N.B., *nota bene*, to call attention to something special, so the Saviour puts here a 'Behold!' 'Look here!' 'See this.' You who have just put on your armour think that you have won the victory. 'Behold, the hour cometh, yea, is now come, that ye shall be scattered, every man to his own, and shall leave me alone.'

I pray you, therefore, brethren, and I speak to myself as well as to you, let us learn the lesson of our frailty; and though we are honestly trusting in Christ tonight, let each one cry, 'Hold thou me up, and I shall be safe.' Let the prayer go up from all of you who are in these galleries, and from all who are sitting downstairs in those pews, from the most experienced and best established of you, as well as from those who have but recently been brought to know the Lord, and let each one cry, 'Lord, keep me, for I cannot keep myself!' Alas! alas! we have seen even the standard-bearers fall; and when that is the case, how sadly do the common soldiers mourn! They who stood like rocks have been made to totter. God keep us! Christ of God, keep us by thy eternal Spirit! Amen.

Now I am going to take you away from that prefatory consideration, keeping still, however, much in the same vein. Let us learn tonight from our Lord, first, *his trial*: 'Ye shall be scattered every man to his own, and shall leave me alone'; secondly, *his confidence*:

'And yet I am not alone, because the Father is with me'; and then, thirdly, *his example*: for in all this, we are to follow his steps. May we, if we have our Lord's trial, also have his confidence because we imitate his example!

I. First, then, notice OUR LORD'S TRIAL, for the like of it may happen to you.

He was left alone. Why, these eleven apostles that are round him, and to whom he is talking, surely they will not leave their Lord! They are so sure that they will stand any fire that may be directed against them; and yet not one of them will stand firm. They will all forsake him and flee. In the garden, the three who are his bodyguard will fall asleep, and the rest of the disciples will do the same; and when he stands before Pilate and Herod, none of them will be there to defend him; not a solitary voice will be lifted up for him.

The sure ones left him whom they so certainly believed; and they were honest men, too, when they spoke so confidently. There was no hypocrisy about what they said, they meant it all; they did each one verily believe that he could go to prison and to death, and that he would do so rather than deny his Lord. In their own esteem, they were not boasting; they were only saying what they really intended to do. Here is the bitterness of your trial, when, in your hour of need, your good, honest friends are gone, your real friends fainting and weary. They cannot go your pace; they cannot confront the storm that you are called upon to face, and they are gone. Alas, for our dear Lord, what grief it was to him! They who were so confident, and they who were really true, yet, nevertheless, were scattered, and he was left alone.

They also really loved Christ. I am sure that Peter's was not a new love when he said, 'Thou knowest all things; thou knowest that I love thee.' He did love his Master. Even when he denied his Lord, there was love in his heart towards him. So was it with the other disciples, they all loved their Lord, yet all of them left him, and poor weak things that they were, they turned their backs in the day of battle. It is a grief to our hearts to be forsaken of good friends and loving friends. I do not know; but if you were sure that they had been hypocrites, you might almost be glad that they were gone; but your very knowledge that they were true at heart, as true as such poor things could be, increases the bitterness that they should leave you. You need not think, when this occurs in your experience that any strange thing has happened to you, for Christ was thus left alone.

Notice, that *he was left by every man*. 'Ye shall be scattered, every man to his own', 'every man'. When the trial comes, does not John remain? Does not he remember that dear breast on which he leaned his head? Is John gone? Yes, 'every man'. Christ looked, and there was none to stand by him. He must confront his accusers without a single witness in his favour; every man was gone. Ah, this was a trial, indeed! But one true friend, a Damon or a Pythias, to be faithful to one another even unto death, and the trial is not so overwhelming. But, no; every man is gone to his own, and Christ is left alone; of the people there is none with him, not even one of those who had been his most intimate friends.

What were they all at? Well, *every man was looking to his own safety*: 'Ye shall be scattered, every man to his own.' Is not that the very essence of selfishness and of meanness, 'Every man to his own'? This is all that Christ received from the best of his followers; they left him, and went every man to his own, to his own house, to see to his own security, to screen his own character, to preserve his own life. 'Every man to his own'. Are these thy friends, O Jesus? Lover of men, are these thy lovers? Do you wonder if, sometimes, you find that your friends would take care of you only that they must take care of themselves? They would keep you, but then you cost too much; you are too 'dear' a friend! The expense of your friendship has to be looked at, and their income will not bear it. 'Every man to his own'. This also the Saviour had to feel.

And, remember this happened *when Christ's special hour was come*. 'The hour cometh', Christ's hour, the hour of the power of darkness. It was then that they left him. When he did not need their friendship, they were his very good friends. When they could do nothing for him if they tried, they were his faithful followers. But the pinch has come; now might they watch with him one hour, now might they go with him amid the rabble throng, and interpose at least the vote of the minority against the masses; but they are gone. Like your swallows, they have disappeared or e'er the first frost has covered the brook. Like the green leaves of summer, where are they now in this wintry time? Alas, alas, for friendship, when it fails when most it is needed! And it did fail the Saviour then.

He was left, also, *in violation of every bond*. These men who left him were pledged to stand by him. They had given him a promise to die with him. These were his choice companions; he had called them from the fishing-smacks of Galilee, and made them his disciples. These were his apostles, the chief men in his new kingdom. They were to sit upon thrones, judging the twelve tribes of Israel. These, he had redeemed unto himself; these were to be partakers of his glory in the day of his appearing. Never were men bound to man as they were bound to Christ; and yet they left him alone. Dear friend, do not expect gratitude from your fellow-creatures; it is a very scarce thing in this world. The more you do for men, the less will be their return. I speak not now like one who thinks ill of my fellows; but I know that it is so, alas! in many instances; and if it be not your lot, you may thank God that it is not, and wonder why you are an exception to the rule. If, by-and-by, you shall come down in the world, and need the help of those you helped in days gone by, they will, as a rule, be the last to help you, and the first to tread you down. Certainly, with our Lord Jesus Christ, those who were nearest and who owed him most fled from him, and he derived from them no succour. It was 'every man to his own'; and they left him alone, to be bound and beaten by his unfeeling adversaries, and to be taken away to prison and to death.

There is the first division of our subject, our Lord's trial. I say again, that a like trial may happen to some here. It has happened often to bold defenders of the faith, to find themselves left to hold the bridge alone; but it is a sharp, stern trial to the man who is called to endure it.

II. More cheery talk shall we have on our second head, which is OUR LORD'S CONFIDENCE. He says, 'Ye shall leave me alone: and yet I am not alone, because the Father is with me.'

Observe, then, that Christ's confidence was confidence that the Father was with him, and this confidence *kept him to his purpose*. See, the disciples flee; they are all scattered, every man to his own. Has Christ gone? Not he. John, Peter, James, Thomas, and all the rest are gone; has Christ gone? Not he. There he stands. They have left him alone; but there he is, still standing to his purpose. He has come to save, and he will save. He has come to redeem, and he will redeem. He has come to overcome the world, and he will overcome it. They have left him alone; they have not taken him away with them. He is no coward. From his purpose he doth never fly, blessed be his name! He stood fast in that dread hour when all forsook him and fled. This was because his confidence was in God.

Next, observe that this confidence in God not only kept him to his purpose, but it *sustained him in the prospect of the trial*. Notice how it runs: 'Ye shall leave me alone: and yet I am not alone.' Christ does not say, 'I shall not be alone.' That was true; but he said, 'I *am not* alone.' I love to read the experience of the child of God in the present tense, the gifts, and graces, and promises of God in the present tense: 'I am not alone.' 'The Lord is my Shepherd', as well as 'I *shall not* want.' 'He *maketh* me to lie down in green pastures; he *leadeth* me beside the still waters.' He is doing everything for me now. The blessed Christ says that the prospect of God's being with him all through the trouble, and the presence of God with him now, is his comfort in the prospect of it. You who were here this morning know what a sad discourse we had from the text, 'My God, my God, why hast thou forsaken me?'[1] I took this text for my evening discourse because it is the counterpart of the one we considered this morning; for our Lord could truly say to his disciples, 'And yet I am not alone, because the Father is with me.'

Our Lord's declaration was *contradicted by appearances*. Did he not have to say to God: 'Why hast thou forsaken me?' How, then, could he say, 'The Father is with me'? It was true; and in a part of my morning sermon I tried to show that, while God forsook him in his official capacity as the Lawgiver and the Executive of the law, yet in his personal relation to him he did not and could not forsake him. The Father was with him. Oh, is it not blessed on the part of Christ to stand to this? He knows that his Father is with him, even when he feels in another sense that the Father has forsaken him. Beloved, if everybody leaves you, and God seems to

---

[1] See Sermon No. 2,133. 'Lama Sabachtani?'

leave you, still hold to your confidence in God. Do not believe that God can forsake his own; do not even dream it; it cannot be. He never did forsake his own; he never can; and he never will. The Father is with Jesus Christ, even when he knows that he will have to say, 'Why hast thou forsaken me?'

Yet, *it was assuredly true* that the Father was with Christ when he was left alone. How was the Father with him, then? Beloved, even when the Father did not look on Christ, or give him one smile, or one word of comfort, he was still with him. How so? Well, he was with him as to his eternal purposes and covenant. They had entered into covenant together for the redemption of men, for the salvation of the elect, and they had crossed hands, and pledged each other to carry out the divine purpose and the everlasting covenant. I remember that passage about Abraham going with Isaac to mount Moriah, where Isaac was to be offered up. It is written, 'So they went both of them together.' So did the Eternal Father and his Well-beloved Son when God was about to give up his own Son to death. There was no divided purpose; they went both of them together. All the work of Christ was the work of the Father, and the Father supported him in it to the very full.

In the design and method of the atonement, the Father and the Son were together. 'God so loved the world that he gave his Only begotten Son'; but Jesus so loved the world that he gave himself. The atonement was the gift of the Father; but it was the work of the Son. In all that he suffered he could say, 'The Father is with me in it. I am doing that which will glorify him and content him.' He went not alone to prison and to death. In all things he did that which pleased the Father, and the Father was with him in it all.

All the decrees of God were at the back of Christ. It is written in the sealed book, but who shall read it except the Christ? Whatever is written there is written in support of Christ. There is not a decree in the book of destiny but works out for Christ's glory, and according to Christ's mind. It is not merely twelve legions of angels that are behind the cross, but the God of the angels is there too. It is not merely the forces of Providence that shall work together to achieve the purpose of the Creator, but the God of Providence, the infinite Jehovah, is in league with Jesus; and he can say it, as he goes out to die, 'I am not alone: because the Father is with me.' Is not this a glorious truth, that our Lord Christ was not alone? So far as earthly companions were concerned, the words written by Isaiah could be literally uttered by Christ, 'I have trodden the winepress alone.' Every man was gone, but God was always with him.

Since then, *it has been made manifest* that God was with Christ. He proved it by raising him from the dead. Did not the Father also prove that he was with the Son by sending the Holy Ghost at Pentecost with various signs and wonders? Jesus is not alone. All the work of the Holy Spirit since, in convincing men of sin, and leading them to Jesus, is a proof that he is not alone. Beloved, all the history of Providence, since the day when Christ was taken up into heaven, proves that he is not alone. Alone? The Christ alone? Why, the beasts of the field are in league with him; the stars in their courses fight for him. Every event of history, give it but time and space, will make his kingdom come. Every turn of yonder enormous wheels of Providence shall make his chariot of triumph come nearer and nearer over the necks of his foes. Even now, by faith, 'we see Jesus, who was made a little lower than the angels for the suffering of death, crowned with glory and honour.'

> Look, ye saints, the sight is glorious,
>   See the 'Man of Sorrows' now;
> From the fight returned victorious,
>   Every knee to him shall bow:
>   Crown him, crown him;
> Crowns become the Victor's brow.

Jesus is the focus of all power and wisdom. God is with him; and the day comes when he shall appear in his glory. In his millennial reign among the sons of God it shall be seen that he is not alone; and when he shall come in the glory of the Father, and all his holy angels with him, then shall he be able to say with even greater emphasis, 'I am not alone: because the Father is with me.' And when he sits upon the great white throne, and divides mankind, his friends to the right, his foes to the left, and pronounces eternal wrath upon rebels, and opens heaven to believers, then shall all worlds know that the Man of Nazareth is not alone. Alone? I seem as if I must laugh at the very thought. All heaven and earth, things present and things to come, time and eternity, life and death, are all with him. Men may forsake him, but he is not alone.

III. Now, I want, in the third place, to teach the lessons of OUR LORD'S EXAMPLE. As my time has nearly gone, I must very briefly speak of these lessons.

First, *learn fidelity when others fail.* Are you a Christian? Do you trust Christ? Do you love him? Then, never desert him. 'Oh! but', says one, 'the current runs the other way now.' Brother, let it run; it will leave off when it has run away. I believe in him who rose again from the dead, whose righteousness doth justify me, whose blood doth wash me whiter than snow. 'But the philosophers tell us that this is not scientific.' I am unscientific, then, and I delight to be unscientific. 'Oh, but the deep thinkers say this is inconsistent with progress!' Well, let it be inconsistent with progress. 'Oh, but all the world denies it!' So much the worse for the world. Let it deny the truth if it will. That was a grand spirit of Athanasius when he said, '*Athanasius contra mundum*'; that is, 'Athanasius against the whole world.' And every Christian may be of this spirit, and ought to be of this spirit. Is this Book true? What matters it though every Tom Fool says that it is a lie! Let Tom Fools say that if they will; but the Bible is true, and hold you to it. If God the Holy Ghost has taught you to trust in Christ, trust you in Christ, whatever other people do. What? Do you live on the breath of other men's nostrils? Do you count heads, and then jump with the larger number? Is that your way? Why, surely such a man as that is hardly worth saving. Is he a man, or is he not a cat that must look before he jumps? Nay, if thou art a man, and thou believest in Christ, stand up for Christ.

> Stand up! Stand up for Jesus!
> Ye soldiers of the cross!
> Lift high his royal banner;
> It must not suffer loss:
> From victory unto victory
> His army shall he lead,
> Till every foe is vanquish'd,
> And Christ is Lord indeed.

Stand up! Stand up for Jesus!
The trumpet-call obey;
Forth to the mighty conflict,
In this his glorious day;
Ye that are men, now serve him,
Against unnumber'd foes;
Your courage rise with danger,
And strength to strength oppose.

And when the many turn aside, stand you the more boldly and the more confidently, for your confidence and boldness are all the more needed at such a time. Your Lord did not forsake his grand errand when all men forsook him. Do not renounce your lifework and your faith, even though all others should renounce theirs.

Next, with your Master, *believe that God is all-sufficient*. Read this: 'Ye shall be scattered, every man to his own, and shall leave me alone: and yet I am not alone, because' – what? 'Because there will be half-a-dozen of you faithful'? No. 'Because three of you will cling to me?' No. 'Because the Father is with me.' Oh, we do not count as we should. There is a million against you. Is God for you? Well, then, you are in the majority. What is a million, after all, but one and so many ciphers? Trust thou in God, and let the millions go their way. God is enough. When he that spoke in the academy found everybody leaving him in his speaking except Plato, he still kept on; and one said, 'Speaker, thou hast no audience but Plato.' 'No audience but Plato?' says he; 'Plato is enough for fifty orators.' So, truly, if thou hast no other helper but God, stand thou where thou art; for God is not only enough for thee, but for all the faithful, weak as they may be.

Next, learn another lesson. *Rest in God, despite appearances*. Art thou very poor? Art thou weak? Art thou slandered? Art thou scourged with God's heaviest rod? Yet kick not thou at him, any more than thy Lord did. He said, 'The Father is with me', even though he had to cry, 'Why hast thou forsaken me?' Believe him when thou canst not see him; believe him when he smiles not; believe him when he frowns; believe him when he smites; believe him when he slays, for that is the climax of it all, to say like Job,

'Though he slay me, yet will I trust in him.' It is his to do what he likes; it is mine to trust him, let him do as he will. I throw my arms about my God, and say, 'My God, my God', even when no sensible joys are felt, and I am obliged to walk by faith.

Lastly, struggling child of God, standing firm for the truth and the right, *expect that thy trouble will not last long.* Did you notice how Christ puts it, 'Behold, the hour cometh'? Only an hour. 'Behold, the hour cometh.' It is not a year, brother, it is not a year; it is not a month; it is not a day; it is but an hour. 'The hour cometh.' To Christ it was a long hour certainly, when he hung upon the cross; but he calls the whole period from the bloody sweat to the death of the cross, 'the hour'. It is the part of faith to shorten days to hours. It is your part, tonight, to recollect that, if you have to suffer, and to stand alone for Christ, it is but for an hour. How willingly have we waited when it has been but for an hour! How cheerfully have we gone on in the dark when we have known that it was only for an hour! Our trial is but for an hour. Literally, before another hour strikes, some of us may be with God; but whether it is so with us, or not, we may still sing,

> Let doubt, then, and danger my progress oppose,
> They only make heaven more sweet at the close:
> Come joy or come sorrow, whate'er may befall,
> An hour with my God will make up for them all.

But if not literally only an hour, yet certainly the longest reign of persecution is but short. It is soon over when we once get home. I think that it will help to make a merry holiday in the land that flows with milk and honey, to sit one of these days by one of those rippling streams, and say, 'I remember when so-and-so forsook me, and I stood fast by the truth as I knew it and believed it. They all forsook me, and it did seem hard to bear at the time; but my loneliness did not last long, it was soon over; and when the Lord said, "Well done, good and faithful servant", it did not seem then that it had been an hour, but only the winking of an eye, or as when, in the night, the candle is blown out, and lighted again by its own smoke, so short was the time of darkness.' So it shall seem in heaven as if we never had suffered anything for Christ. The martyr shall go in the red-hot chariot from the stake; and when he gets to heaven, he shall have forgotten that he burned to death, in the exceeding joy of beholding his Master. It is but an hour, and we shall meet before the golden throne, and stand upon the sea of glass, and sing for ever, 'Unto him that loved us, and washed us from our sins in his own blood, and hath made us kings and priests unto God and his Father; to him be glory and dominion for ever and ever. Amen.'

7

CHRIST'S PASTORAL PRAYER FOR HIS PEOPLE [1]

'I pray for them: I pray not for the world, but for them
which thou hast given me; for they are thine. And all mine
are thine, and thine are mine; and I am glorified in them.'
JOHN 17:9–10

TO BEGIN WITH, I REMARK that our Lord Jesus pleads for his
own people. When he puts on his priestly breastplate, it is for the
tribes whose names are there. When he presents the atoning
sacrifice, it is for Israel whom God hath chosen; and he utters this
great truth, which some regard as narrow, but which we adore, 'I
pray for them: I pray not for the world.' The point to which I want
to call attention is this, the reason why Christ prays not for the
world, but for his people. He puts it, 'For they are thine', as if they
were all the dearer to him because they were the Father's: 'I pray
for them: I pray not for the world, but for them which thou hast
given me, for they are thine.' We might have half thought that Jesus
would have said, 'They are mine, and therefore I pray for them.' It
would have been true; but there would not have been the beauty
of truth about it which we have here. He loves us all the better,
and he prays for us all the more fervently, because we are the
Father's. Such is his love to his Father, that our being the Father's
sheds upon us an extra halo of beauty. Because we belong to the
Father, therefore does the Saviour plead for us with all the greater
earnestness at the throne of the heavenly grace.

[1] Sermon No. 2,331. Preached at the Metropolitan Tabernacle on Sunday evening,
1 September 1889.

But this leads us on to remember that our Lord had undertaken suretyship engagements on account of his people; he undertook to preserve the Father's gift: 'Those that thou gavest me I have kept, and none of them is lost.' He looked upon the sheep of his pasture as belonging to his Father, and the Father had put them into his charge, saying to him, 'Of thine hand will I require them.' As Jacob kept his uncle's flocks, by day the heat devoured him, and at night the frost but he was more careful over them because they were Laban's than if they had been his own; he was to give in an account of all the sheep committed to him, and he did so, and he lost none of Laban's sheep; but his care over them was partly accounted for by the fact that they did not belong to himself, but belonged to his uncle Laban.

Understand this twofold reason, then, for Christ's pastoral prayer for his people. He first prays for them because they belong to the Father, and therefore have a peculiar value in his eye; and next, because they belong to the Father, he is under suretyship engagements to deliver them all to the Father in that last great day when the sheep shall pass under the rod of him that telleth them. Now you see where I am bringing you tonight. I am not going to preach at this time to the world any more than Christ upon this occasion prayed for the world; but I am going to preach to his own people as he in this intercessory prayer pleaded for them. I trust that they will all follow me, step by step, through this great theme; and I pray the Lord that, in these deep central truths of the gospel we may find real refreshment for our souls tonight.

I. In calling your attention to my text, I want you to notice, first, THE INTENSITY OF THE SENSE OF PROPERTY WHICH CHRIST HAS IN HIS PEOPLE.

Here are six words setting forth Christ's property in those who are saved: 'Them which thou hast *given me*' – (that is one); 'for they are *thine*. And all *mine* are *thine*, and *thine* are *mine*; and I am glorified in them.' There are certain persons so precious to Christ that they are marked all over with special tokens that they belong to him; as I have known a man write his name in a book which he has greatly valued, and then he has turned over some pages, and he has written his name again; and as we have sometimes known persons, when they have highly valued a thing, to put their mark, their seal, their stamp, here, there, and almost everywhere upon it. So, notice in my text how the Lord seems to have the seal in his hand, and he stamps it all over his peculiar possession: 'They are thine. And all mine are thine, and thine are mine.' It is all possessive pronouns, to show that God looks upon his people as his portion, his possession, his property. 'They shall be mine, saith the Lord of hosts, in that day when I make up my jewels.' Every man has something or other which he values above the rest of his estate; and here the Lord, by so often reiterating the words which signify possession, proves that he values his people above everything. Let us show that we appreciate this privilege of being set apart unto God; and let us each one say to him –

> Take my poor heart, and let it be
> For ever closed to all but thee!
> Seal thou my breast, and let me wear
> That pledge of love for ever there.

I call your attention, next, to the fact that, while there are these six expressions here, they are all applied to the Lord's own people. 'Mine' (that is, the saints) are thine (that is, the saints); 'and thine' (that is, the saints) are mine (that is, the saints). These broad arrows of the King of kings are all stamped upon his people. While the marks of possession are numerous, they are all set upon one object. What, doth not God care for anything else? I answer, No; as compared with his own people, he cares for nothing else. 'The Lord's portion is his people: Jacob is the lot of his inheritance.' Has not God other things? Ah, what is there that he has not? The silver and the gold are his, and the cattle on a thousand hills. All things are of God; of him, and by him, and through him, and to him are all things; yet he reckons them not in comparison with his people. You know how you, dearly beloved, value your children much more than you do anything else. If there were a fire in your house tonight, and you could only carry one thing out of it, mother, would you hesitate a moment as to what that one thing should be? You would carry your babe, and let everything else be consumed in the flames; and it is so with God. He cares for his people beyond everything else. He is the Lord God of Israel, and in Israel he hath set his name, and there he takes his delight. There doth he rest in his love, and over her doth he rejoice with singing.

I want you to notice these different points, not because I can fully explain them all to you; but if I can only give you some of these great truths to think about, and to help you to communion with Christ tonight, I shall have done well. I want you to remark yet further, concerning these notes of possession, that they occur in the private intercourse between the Father and the Son. It is in our Lord's prayer, when he is in the inner sanctuary speaking with the Father, that we have these words, 'All mine are thine, and thine are mine.' It is not to you and to me that he is talking now; the Son of God is speaking with the Father when they are in very near communion one with the other. Now, what does this say to me but that the Father and the Son greatly value believers? What people talk about when they are alone, not what they say in the market, not what they talk of in the midst of the confused mob, but what they say when they are in private, that lays bare their heart. Here is the Son speaking to the Father, not about thrones and royalties, nor cherubim and seraphim, but about poor men and women, in those days mostly fishermen and peasant folk, who believed on him. They are talking about these people, and the Son is taking his own solace with the Father in their secret privacy by talking about these precious jewels, these dear ones that are their peculiar treasure. You have not any notion how much God loves you. Dear brother, dear sister, you have never yet had half an idea, or the tithe of an idea, of how precious you are to Christ. You think, because you are so imperfect, and you fall so much below your own ideal, that, therefore, he does not love you much; you think that he cannot do so. Have you ever measured the depth of Christ's agony in Gethsemane, and of his death on Calvary? If you have tried to do so, you will be quite sure that, apart from anything in you or about you, he loves you with a love that passeth knowledge. Believe it. 'But I do not love him as I should', I think I hear you say. No, and you never will unless you first know his love to you. Believe it; believe it to the highest degree, that he so loves you that, when there is no one who can commune with him but the Father, even then their converse is about their mutual estimate of you, how much they love you: 'All mine are thine, and thine are mine.'

Only one other thought under this head, and I do but put it before you, and leave it with you, for I cannot expound it tonight. All that Jesus says is about all his people, for he says, 'All mine are thine, and thine are mine.' These high, secret talks are not about some few saints who have reached a 'higher life', but about all of us who belong to him. Jesus bears all of us on his heart, and he speaks of us all to the Father: 'All mine are thine.' 'That poor woman who could never serve her Lord except by patient endurance, she is mine', says Jesus. 'She is thine, great Father.' 'That poor girl, newly-converted, whose only spiritual life was spent upon a sick-bed, and then she exhaled to heaven, like a dewdrop of the morning, she is mine, and she is thine. That poor child of mine, who often stumbles, who never brought much credit to the sacred name, he is mine, and he is thine. All mine are thine.' I seem as if I heard a silver bell ringing out; the very tones of the words are like the music from the harps of angels: 'Mine – thine; thine – mine.' May such sweet risings and fallings of heavenly melodies charm all our ears!

I think that I have said enough to show you the intensity of the sense of property which Christ has in his people: 'All mine are thine, and thine are mine.'

II. The next head of my discourse is, THE INTENSITY OF UNITED INTEREST BETWEEN THE FATHER AND THE SON CONCERNING BELIEVERS.

First, let me say that *Jesus loves us because we belong to the Father*. Turn that truth over. 'My Father has chosen them, my Father loves them; therefore', says Jesus, 'I love them, and I lay down my life for them, and I will take my life again for them, and live throughout eternity for them. They are dear to me because they are dear to my Father.' Have you not often loved another person for the sake of a third one upon whom all your heart was set? There is an old proverb, and I cannot help quoting it just now; it is, 'Love me, love my dog.' It is as if the Lord Jesus so loved the Father that even such poor dogs as we are get loved by him for his Father's sake. To the eyes of Jesus we are radiant with beauty because God hath loved us.

Now turn that thought round the other way, *the Father loves us because we belong to Christ*. At first, the Father's love in election was sovereign and self-contained; but now, today, since he has given us over to Christ, he takes a still greater delight in us. 'They are my Son's sheep', says he; 'he bought them with his blood.' Better still, 'That is my Son's spouse', says he, 'that is my Son's bride. I love her for his sake.' There was that first love which came fresh from the Father's heart, but now, through this one channel of love to Jesus, the Father pours a double flood of love on us for his dear Son's sake. He sees the blood of Jesus sprinkled on us; he remembers the token, and for the sake of his beloved Son he prizes us beyond all price. Jesus loves us because we belong to the Father, and the Father loves us because we belong to Jesus.

Now come closer still to the central thought of the text, 'All mine are thine.' *All who are the Son's are the Father's.* Do we belong to Jesus? Then we belong to the Father. Have I been washed in the precious blood? Can I sing tonight –

> The dying thief rejoiced to see
> That fountain in his day;
> And there have I, though vile as he,
> Washed all my sins away?

Then, by redemption I belong to Christ; but at the same time I may be sure that I belong to the Father: 'All mine are thine.' Are you trusting in Christ? Then you are one of God's elect. That high and deep mystery of predestination need trouble no man's heart if he be a believer in Christ. If thou believest in Christ, Christ hath redeemed thee, and the Father chose thee from before the foundation of the world. Rest thou happy in that firm belief, 'All mine are thine.' How often have I met with people puzzling themselves about election! They want to know if they are elect. No man can come to the Father but by Christ; no man can come to election except through redemption. If you have come to Christ, and are his redeemed, it is certain beyond all doubt that you were chosen of God, and are the Father's elect. 'All mine are thine.'

So, if I am bought by Christ's precious blood, I am not to sit down, and say how grateful I am to Christ as though he were apart from the Father, and more loving and more tender than the Father. No, no; I belong to the Father if I belong to Christ; and I have for the Father the same gratitude, the same love, and I would render the same service as to Jesus; for Jesus puts it, 'All mine are thine.'

If, tonight, also, I am a servant of Christ, if, because he bought me, I try to serve him, then I am a servant of the Father if I am a servant of the Son. 'All mine, whatever position they occupy, belong to thee, great Father', and they have all the privileges which come to those who belong to the Father. I hope that I do not weary you; I cannot make these things entertaining to the careless. I do not try to do so; but you who love my Lord, and his truth, ought to rejoice tonight to think that, in being the property of Christ, you are assured that you are the property of the Father. 'All mine are thine.'

> With Christ our Lord we share our part
> In the affections of his heart;
> Nor shall our souls be thence removed
> Till he forgets his first-beloved.

But now you have to look at the other part of it: 'and thine are mine.' *All who are the Father's are the Son's.* If you belong to the Father, you belong to the Son. If you are elect, and so the Father's, you are redeemed, and so the Son's. If you are adopted, and so the Father's, you are justified in Christ, and so you are the Son's. If you are regenerated, and so are begotten of the Father, yet still your life is dependent upon the Son. Remember that, while one biblical figure sets us forth as children who have each one a life within himself, another equally valid figure represents us as branches of the vine, which die unless they continue united to the stem. 'All thine are mine.' If you are the Father's, you must be Christ's. If your life is given you of the Father, it still depends entirely upon the Son. What a wonderful mixture all this is! The Father and the Son are one, and we are one with the Father and with the Son. A mystic union is established between us and the Father, by reason of our union with the Son, and the Son's union with the Father. See to what a glorious height our humanity has risen through Christ. By the grace of God, ye who were like stones

95

in the brook are made sons of God. Lifted out of your dead materialism you are elevated into a spiritual life and you are united unto God. You have not any idea tonight of what God has already done for you, and truly it doth not yet appear what you shall be. A Christian man is the noblest work of God. God has here reached the fullness of his power and his grace, in making us to be one with his own dear Son, and so bringing us into union and communion with himself. Oh, if the words that I speak could convey to you the fullness of their own meaning, you might spring to your feet, electrified with holy joy to think of this, that we should be Christ's, and the Father's, and that we should be thought worthy to be the object of intricate transactions and inter-communions of the dearest kind between the Father and the Son! We, even we, who are but dust and ashes at our very best, are favoured as angels never were; therefore let all praise be ascribed to sovereign grace!

III. And now I shall only detain you a few minutes longer while I speak upon the third part of our subject, that is, THE GLORY OF CHRIST: 'And I am glorified in them.' I must confess that, while the former part of my subject was very deep, this third part seems to me to be deeper still, 'I am glorified in them.'

If Christ had said, 'I will glorify them', I could have understood it. If he had said, 'I am pleased with them', I might have set it down to his great kindness to them; but when he says, 'I am glorified in them', it is very wonderful. The sun can be reflected, but you need proper objects to act as reflectors; and the brighter they are, the better will they reflect. You and I do not seem to have the power of reflecting Christ's glory; we break up the glorious rays that shine upon us; we spoil, we ruin so much of the good that falls upon us. Yet Christ says that he is glorified in us. Take these words home, dear friend, to yourself, and think that the Lord Jesus met you tonight, and as you went out of the Tabernacle, said to you, 'Thou art mine, thou art my Father's; and I am glorified in thee.' I dare not say that it would be a proud moment for you; but I dare to say that there would be more in it to make you feel exalted for him to say, 'I am glorified in you', than if you could have all the honours that all the kings can put upon all men in the world. I think that I could say, 'Lord, now lettest thou thy servant depart in peace, according to thy word', if he would but say to me, 'I am glorified in thy ministry.' I hope that he is; I believe that he is; but, oh, for an assuring word, if not spoken to us personally, yet spoken to his Father about us, as in our text, 'I am glorified in them'!

How can this be? Well, it is a very wide subject. Christ is glorified in his people in many ways. *He is glorified by saving such sinners*, taking these people, so sinful, so lost, so unworthy. When the Lord lays hold upon a drunkard, a thief, an adulterer, when he arrests one who has been guilty of blasphemy, whose very heart is reeking with evil thoughts, when he picks up the far-off one, the abandoned, the dissolute, the fallen, as he often does, and when he says, 'These shall be mine; I will wash these in my blood; I will use these to speak my word', oh, then, he is glorified in them!

Read the lives of many great sinners who have afterwards become great saints, and you will see how they have tried to glorify him, not only she who washed his feet with her tears, but many another like her. Oh, how they have loved to praise him! Eyes have wept tears, lips have spoken words, but hearts have felt what neither eyes nor lips could speak, of adoring gratitude to him. 'I am glorified in them.' Great sinners, Christ is glorified in you. Some of you Pharisees, if you were to be converted, would not bring Christ such glory as he gets through saving publicans and harlots. Even if you struggled into heaven, it would be with very little music for him on the road, certainly no tears and no ointment for his feet, and no wiping them with the hairs of your head. You are too respectable ever to do that; but when he saves great sinners, he can truly say, 'I am glorified in them', and each of them can sing –

> It passeth praises, that dear love of thine,
> My Jesus, Saviour: yet this heart of mine
> Would sing that love, so full, so rich, so free,
> Which brings a rebel sinner, such as me,
>   Nigh unto God.

And *Christ is glorified by the perseverance which he shows in the matter of their salvation*. See how he begins to save, and the man resists. He follows up his kind endeavour, and the man rebels.

97

He hunts him, pursues him, dogs his footsteps. He will have the man, and the man will not have him. But the Lord, without violating the free will of man, which he never does, yet at length brings the one who was most unwilling to lie at his feet, and he that hated most begins to love, and he that was most stout-hearted bows the knee in lowliest humility. It is wonderful how persevering the Lord is in the salvation of a sinner; ay, and in the salvation of his own, for you would have broken loose long ago if your great Shepherd had not penned you up within the fold. Many of you would have started aside, and have lost yourselves, if it had not been for constraints of sovereign grace which have kept you to this day, and will not let you go. Christ is glorified in you. Oh, when you once get to heaven, when the angels know all that you were, and all that you tried to be, when the whole story of almighty, infinite grace is told, as it will be told, then will Christ be glorified in you!

Beloved, *we actively glorify Christ when we display Christian graces.* You who are loving, forgiving, tender-hearted, gentle, meek, self-sacrificing, you glorify him; he is glorified in you. You who are upright, and who will not be moved from your integrity, you who can despise the sinner's gold, and will not sell your conscience for it, you who are bold and brave for Christ, you who can bear and suffer for his name's sake, all your graces come from him. As all the flowers are bred and begotten of the sun, so all that is in you that is good comes from Christ, the Sun of righteousness; and therefore he is glorified in you.

But, beloved, God's people have glorified Christ in many other ways. *When they make him the object of all their trust, they glorify him,* when they say, 'Though I am the chief of sinners, yet, I trust him; though my mind is dark, and though my temptations abound, I believe that he can save to the uttermost, I do trust him.' Christ is more glorified by a sinner's humble faith than by a seraph's loudest song. If thou believest, thou dost glorify him. Child of God, are you tonight very dark, and dull, and heavy? Do you feel half dead, spiritually? Come to your Lord's feet, and kiss them, and believe that he can save, nay, that he has saved you, even you; and thus you will glorify his holy name. 'Oh!' said a believer, the other day, 'I know whom I have believed; Christ is mine.' 'Ah!' said another, 'that is presumption.' Beloved, it is nothing of the kind; it is not presumption for a child to own his own father; it might be pride for him to be ashamed of his father; it is certainly great alienation from his father if he is ashamed to own him. 'I know whom I have believed.' Happy state of heart, to be absolutely sure that you are resting upon Christ, that he is your Saviour, that you believe in him, for Jesus said, 'He that believeth on me hath everlasting life.' I believe on him, and I have everlasting life. 'He that believeth on him is not condemned.' I believe on him, and I am not condemned. Make sure work of this, not only by signs and evidences, but do even better; make the one sign and the one evidence to be this, 'Jesus Christ came into the world to save sinners; I, a sinner, accept his great sacrifice, and I am saved.'

Especially, I think that *God's people glorify Christ by a cheerful conversation.* If you go about moaning and mourning, pining and complaining, you bring no honour to his name; but if, when thou fastest, thou appear not unto men to fast, if thou canst wear a cheerful countenance, even when thy heart is heavy, and if, above all, thou canst rally thy spirit out of its depths, and begin to bless God when the cupboard is empty, and friends are few, then thou wilt indeed glorify Christ.

Many are the ways in which this good work may be done; let us try to do it. 'I am glorified in them', says Christ; that is, *by their bold confession of Christ.* Do I address myself to any here who love Christ, but who have never owned it? Do come out, and come out very soon. He deserves to have all the glory that you can give him. If he has healed you, be not like the nine who forgot that Christ had healed their leprosy. Come and praise the name of the great Healer, and let others know what Christ can do. I am afraid that there are a great many here tonight who hope that they are Christians, but they have never said so. What are you ashamed of? Ashamed of your Lord? I am afraid that you do not, after all, love him.

Now, at this time, at this particular crisis of the history of the church and the world, if we do not publicly take sides with Christ, we shall really be against him. The time is come now when we cannot afford to have go-betweens. You must be for him or for his enemies; and tonight he asks you if you are really his, to say it.

Come forward, unite yourself with his people, and let it be seen by your life and conversation that you do belong to Christ. If not, how can it be true, 'I am glorified in them'? Is Christ glorified in a non-confessing people, a people that hope to go slinking into heaven by the by-roads or across the fields, but dare not come into the King's highway, and travel with the King's subjects, and own that they belong to him?

Lastly, I think that *Christ is glorified in his people by their efforts to extend his kingdom*. What efforts are you making? There is a great deal of force in a church like this; but I am afraid that there is a great deal of waste steam, waste power here. The tendency is, so often, to leave everything to be done by the minister, or else by one or two leading people; but I do pray you, beloved, if you be Christ's, and if you belong to the Father, if, unworthy though you be, you are claimed with a double ownership by the Father and the Son, do try to be of use to them. Let it be seen by your winning others to Christ that he is glorified in you. I believe that, by diligent attendance to even the smallest Sabbath-school class, Christ is glorified in you. By that private conversation in your own room, by that letter which you dropped into the post with many a prayer, by anything that you have done with a pure motive, trusting in God in order to glorify Christ, he is glorified in you. Do not mistake my meaning with regard to serving the Lord. I think it exceedingly wrong when I hear exhortations made to young people, 'Quit your service as domestics, and come out into spiritual work. Business men, leave your shops. Workmen, give up your trades. You cannot serve Christ in that calling, come away from it altogether.' I beg to say that nothing will be more pestilent than such advice as that. There are men called by the grace of God to separate themselves from every earthly occupation, and they have special gifts for the work of the ministry; but ever to imagine that the bulk of Christian people cannot serve God in their daily calling, is to think altogether contrary to the mind of the Spirit of God. If you are a servant, remain a servant. If you are a waiter, go on with your waiting. If you are a tradesman, go on with your trade. Let every man abide in the calling wherein he is called, unless there be to him some special call from God to devote himself to the ministry. Go on with your employment, dear Christian people, and do not imagine that you are to turn hermits, or monks, or nuns. You would not glorify God if you did so act. Soldiers of Christ are to fight the battle out where they are. To quit the field, and shut yourselves up alone, would be to render it impossible that you should get the victory. The work of God is as holy and acceptable in domestic service, or in trade, as any service that can be rendered in the pulpit, or even by the foreign missionary. We thank God for the men specially called and set apart for his own work; but we know that they would do nothing unless the salt of our holy faith should permeate the daily life of other Christians. You godly mothers, you are the glory of the church of Christ. You hard-working men and women, who endure patiently 'as seeing him who is invisible', are the crown and glory of the church of God. You who do not shirk your daily labour, but stand manfully to it, obeying Christ in it, are proving what the Christian religion was meant to do. We can, if we are truly priests unto God, make our everyday garments into vestments, our meals into sacraments, and our houses into temples for God's worship. Our very beds will be within the veil, and our inmost thoughts will be as a sweet incense perpetually smoking up to the Most High.

Dream not that there is anything about any honest calling that degrades a man, or hinders him in glorifying God; but sanctify it all, till the bells, upon the horses shall ring out, 'Holiness to the Lord', and the pots in your houses shall be as holy as the vessels of the sanctuary.

Now, I want that we should so come to the communion table tonight, that even here Christ may be glorified in us. Ah, you may sit at the Lord's table wearing a fine dress or a diamond ring, and you may think that you are somebody of importance, but you are not! Ah, you may come to the Lord's table, and say, 'Here is an experienced Christian man who knows a thing or two.' You are not glorifying Christ that way; you are only a nobody. But if you come tonight saying, 'Lord, I am hungry, thou canst feed me'; that is glorifying him. If you come saying, 'Lord, I have no merit, and no worthiness, I come because thou hast died for me, and I trust thee', you are glorifying him. He glorifies Christ most who takes most from him, and who then gives most back to him. Come, empty pitcher, come and be filled; and, when thou art filled, pour all out at the dear feet of him who filled thee. Come, trembler, come and let him touch thee with his strengthening hand, and then go out and work, and use the strength which he has given thee. I fear that I have not led you where I wanted to bring you, close to my Lord and to the Father, yet I have done my best. May the Lord forgive my feebleness and wandering, and yet bless you for his dear name's sake! Amen.

8

THE GARDEN OF THE SOUL[1]

'A place called Gethsemane'
MATTHEW 26:36

THOUGH I HAVE TAKEN ONLY THESE FEW WORDS for my text, I shall endeavour to bring the whole narrative before your mind's eye. It is a part of the teaching of Holy Writ that man is a composite being; his nature being divisible into three parts – 'spirit', 'soul', and 'body'. I am not going to draw any nice distinctions tonight between the spirit and the soul, or to analyse the connecting link between our immaterial life and consciousness and the physical condition of our nature and the materialism of the world around us. Suffice it to say, that whenever our vital organization is mentioned, this triple constitution is pretty sure to be referred to. If you notice it carefully, you will see in our Saviour's sufferings on our behalf that the passion extended to his spirit, soul, and body; for although at the last extremity upon the cross it were hard to tell in which respect he suffered most, all three being strained to the utmost, yet it is certain there were three distinct conflicts in accordance with this threefold endowment of humanity.

The first part of our Lord's dolorous pain fell upon his spirit. This took place at the table, in that upper chamber where he ate the Passover with his disciples. Those of you who have read the narrative attentively, will have noticed these remarkable words in the thirteenth chapter of John and the twenty-first verse: 'When Jesus had thus said, he was troubled in spirit, and testified, and said, Verily, verily, I say unto you, that one of you shall betray me.'

[1] Sermon No. 693. Preached at the Metropolitan Tabernacle, date unknown.

Of that silent conflict in the Saviour's heart whilst he was sitting at table no one was a spectator. Into any man's spiritual apprehensions it were beyond the power of any other creature to penetrate; how much less into the spiritual conflicts of the man Christ Jesus! No one could by any possibility have gazed upon these veiled mysteries. He seems to have sat there for a time like one in the deepest abstraction. He fought a mighty battle within himself. When Judas rose and went out it may have been a relief. The Saviour gave out a hymn as if to celebrate his conflict; then, rising up, he went forth to the Mount of Olives. His discourse with his disciples there is recorded in that wonderful chapter, the fifteenth of John, so full of holy triumph, beginning thus, 'I am the true vine.' He went to the agony in the same joyous spirit like a conqueror, and oh! how he prayed! That famous prayer, what a profound study it is for us! It ought, properly, to be called 'The Lord's Prayer'. The manner and the matter are alike impressive. 'These words spake Jesus, and lifted up his eyes to heaven and said, Father, the hour is come; glorify thy Son, that thy Son also may glorify thee.' He seems to have been chanting a melodious paean just then at the thought that his first battle had been fought, that his spirit, which had been troubled, had risen superior to the conflict, and that he was already victorious in the first of the three terrible struggles. As soon as this had occurred there came another hour, and with it the power of darkness, in which not so much the spirit as the soul of our blessed Lord was to sustain the shock of the encounter. This took place in the garden. You know that after he had come forth triumphant in this death-struggle he went to the conflict more expressly in his body, undergoing in his physical nature the scourging, and the spitting, and the crucifixion; although in that third case there was a grief of spirit and an anguish of soul likewise, which mingled their tributary streams. We would counsel you to meditate upon each separately, according to the time and the circumstance in which the pre-eminence of any one of these is distinctly adverted to.

This second conflict which we have now before us well deserves our most reverent attention. I think it has been much misunderstood. Possibly a few thoughts may be given us tonight which shall clear away the mist from our understanding, and open some of the mystery to our hearts. It seems to me that the agony in the garden was a repetition of the temptation in the wilderness. These two contests with the prince of darkness have many points of exact correspondence. If carefully pondered, you may discover that there is a singular and striking connection between the triple temptation and the triple prayer. Having fought Satan at the first in the wilderness, on the threshold of his public ministry, our Lord now finds him at the last in the garden as he nears the termination of his mediatorial work on the earth. Keep in mind that it is the soul of Jesus of which we now have to speak, while I take up the several points consecutively, offering a few brief words on each.

THE PLACE OF CONFLICT has furnished the theme of so many discourses that you can hardly expect anything new to be said upon it. Let us, however, stir up your minds by way of remembrance. Jesus went to the GARDEN, there to endure the conflict, because it was the place of meditation. It seemed fit that his mental conflict should be carried on in the place where man is most at home in the pensive musings of his mind –

> The garden contemplation suits.

As Jesus had been accustomed to indulge himself with midnight reveries in the midst of those olive groves, he fitly chooses a place sacred to the studies of the mind to be the place memorable for the struggles of his soul –

> In a garden man became
> Heir of endless death and pain.

It was there the first Adam fell, and it was meet that there

> The second Adam should restore
> The ruins of the first.

He went to that particular garden, it strikes me, because it was within the boundaries of Jerusalem. He might have gone to Bethany that night as he had on former nights, but why did he not? Do you not know that it was according to the Levitical law that the Israelites should sleep within the boundaries of Jerusalem, on the Paschal night? When they came up to the temple to keep the Passover they must not go away till that Paschal night was over. So our Lord selected a rendezvous within the liberties of the city, that he might not transgress even the slightest jot or tittle of the law. And again, he chose that garden, amongst others contiguous to Jerusalem, because Judas knew the place. He wanted retirement, but he did not want a place where he could skulk and hide himself. It was not for Christ to give himself up – that were like suicide; but it was not for him to withdraw and secrete himself – that were like cowardice. So he goes to a place which he is quite sure that Judas, who was aware of his habitudes, knows he is accustomed to visit; and there, like one who, so far from being afraid to meet his death, pants for the baptism with which he is to be baptized, he awaits the crisis that he had so distinctly anticipated. 'If they seek me', he seemed to say, 'I will be where they can readily find me, and lead me away.' Every time we walk in a garden I think we ought to recollect the garden where the Saviour walked, and the sorrows that befell him there. Did he select a garden, I wonder, because we are all so fond of such places, thus linking our seasons of recreation with the most solemn mementoes of himself? Did he recollect what forgetful creatures we are, and did he therefore let his blood fall upon the soil of a garden, that so often as we dig and delve therein we might lift up our thoughts to him who fertilised earth's soil, and delivered it from the curse by virtue of his own agony and griefs?

Our next thought shall be about the WITNESSES.

Christ's spiritual suffering was altogether within the veil. As I have said, no one could descry or describe it. But his soul-sufferings had some witnesses. Not the rabble, not the multitude; when they saw his bodily suffering, that was all they could understand, therefore it was all they were permitted to see. Just so, Jesus had often shown them the flesh as it were, or the carnal things of his teaching, when he gave them a parable; but he had never shown them the soul, the hidden life of his teaching, this he reserved for his disciples. And thus it was in his passion; he let the Greek and the Roman gather around in mockery, and see his flesh torn, and rent, and bleeding, but he did not let them go into the garden with him to witness his anguish or his prayer. Within that enclosure none came but the disciples. And mark, my brethren, not all the disciples were there. There were a hundred and twenty of his disciples, at least, if not more, but only eleven bore him company then. Those eleven must cross that gloomy brook of Kedron with him, and eight of them are set to keep the door, their faces towards the world, there to sit and watch; only three go into the garden, and those three see something of his sufferings; they behold him when the agony begins, but still at a distance. He withdraws from them a stone's cast, for he must tread the wine-press alone, and it is not possible that the priestly sufferer should have a single compeer in the offering which he is to present to his God. At last it came to this, that there was only one observer. The chosen three had fallen asleep, God's unsleeping eye alone looked down upon him. The Father's ear alone was attentive to the piteous cries of the Redeemer.

> He knelt, the Saviour knelt and pray'd,
> When but his Father's eye
> Look'd through the lonely garden's shade
> On that dread agony:
> The Lord of all above, beneath,
> Was bow'd with sorrow unto death!

Then there came an unexpected visitor. Amazement wrapped the sky, as Christ was seen of angels to be sweating blood for us. 'Give strength to Christ', the Father said as he addressed some strong-winged spirit.

> The astonish'd seraph bow'd his head,
> And flew from worlds on high.

He stood to strengthen, not to fight, for Christ must fight alone; but applying some holy cordial, some sacred anointing to the oppressed Champion who was ready to faint, he, our great Deliverer, received strength from on high, and rose up to the last of his fights. Oh! my dear friends, does not all this teach us that the outside world knows nothing about Christ's soul-sufferings? They draw a picture of him; they carve a piece of wood or ivory, but they do not know his soul sufferings; they cannot enter into them. Nay, the mass of his own people even do not know them, for they are not made conformable to those sufferings by a spiritual fellowship. We have not that keen sense of mental things to sympathize with such grievings as he had, and even the favoured ones, the three, the elect out of the elect, who have the most of spiritual graces and who have therefore the most of suffering to endure, and the most of depression of spirits, even they cannot pry into the fullness of the mystery. God only knows the soul-anguish of the Saviour when he sweat great drops of blood; angels saw it, but yet they understood it not. They must have wondered more when they saw the Lord of life and glory sorrowful with exceeding sorrowfulness, even unto death, than when they saw this round world spring into beautiful existence from nothingness, or when they saw Jehovah garnish the heavens with his Spirit, and with his hand form the crooked serpent. Brethren, we cannot expect to know the length and breadth and height of these things, but as our own experience deepens and darkens we shall know more and more of what Christ suffered in the garden.

Having thus spoken about the place and the witnesses, let us say a little concerning THE CUP ITSELF.

What was this 'cup' about which our Saviour prayed – 'If it be possible let this cup pass from me'? Some of us may have entertained the notion that Christ desired, if possible, to escape from the pangs of death. You may conjecture that, although he had undertaken to redeem his people, yet his human nature flinched and started back at the perilous hour. *I* have thought so myself in times past, but on more mature consideration, I am fully persuaded that such a supposition would reflect upon the Saviour a dishonour. I do not consider that the expression 'this cup' refers to death at all. Nor do I imagine that the dear Saviour meant for a single moment to express even a particle of desire to escape from the pangs, which were necessary for our redemption. This 'cup', it appears to me, relates to something altogether different – not to the last conflict, but to the conflict in which he was then engaged. If you study the words – and especially the Greek words – which are used by the various evangelists, I think you will find that they all tend to suggest and confirm this view of the subject. The Saviour's spirit having been vexed and having triumphed, there was next an attack made by the Evil Spirit upon his mental nature, and this mental nature became in consequence thereof most horribly despondent and cast down. As when on the pinnacle of the temple the Saviour felt the fear of falling, so when in the garden he felt a sinking of soul, an awful despondency, and he began to be very heavy. The cup, then, which he desired to pass from him was, I believe, that cup of despondency, and nothing more. I am the more disposed so to interpret it, because not a single word recorded by any of the four evangelists seems to exhibit the slightest wavering on the part of our Saviour as to offering himself up as an atoning sacrifice. Their testimony is frequent and conclusive: 'He set his face to go towards Jerusalem'; 'I have a baptism to be baptized with, and how am I straitened till it be accomplished'; 'The Son of man goeth, as it is written of him.' You never hear a sentence of reluctance or hesitancy. It does not seem to be consistent with the character of our blessed Lord, even as man, to suppose that he desired that final cup of his sufferings to pass away from him at all.

Moreover, there is this, which I take to be a strong argument. The apostle tells us that he was 'heard in that he feared'. Now, if he feared to die, he was not heard, for he did die. If he feared to bear the wrath of God, or the weight of human sin, and really desired to escape therefrom, then he was not heard, for he did feel the weight of sin, and he did suffer the weight of his Father's vindictive wrath. Thus it appears to me that what he feared was that dreadful depression of mind, which had suddenly come upon him, so that his soul was very heavy.

He prayed his Father that that cup might pass away; and so it did, for I do not see in all the Saviour's griefs afterwards that singular overwhelming depression he endured when in the garden. He suffered much in Pilate's hall, he suffered much upon the tree; but there was, I was almost about to say, a bold cheerfulness about him even to the last, when for the joy that was set before him he endured the cross; yea, when he cried, 'I thirst', and, 'My God, my God, why hast thou forsaken me?' I think I notice a holy force and vigour about the words and thoughts of the sufferer which not the weak and trembling state of his body could extinguish. The language of that Twenty-Second Psalm, which seems to have struck the key-note, if I may so speak, of his devotion on the cross, is full of faith and confidence. If the first verse contains the bitterest of woe, the twenty-first verse changes the plaintive strain. 'Thou hast heard (or answered) me' marks a transition from suffering to satisfaction which it is delightful to dwell upon.

Now, perhaps some of you may think, that if this cup only meant depression of the spirits and dismay of the soul it was nothing of much moment or significance, or at least it weakens the spell of those unwonted words and deeds which twine around Gethsemane. Permit me to beg your pardon. Personally I know that there is nothing on earth that the human frame can suffer to be compared with despondency and prostration of mind. Such is the dolefulness and gloom of a heavy soul, yea, a soul exceeding heavy even unto death, that I could imagine the pangs of dissolution to be lighter. In our latest hour joy may light up the heart, and the sunshine of heaven within may bear up the soul when all without is dark.

But when the iron entereth into a man's soul, he is unmanned indeed. In the cheerlessness of such exhausted spirits the mind is confounded; well can I understand the saying that is written, 'I am a worm and no man', of one that is a prey to such melancholy. Oh that cup! When there is not a promise that can give you comfort, when everything in the world looks dark, when your very mercies affright you, and rise like hideous spectres and portents of evil before your view, when you are like the brethren of Benjamin as they opened the sacks and found the money, but instead of being comforted thereby said, 'What is this that God hath done unto us?' when everything looks black, and you seem, through some morbid sensitiveness into which you have fallen, to distort every object and every circumstance into a dismal caricature, let me say to you, that for us poor sinful men this is a cup more horrible than any which inquisitors could mix.

I can imagine Anne Askew on the rack, braving it out, like the bold woman she was, facing all her accusers, and saying:

> 'I am not she that lyst
> My anchor to let fall;
> For every dryzzling myst
> My ship's substantiall',

but I cannot think of a man in the soul-sickness of such depression of spirits as I am referring to, finding in thought or song a palliative for his woe. When God touches the very secret of a man's soul, and his spirit gives way, he cannot bear up very long; and this seems to me to have been the cup which the Saviour had to drink just then, from which he prayed to be delivered, and concerning which he was heard.

Consider for a moment what he had to depress his soul. Everything, my brethren, everything was draped in gloom, and overcast with darkness that might be felt. There was *the past*. Putting it as I think he would look at it, his life had been unsuccessful. He could say with Isaiah, 'Who hath believed our report, and to whom is the arm of the Lord revealed?' 'He came unto his own, and his own received him not.' And how poor was that little success he did have! There were his twelve disciples; one of them he knew to be on the way to betray him; eight of them were asleep at the entrance to the garden, and three asleep within the garden! He knew that they would all forsake him, and one of them would deny him with oaths and curses! What was there to comfort him? When a man's spirit sinks he wants a cheerful companion; he wants somebody to talk to him. Was not this felt by the Saviour? Did not he go three times to his disciples? He knew they were but men; but then a man can comfort a man in such a time as that. The sight of a friendly face may cheer one's own countenance, and enliven one's heart. But he had to shake them from their slumbers, and then they stared at him with unmeaning gaze. Did he not return back again to prayer because there was no eye to pity, and none that could help? He found no relief. Half a word sometimes, or even a smile, even though it be only from a child, will help you when you are sad and prostrate. But Christ could not get even that. He had to rebuke them almost bitterly. Is not there a tone of irony about his remonstrance? 'Sleep on now and take your rest.' He was not angry, but he did feel it. When a man is low-spirited he feels more keenly and acutely than at other times; and although the splendid charity of our Lord made that excuse – 'The spirit is willing but the flesh is weak', yet it did cut him to the heart, and he had an anguish of soul like that which Joseph felt when he was sold into Egypt by his brethren. You will see, then, that both the past and the present were sufficient to depress him to the greatest degree. But there was *the future*; and as he looked forward to that, devoted as his heart was, and unfaltering as was the courage of his soul (for it were sacrilege and slander methinks to impute even a thought of flinching to him), yet his human heart quailed; he seemed to think – 'Oh! how shall I bear it?' The mind started back from the shame, and the body started back from the pain, and the soul and body both started back from the thought of death, and of death in such an ignominious way:

> He proved them all – the doubt, the strife,
> The faint, perplexing dread;
> The mists that hang o'er parting life
> All gathered round his head:
> That he who gave man's breath might know
> The very depths of human woe.

Brethren, none of us have such cause for depression as the Saviour had. We have not his load to carry; and we have a helper to help us whom he had not, for God who forsook him will never forsake us. Our soul may be cast down within us, but we can never have such great reason for it, nor can we ever know it to so great an extent as our dear Redeemer did. I wish I could picture to you that lovely man, friendless like a stag at bay, with the dogs compassing him round about, and the assembly of the wicked enclosing him; foreseeing every incident of his passion, even to the piercing of his hands and his feet, the parting of his garments, and the lots cast upon his vesture, and anticipating that last death-sweat without a drop of water to cool his lips! I can but conceive that his soul must have felt within itself a solemn trembling, such as might well make him say, 'I am exceeding sorrowful even unto death.'

This, then, seems to me to be the cup which our Lord Jesus Christ desired to have passed from him, and which did pass from him in due time.

Advancing a little further, I want you to think of the AGONY. We have been accustomed so to call this scene in the garden. You all know that it is a word, which signifies 'wrestling'. Now, there is no wrestling where there is only one individual. To this agony, therefore, there must have been two parties. Were there not, however mystically speaking, two parties in Christ? What do I see in this King of Sharon but, as it were, two armies? There was the stern resolve to do all, and to accomplish the work which he had undertaken; and there was the mental weakness and depression which seemed to say to him, 'You cannot; you will never accomplish it.' 'Our fathers trusted in thee, and thou didst deliver them. They cried unto thee and were delivered; they trusted in thee and were not confounded'; 'but I am a worm and no man, a reproach of men, and despised of the people'; so that the two thoughts come into conflict – the shrinking of the soul, and yet the determination of his invincible will to go on with it, and to work it out. He was in an agony in that struggle between the overwhelming fear of his mind and the noble eagerness of his spirit. I think, too, that Satan afflicted him; that the powers of darkness were permitted to use their utmost craft in order to drive the Saviour to absolute despair. One expression used to depict it I will handle very delicately; a word that, in its rougher sense, means, and has been applied to, persons out of their mind and bereft for awhile of reason. The term used concerning the Saviour in Gethsemane can only be interpreted by a word equivalent to our 'distracted'. He was like one bewildered with an overwhelming weight of anxiety and terror. But his divine nature awakened up his spiritual faculties and his mental energy to display their full power. His faith resisted the temptation to unbelief. The heavenly goodness that was within him so mightily contended with the Satanic suggestions and insinuations which were thrown in his way that it came to a wrestling. I should like you to catch the idea of wrestling, as though you saw two men trying to throw one another, struggling together till the muscles stand out and the veins start like whipcord on their brows. That were a fearful spectacle when two men in desperate wrath thus close in with each other. But the Saviour was thus wrestling with the powers of darkness, and he grappled with such terrible earnestness in the fray that he sweat, as it were, great drops of blood:

> The powers of hell united prest,
>   And squeezed his heart, and bruised his breast,
> What dreadful conflicts raged within,
> When sweat and blood forced through his skin!

Observe the way in which Christ conducted the agony. It was by prayer. He turned to his Father three times with the self-same words. It is an index of distraction when you repeat yourself. Three times with the self-same words he approached his God – 'My Father, let this cup pass from me.' Prayer is the great cure-all for depression of spirit. 'When my spirit is overwhelmed within me, I will look to the rock that is higher than I.' There will be a breaking up altogether, and a bursting of spirit, unless you pull up the sluices of supplication, and let the soul flow out in secret communion with God. If we would state our griefs to God they would not fret and fume within, and wear out our patience as they are sometimes wont to do. In connection with the agony and the prayer there seems to have been a bloody sweat. It has been thought by some that the passage only means that the sweat was like drops of blood; but then the word 'like', is used in Scripture to signify not merely resemblance but the identical thing itself. We believe that the Saviour did sweat from his entire person, great drops of blood falling down to the ground. Such an occurrence is very rare indeed among men. It has happened some few times. Books of surgery record a few instances, but I believe that the persons who under some horrifying grief experience such a sweat never recover; they have always died. Our Saviour's anguish had this peculiarity about it, that though he sweat as it were great drops of blood falling to the ground, so copiously as if in a crimson shower, yet he survived.

His blood must needs be shed by the hands of others, and his soul poured out unto death in another form. Remembering the doom of sinful man – that he should eat his bread in the sweat of his face, we see the penalty of sin exacted in awful measure of him who stood surety for sinners. As we eat bread this day at the table of the Lord we commemorate the drops of blood that he sweat. With the perspirings on his face, and huge drops on his brow man toils for the bread that perishes; but bread is only the staff of life: when Christ toiled for life itself to give it to men he sweat, not the common perspiration of the outward form, but the blood which flows from the very heart itself.

Would that I had words to bring all this before you. I want to make you see it; I want to make you feel it. The heavenly Lover who had nought to gain except to redeem our souls from sin and Satan, and to win our hearts for himself, leaves the shining courts of his eternal glory and comes down as a man, poor, feeble, and despised. He is so depressed at the thought of what is yet to be done and suffered, and under such pressure of Satanic influence, that he sweat drops of blood, falling upon the cold frosty soil in that moon-lit garden. Oh the love of Jesus! Oh the weight of sin! Oh the debt of gratitude which you and I owe to him!

> Were the whole realm of nature mine,
> That were a present far too small:
> Love so amazing, so divine,
> Demands my soul, my life, my all.

We must proceed with the rich narrative to meditate upon our SAVIOUR CONQUERING.

Our imagination is slow to fix upon this precious feature of the dolorous history. Though he had said, 'If it be possible let this cup pass from me'; yet presently we observe how tranquil and calm he is when he rises up from that scene of prostrate devotion! He remarks, as though it were in an ordinary tone of voice he announced some expected circumstance – 'He is at hand that shall betray me; rise, let us be going.' There is no distraction now, no hurry, no turmoil, no exceeding sorrow even unto death. Judas comes, and Jesus says, 'Friend, wherefore art thou come?' You would hardly know him to be the same man that was so sorrowful just now. One word with an emanation of his Deity suffices to make all the soldiery fall backwards. Then he turns round and touches the ear of the high priest's servant, and heals it as in happier days he was wont to heal the diseases and the wounds of the people that flocked round him in his journeys. Away he goes, so calm and collected that unjust accusations cannot extort a reply from him; and though beset on every hand yet is he led as a lamb to the slaughter, and as a sheep before her shearers is dumb, so he opens not his mouth. That was a magnificent calmness of mind that sealed his lips, and kept him passive before his foes. You and I could not have done it. It must have been a deep profound peace within which enabled him to be thus mute and still amidst the hoarse murmur of the council and the boisterous tumult of the multitude. I believe that having fought the enemy within, he had achieved a splendid victory; he was heard in that he feared, and was now able in the fullness of his strength to go out to the last tremendous conflict in which he met the embattled hosts of earth and hell; and yet unabashed after he had encountered them all, to wave the banner of triumph, and to say, 'It is finished.'

What, then, let us ask in drawing to a conclusion, is the LESSON FROM ALL THIS? I think I could draw out twenty lessons, but if I did they would not be so good and profitable as the one lesson which the Saviour draws himself. What was the lesson, which he particularly taught to his disciples? Now, Peter, and James, and John, open your ears; and thou, Magdalene, and thou, Mary, and thou, the wife of Herod's steward, and other gracious women, listen for the inference which I am going to draw. It is not mine; it is that of our Lord and Master himself. With how much heed should we treasure it up! 'What I say unto you I say unto all, Watch.' 'Watch'; and yet again, 'Watch and pray lest ye enter into temptation.' I have been turning this over in my mind to make out the connection. Why on this particular occasion should he exhort them to watch? It strikes me that there were two sorts of watching. Did you notice that there were eight disciples at the garden gate? They were watching, or ought to have been; and three were inside the garden; they were watching, or ought to have been. But they watched differently. Which way were the eight looking? It strikes me that they were set there to look outwards, to watch lest Christ should be surprised by those who would attack him. That was the object of their being put there? The other three were set to watch his actions and his words; to look at the Saviour and see if they could help, or cheer, or encourage him. Now, you and I have reason to look both ways, and the Saviour seems to say as we look upon the agony – 'You will have to feel something like this, therefore watch'; watch outwards; be always on your watch-tower, lest sin surprise you. It is through trespasses that you will be brought into this agony; it is by giving Satan an advantage over you that the sorrows of your soul will be multiplied. If your foot slip your heart will become the prey of gloom. If you neglect communion with Jesus, if you grow cold or lukewarm in your affections, if you do not live up to your privileges, you will become the prey of darkness, dejection, discouragement, and despair; therefore, watch, lest ye enter upon this great and terrible temptation. Satan cannot bring strong faith, when it is in healthy exercise, into such a state of desolation. It is when your faith declines and your love grows negligent, and your hope is inanimate, that he can bring you into such disconsolate heaviness that you see not your signs, nor know whether you are a believer or not. You will not be able to say, 'My Father', for your soul will doubt whether you are a child of God at all. When the ways of Zion mourn, the harps of the sons and daughters of Zion are unstrung. Therefore, keep good watch, ye who like the eight disciples are charged as sentinels at the threshold of the garden.

But ye three, watch inward. Look at Christ. 'Consider him that endured such contradiction of sinners against himself.' Watch the Saviour, and watch with the Saviour. Brethren and sisters, I should like to speak this to you so emphatically that you would never forget it. Be familiar with the passion of your Lord. Get right up to the cross. Do not be satisfied with that, but get the cross on your shoulders; get yourself bound to the cross in the spirit of the apostle when he said, 'I am crucified with Christ, nevertheless I live.' I do not know that I have had sweeter work to do for a long time than when a few weeks ago I was looking over all the hymn-writers and all the poets I knew of for hymns upon the passion of the Lord. I tried to enjoy them as I selected them, and to get into the vein in which the poets were when they sung them. Believe me, there is no fount that yields such sweet water as the fount that springs from Calvary just at the foot of the cross. Here it is that there is a sight to be seen more astounding and more ravishing than even from the top of Pisgah. Get into the side of Christ; it is a cleft of the rock in which you may hide until the tempest is overpassed. Live in Christ; live near to Christ; and then, let the conflict come, and you will overcome even as he overcame, and rising up from your sweat and from your agony you will go forth to meet even death itself with a calm expression on your brow, saying, 'My Father, not as I will, but as thou wilt.'

My God, I love thee; not because
 I hope for heaven thereby,
Nor because they who love thee not
 Must burn eternally.

Thou, O my Jesus, thou didst me
 Upon the cross embrace;
For me didst bear the nails and spear,
 And manifold disgrace;

And griefs and torments numberless,
 And sweat of agony;
Yea, death itself – and all for me
 Who was thine enemy.

Then why, O blessed Jesu Christ,
 Should I not love thee well?
Not for the hope of winning heaven,
 Nor of escaping hell;

Not with the hope of gaining aught,
 Nor seeking a reward
But as thyself hast loved me,
 O ever-loving Lord.

E'en so I love thee, and will love,

> And in thy praise will sing;
> Because thou art my loving God,
> And my Eternal King.

I hope that this meditation may be profitable to some tried Christians, and even to impenitent sinners likewise. Oh that the pictures I have been trying to draw might be seen by some who will come and trust in this wondrous Man, this wondrous God, who saves all who trust in him. Oh, rest on him! 'Though your sins be as scarlet, they shall be as white as snow; though they be red like crimson, they shall be as wool.' Do but trust him, and you are saved. I do not say you shall be saved another day, but you are saved tonight. The sin which was on your shoulder heavy as a burden when you came into this house shall all be gone. Look now to him in the garden, on the cross, and on the throne. Trust him; trust him; trust him now; trust him only; trust him wholly;

> Let no other trust intrude;
> None but Jesus, none but Jesus
> Can do helpless sinners good.

May the Lord bless you, every one in this assembly, and at the table may you have his presence. Amen.

9

JESUS IN GETHSEMANE [1]

'When Jesus had spoken these words, he went forth
with his disciples over the brook Kedron, where was a
garden, into the which he entered, and his disciples.
And Judas also, which betrayed him, knew the place;
for Jesus ofttimes resorted thither with his disciples.'
JOHN 18:1–2

I REMEMBER TO HAVE READ somewhere, though I cannot just
now recall the authority, that Bethany – to which place one would
have thought the Saviour would have gone to spend the night, at
the house of Mary and her sister Martha, was over the brow of
the Mount of Olives, and was out of the bounds of the city of
Jerusalem. Now, at the Passover, it was incumbent that all who
kept the feast should spend the whole night within the bounds of
the city; and our Divine Lord and Master, scrupulous to observe
every point of the old law, did not go over the hill, but stayed within
the area which was technically considered to be part and parcel of
Jerusalem; so that his going to Gethsemane was, in part, a
fulfilment of the ceremonial law; and, for that reason, he went no
further, and sought no other shelter.

Our Lord also knew that, on that particular night, he would be
betrayed into the hands of his enemies; and, therefore, he would
need to be prepared, by a special season of devotion, for the terrible
ordeal he was about to endure. That Passover night was a night to
be remembered on this account, and he would, therefore, keep it
peculiarly sacred; but it was to be made still more memorable as

[1] Sermon No. 2,767. Preached at the Metropolitan Tabernacle on Sunday evening,
6 March 1881.

the time of the commencement of his passion sufferings, so he determined to spend the whole night in prayer to his Father. In this act, he reminds us of Jacob by the brook Jabbok; when he had to face trouble on the morrow, he spent the night in wrestling prayer; and this greater Jacob spent his night, not by Jabbok, but by the black, foul brook of Kedron, and there wrestled with mightier power even than the patriarch put forth in his notable night struggle with the Angel of the covenant. I want you to try, in thought, to go as far as Gethsemane, and I think you ought to be encouraged to go there because our text says 'Jesus ofttimes resorted thither with his disciples.'

I. And, first, so far as we can in thought, LET US VIEW THE PLACE. I have never seen the garden of Gethsemane; many travellers tell us that they have done so, and they have described what they saw there. My impression is, that not one of them ever saw the real spot, and that not a trace of it remains. There are certain old olive trees, within an enclosure, which are commonly thought to have been growing at the time of the Saviour; but that seems scarcely possible, for Josephus tells us that the whole of the trees round about Jerusalem were cut down, many of them to be made into crosses for the crucifixion of the Jews, others of them to assist in building the bulwarks with which the Roman emperor surrounded the doomed city. There does not seem to have been scarcely anything left that would be a true relic of the old city, and I cannot imagine that the olive trees would be spared. From what I have heard from brethren who have gone to the reputed garden of Gethsemane, I conclude that it is not very helpful to one's devotions to go there at all. One, who thought to spend a part of his Sabbath there, and who hoped to enjoy much fellowship with Christ in the place, said that he was made very bitterly to learn the meaning of our Saviour's words to the woman at the well of Sychar, 'The hour cometh, when ye shall neither in this mountain, nor yet at Jerusalem, worship the Father ... The hour cometh, and now is, when the true worshippers shall worship the Father in spirit and in truth: for the Father seeketh such to worship him.'

I do not want to find out exactly where Gethsemane was; it is enough for me to know that it was at the side of Mount Olivet, and that *it was a very retired spot*. My conception of it is the result of having, for many winters, resided in a little town in the South of France where olive trees grow to perfection; and where, on the side of the hills, I have often sat me down in olive groves, and I have said to myself, 'Gethsemane was a place just like this.' I am sure it was so, because one olive garden, on the side of a hill, must necessarily be very like another. The hills are lined out in terrace above terrace, each one seldom above eight, ten, or twelve feet wide; then you rise, say, five, six, seven, or eight feet, and there is another terrace, and so on right up the hill; and on these terraces the olive trees grow.

One of the charms of an olive garden of that kind is that, as soon as you get into it, you may sit down under the lee of the bank at the back of the terrace – perhaps in an angle where you are sheltered from the wind – and you will be completely hidden from all observers. I have had persons sitting within a few yards of me, of whose presence I had no idea. One Sabbath day, when we had been spending a little time in prayer together, I saw what appeared to be an Englishman's tall hat moving away, at a little distance, just above one of the terraces. By-and-by, I recognized the head that was under the hat as that of a Christian brother whom I knew, and I found that he had been walking up and down there, studying his sermon for the afternoon. He had not noticed us, except that he had heard some sounds that seemed to him like prayer and praise. Many of you might be in an olive garden; but, unless you made some sign of recognition to your friends, they would scarcely know that anybody else was there; and under the thick yet light foliage, with the glints of sunlight shining through, or at night, under the kind of ashy, grey colour, with the moonlight glimmering through with its silvery beams, I cannot imagine a more delightful place of retreat – a place where one would feel surer of being quite alone, even though somebody might be near you – a place where you might feel free to express your thoughts and your prayers; because, at any rate, to your own consciousness, you would seem to be entirely alone.

I cannot help thinking that our Saviour also loved to get among the olive trees, *because of the very congenial form of the olive*. It twists and winds and turns about as though it were in an agony. It has to draw up oil out of the flinty rock, and it seems to do so with labour and travail; the very shape of many olive trees seems to suggest that thought. So, an olive garden is a place of painful pleasure and of fruitful toil, where the oil is rich and fat, but where much effort has to be expended in the extraction of it out of the hard soil on which the olive stands. I believe that others have felt about this matter as I have felt, namely, that there is no tree which seems more suggestive of a fellow-feeling with the sufferer than an olive, no shade that is more sweetly pensive, more suitable to the season of sorrow, and the hour of devout meditation. I marvel not, therefore, that Jesus sought the garden of Gethsemane that he might be quite alone – that he might pour out his soul before God, and yet might have some companions within call without being disturbed by their immediate presence.

One reason for his going to that particular garden was, because he had gone there so often that *he loved to be in the old familiar place*. Do you not feel something of that in your own special place of prayer? I do not like reading out of other people's Bibles so well as out of my own. I do not know how it is, but I like my own study Bible best of all; and if I must have a smaller one, I prefer one that has the words on the same page as in my Bible, so that I may easily find them; and I do not know whether you feel the same, but I can usually pray best in one place. There are certain spots where I delight to be when I draw near to God; there is some association, connected with them, of former interviews with my heavenly Father, that makes the old arm-chair to be the very best place at which one can kneel. So, I think, the Saviour loved Gethsemane, because he had oftentimes resorted thither with his disciples; and, therefore he makes that the sacred spot where his last agony of prayer shall be poured out before his Father.

II. That, however, is only the introduction to the main matter of our meditations; so, now, LET US VIEW THE SAVIOUR IN GETHSEMANE, THAT WE MAY IMITATE HIM.

And, first, our blessed Lord is to be imitated by us in that *he frequently sought and enjoyed retirement*. His was a very busy life; he had much more to do than you and I have; yet he found abundant time for private prayer. He was much holier than any of us are; yet he realized his need of private prayer and meditation. He was much wiser than we shall ever be; yet he felt the necessity for retiring into solitude for communion with his Father. He had much power over himself, he could control and compose himself far more readily than we can; yet, amid the distractions of the world, he felt that he must frequently get away alone. It would be well for us if we were more often alone; we are so busy – so taken up with this or that committee meeting, working-class, Sunday-school, preaching, talking, visiting, gossiping – all sorts of things, good, bad, or indifferent – that we have no leisure for the due cultivation of our spiritual life. We rush from pillar to post, without proper time for rest; but, brothers and sisters, if we want to be strong, if we mean to be like Jesus our Lord and Saviour, we must have our Gethsemane, our place for secret retirement, where we can get alone with our God. I think it was Luther who said, 'I have a hard day's work before me today; it will take me many hours, and there will be a stern struggle, so I must have at least three hours' prayer, that I may gain the necessary strength for my task.' Ah! we do not act in that wise fashion nowadays; we feel as if we cannot spare the time for private prayer; but, had we more communion with God, we should have more influence with men.

But our blessed Master is especially to be imitated in that he sought retirement when *he was about to enter upon the great struggle of his life*. Just then, when Judas was about to give the traitor's kiss – when scribes and Pharisees were about to hound him to the cross – it was then that he felt that he must get away to Gethsemane, and be alone in prayer with his Father. What did you do, my dear brother, when you apprehended trial? Why, you sought out a sympathizing friend. I shall not blame you for desiring the consolations of true friendship, but I shall not commend you if you put them into the place of communion with God. Are you, even now, dreading some approaching calamity? What are you doing to meet it? I will not suggest that you should neglect certain precautions, but I would admonish you that the first and best precaution is to get away to your God in prayer. As the feeble conies find their shelter in the solid rock, and as the doves fly away to their home in the dovecot, so should Christians, when they expect trouble, fly straight away to their God upon the wings of fear and faith. Your great strength does not lie in your hair, else might you feel as proud as Samson was in the days of his victories; your great strength lies in your God. Wherefore, flee away to him with all speed, and ask from him help in this your hour of need.

Some of you pray when you are, as it were, at Calvary, but not at Gethsemane. I mean, you pray when the trouble comes upon you, but not when it is on the road; yet your Master here teaches you that to conquer at your Calvary, you must commence by wrestling at your Gethsemane. When as yet it is but the shadow of your coming trial that spreads its black wings over you, cry unto God for help. When you are not emptying the bitter cup – when you are only sipping the first drops of the wormwood and the gall, begin even then to pray, 'Not as I will, but as thou wilt, O my Father!' You will thus be the better able to drink of the cup to its very dregs when God shall place it in your hand.

We may also imitate our Lord – as far as it would be in our line, *in his taking his disciples with him.* At any rate, if we do not imitate him in this respect, we may certainly admire him; for he took the disciples with him, I think, for two purposes. First, for their good. Remember, brethren and sisters, that the morrow was to be a day of trial for them as well as for himself. He was to be taken to trial and condemnation; but they were to be severely tried, in their fidelity to him, by seeing their Lord and Master put to a shameful death. So he took them with him that they also might pray – that they might learn how to pray by hearing his wondrous prayers – that they might watch and pray, lest they should enter into temptation. Now, sometimes, in your special hour of trouble, I believe that it will be for the good of others for you to communicate to them the story of your distress, and ask them to join you in prayer concerning it. I have often done this, so I can urge you to do the same. I found it a great blessing, on one dark day of my life, to ask my sons, though they were but lads, to come into my room, and pray with their father in his time of trouble. I know that it was good for them, and their prayers were helpful to me; but I acted as I did in part that they might realize their share in domestic responsibilities, that they might come to know their father's God, and might learn to trust him in their time of trouble.

But our Saviour also took his disciples with him to Gethsemane that they might assist to comfort him; and, in this respect, he is to be imitated by us because of his wonderful humility. If those disciples had all done their best, what would it have been worth? But what they really did was most discouraging to Christ, instead of being at all helpful to him. They went to sleep when they should have watched with their Lord, and they did not assist him with their prayers as they might have done. It is noteworthy that he did not ask them to pray with him; he bade them watch and pray, lest they should enter into temptation, but he said to them, 'What, could ye not watch with me one hour?' He did not say, 'What, could ye not pray with me one hour?' He knew that they could not do that. What mortal man could pray at such a time as that, when great drops of bloody sweat punctuated every paragraph of his petition? No; they could not pray with him, but they might have watched with him; yet that they did not do. Sometimes, dear friends, when a very great trial comes upon you, it will be well for you to ask some brothers and sisters, who cannot do much, but who can do something to come and watch with you, and pray with you. If it does not do any good to you, it will be good for them; but it will do good to you also, I feel sure. Often – I have to confess it – I have got two brethren to kneel with me in prayer, when I have been depressed through this late illness of mine, and their honest, earnest, hearty prayers in my study have often lifted me right up into joy and peace. I believe it has done them good also; I know it has done me good, and I feel sure that you might often be a blessing to others if you did not mind confessing to them when you are depressed and sad at heart. Say, 'Come into my room, and watch with me one hour'; and you may add to that request this other one, 'Come and pray with me', for some of them can pray as well as you can, and even better. So imitate the Saviour in endeavouring not only to pray yourself, but to call to your assistance the praying legion of God's elect ones when a great trial is impending.

Still, our Lord's example may mainly be followed in another direction, namely, when we do pray in the presence of a great trouble, *it is well to pray with much importunity.* Our Saviour prayed in Gethsemane three times, using the same words. He prayed with such intensity of desire that his heart seemed to burn with anguish. The canals overflowed their banks, and the red streams came bursting down in bloody drops that fell upon the earth in that rightly-named 'olive-press'. Ah! that is the way to pray – if not actually unto a bloody sweat, as we may not have to do, or be able to do, yet with such intensity of hearty earnestness as we can, and as we ought, when God the Holy Spirit is working mightily in us. We cannot expect to be helped in our time of trouble unless it is intense prayer that we send up to heaven.

But imitate Christ also in *the matter of your prayer*. I feel sure that he only softly whispered the request, 'O my Father, if it be possible, let this cup pass from me.' You also may present that petition, but mind that you say it very softly. Yet I feel certain that it was with all his might that our Saviour said, 'Nevertheless not as I will, but as thou wilt.' In the presence or in the prospect of a great trouble, make this your prayer to God, 'Thy will be done.' Brace up your soul to this point – having asked the Lord to screen you, if it should seem good in his sight, resign yourself absolutely into his hands, and say, 'Nevertheless, O my Father, not as I will, but as thou wilt!'

It is prevailing prayer when one gets as far as that; a man is prepared to die when he knows how to present that petition. That is the best preparation for any cross that may come upon your shoulders. You can die a martyr's death, and clap your hands even in the midst of the fire, if you can, with all your soul, really pray as Jesus prayed, 'Not as I will, but as thou wilt.' This is the object which I set before you, my brothers and sisters in Christ – that, if you are expecting sickness – if you are fearing loss – if you are anticipating bereavement – if you are dreading death – let this be your great ultimatum, go to God now, in the time of your distress, and, by mighty prevailing prayer, with such prayerful sympathy as others can give you, breathe out this one petition, 'Thy will be done, O my Father! Thy will be done; help me to do it; help me to bear it; help me to go through with it all, to thy honour and glory. Let me be baptized with thy baptism, and drink of thy cup, even to the dregs.'

Sometimes, dear friends, you may wish, in your hearts, that the Lord would make great use of you, and yet perhaps he may not do so. Well, a man who holds his tongue, when Christ tells him to do so, is glorifying Christ more than if he opened his mouth, and broke the Master's commandment. There are some of the Lord's people who, by a quiet, holy, consistent manifestation of what the Lord has done for them, glorify him more than they would do if they went from place to place telling out his gospel in a way which would make the gospel itself disgusting to those who heard it. That is quite possible, for some people do it. If my Lord puts me in the front rank, blessed be his name for it, and I must fight for him there as best I can. But if he says to me, 'Lie in bed! Be bed-ridden for seven years, and never get up!' – I have nothing to do but to glorify him in that way. He is the best soldier who does exactly what his captain bids him.

III. Now, in the third place, and only briefly, LET US VIEW THE DISCIPLES IN GETHSEMANE, BY WAY OF INSTRUCTION TO OURSELVES.

Probably, *the disciples had often been with their Master to Gethsemane* – I suppose, sometimes by day, and oftentimes by night, in secret conclave they had been instructed in the olive garden. It had been their Academy; there they had been with the Master in prayer; no doubt, each one praying, and learning how to pray better from his divine example. Dear brothers and sisters, I recommend you oftentimes to get to the place where you can best commune with your God.

But, now, the disciples came to Gethsemane *because a great trouble was impending.* They were brought there that they might watch and pray. So, get you to the place of prayer, at this time of trouble, and at all other times of trial that shall come upon you throughout your whole life. Whenever you hear the knell ringing out all earthly joy, let it ring you into the garden of prayer. Whenever there is the shadow of a coming trouble looming before you, let there also be the substance of more intense communion with God. These disciples were, however, at this time, called to enter into fellowship with their Master in the thicker, deeper darkness that was coming over him – far denser than any that was coming over them. And you are called, dear brothers and sisters, each in your measure, to be baptized unto Jesus in the cloud and in the sea, that you may have fellowship with him in his sufferings. Be not ashamed to go even to Gethsemane with Christ, entering into a knowledge of what he suffered by being made, according to your capacity, to suffer in the selfsame manner. All his true followers have to go there, some have only to stand at the outside gate, and keep watch; but his highly-favoured ones have to go into the denser gloom, and to be nearer to their Lord in his greatest agonies; but, if we are his true disciples, we must have fellowship with him in his sufferings.

Our difficulty is, that the flesh shrinks from this trial, and that, like the disciples, *we sleep when we ought to watch*. When the time of trial comes, if we get depressed in spirit about it, we are apt not to pray with that fervour and vigour which greater hopefulness would have begotten; and when we come to feel something of what the Saviour endured, we are too apt to be overwhelmed by it rather than stimulated by it; and so, when he comes to us, he finds us, like the disciples, 'sleeping for sorrow'. The Master gently said, 'The spirit indeed is willing, but the flesh is weak'; but I do not suppose that one of the disciples made any excuse for himself. I feel, if I may judge them from myself, that I should always have said, 'I never can forgive myself for going to sleep that night; how could I fall asleep when he said, "Watch with me"? And when he came again, with his face red with bloody sweat, and with that disappointed look upon his countenance, said, "What, could ye not watch with me one hour?" how could I go to sleep a second time? and, then, how could I go to sleep a third time?' Oh, I think that Simon Peter must ever have remembered that his Saviour said to him, 'Simon, couldst not thou watch with me one hour?' That question must have stuck by him all his life; and James and John must have felt the same. Brethren and sisters, are any of you sleeping under similar circumstances – while Christ's church is suffering – while Christ's cause is suffering – while Christ's people are suffering – while a trial is coming upon you to help you into fellowship with him? Are you, instead of being aroused to a higher and intenser devotion, sinking into deeper sleep? If so, Christ may in his great love excuse you, but I beg you not to begin making excuses for yourself. Nay, rouse ye, brethren, and 'watch and pray, lest ye enter into temptation.'

That slumber of theirs must have been *greatly rebuked by their Saviour's kindness to them*. As I understand the narrative, our Lord came to his disciples three times, and on the third occasion he found them still heavy with sleep, so he sat down beside them, and said to them, 'Sleep on now, and take your rest.' There he sat, patiently waiting for the traitor's arrival – not expecting any help or sympathy from his disciples, but just watching over them as they would not watch with him, praying for them as they would not pray for themselves, and letting them take another nap while he made himself ready to meet Judas and the rabble throng that would so soon surround him. Our Master, in his great tenderness, sometimes indulges us with such sleeps as these; yet we may have to regret them, and to wish that we had had sufficient strength of mind and earnestness of heart to keep awake, and watch with him in his season of sorrow. It appears to me that, of all the eleven good disciples, there was not one who kept awake. There was one vile traitor, and he was wide-awake. He never went to sleep – he was awake enough to sell his Master, and to act as guide to those who came to capture him.

I think also that, at least partly in consequence of that slumber of the disciples, within a short time, '*they all forsook him, and fled.*' They seem, for the time, to have slept away their attachment to their Lord, and waking, as from a disturbed dream, they scarcely knew what they did, and helter-skelter away they fled. The sheep were all scattered, and the Shepherd was left alone, thus fulfilling the ancient prophecy, 'Smite the Shepherd, and the sheep shall be scattered'; and that other word, 'I have trodden the winepress alone; and of the people there was none with me.' Wake up, brothers and sisters, else you too may forsake your Master; and in the hour when you ought most to prove your fidelity, it may be that your slumbering state of heart will lead on to backsliding, and to forsaking of your Lord. God grant that it may not!

IV. Now I close with a word of warning which I have almost anticipated. LET US, IN THOUGHT, GO TO GETHSEMANE TO TAKE WARNING FROM JUDAS. Let me read to you the latter part of the text: 'Judas also, which betrayed him, knew the place: for Jesus ofttimes resorted thither with his disciples.'

'Judas also, which betrayed him, knew the place.' Yes, *he had probably, many times, been there all night with Christ.* He had sat with the other disciples in a circle round their Lord on one of those olive-clad terraces, and he had listened to his wondrous words in the soft moonlight. He had often heard his Master pray there. 'Judas also, which betrayed him', had heard him pray in Gethsemane. He knew the tones of his voice, the pathos of his pleading, the intense agony of that great heart of love when it was poured out in prayer. He had, no doubt, joined with the other disciples when they said, 'Lord, teach us to pray.'

'Judas also, which betrayed him, knew the place.' He could have pointed out to us the very spot where the Saviour most loved to be – that angle in the terrace, that little corner out of the way, where the Master was wont to find a seat when he sat down, and taught the chosen band around him. Yes, Judas knew the place; and it was because he knew the place that he was able to betray Christ; for, if he had not known where Jesus was, he could not have taken the soldiers there.

It does seem, to me, very dreadful that *familiarity with Christ should have qualified this man to become a traitor*; and it is still true that, sometimes, familiarity with religion may qualify men to become apostates. Oh, if there be a Judas here, I would speak very solemnly to you! You know the place; you know all about church government and church order, and you can go and tell pretty tales about the mistakes made by some of God's servants, who would not err if they could help it. Yes; you know the church members; you know where there are any flaws of character and infirmity of spirit; you know how to go and spread the story of them among worldlings, and you can make such mischief as you could not make if you had not known the place. Yes; and you know the doctrines of grace, at least with a measure of head-knowledge, and you know how to twist them, so as to make them seem ridiculous, even those eternal verities, which ravish the hearts of angels and of the redeemed from among men. Because you know them so well, you know how to parody them, and to caricature them, and to make the grace of God itself seem to be a farce. Yes, you know the place; you have been to the Lord's table, and you have heard the saints speak of their raptures and their ecstasies; and you pretended that

131

you were sharing them. So you know how to go back to the world and to represent true godliness as being all cant and hypocrisy; and you make rare fun out of those most solemn secrets of which a man would scarcely speak to his fellow because they are the private transactions between his soul and his God.

I can hardly realize how terrible will be the doom of those who, after making a profession of religion, have prostituted their knowledge of the inner working of the church of God, and made it the material for novels in which Christ's gospel is held up to scorn. Yet there have been such men, who have not been content to be like birds that have fouled their own nests, for they have also gone forth, and tried also to foul the nest of every believing heart that they could reach. What a dreadful thing it will be if any one of us, here, should know the place, and therefore should betray the Saviour! Do you know the place of private prayer, or do you think you do? Do you know the place where men go when the shadow of a coming trial is looming before them? Do you think you know something about fellowship with Christ in his sufferings? But, what if the greed of gold should overmaster in you, as it did in Judas, such natural attachment as you feel towards Christ and better things? And what if even Gethsemane should, like a pit, open wide its mouth to swallow you up? It is terrible to contemplate, yet it may be true, for 'Judas also, which betrayed him, knew the place.' I cannot bear to think that any one of you should be familiar with the ins and outs of this Tabernacle, and yet should betray Christ – that you should be one of those who gather around this communion table, that you should be familiar with all the loving and tender expressions which we are wont to use here, and yet, after all, should forsake our Lord and Saviour, Jesus Christ. Pass the disciples' question round, and each one ask it, 'Lord, is it I? Is it I?'

> When any turn from Zion's way,
>   (Alas, what numbers do!)
> I think I hear my Saviour say,
>   'Wilt thou forsake me too?'
>
> Ah Lord! with such a heart as mine,
>   Unless thou hold me fast,

I feel I must, I shall decline,
And prove like them at last.

Therefore, hold thou me up, O Lord, and I shall be safe; keep
me even to the end, for thy dear Son's sake! Amen.

IO

THE WEAKENED CHRIST STRENGTHENED [1]

'And there appeared an angel unto him from heaven,
strengthening him.'
LUKE 22:43

I SUPPOSE THAT THIS INCIDENT happened immediately after
our Lord's first prayer in the garden of Gethsemane. His pleading
became so fervent, so intense, that it forced from him a bloody
sweat. He was, evidently, in a great agony of fear as he prayed and
wrestled even unto blood. We are told, by the writer of the Epistle
to the Hebrews, that he 'was heard in that he feared'. It is probable
that this angel came in answer to that prayer. This was the Father's
reply to the cry of his fainting Son, who was enduring an infinity
of sorrow because of his people's sin; and who must, therefore, be
divinely upheld as to his manhood, lest he should be utterly
crushed beneath the terrible weight that was pressing upon his holy
soul.

Scarcely had our Saviour prayed before the answer to his petition
came. It reminds us of Daniel's supplication, and of the angelic
messenger who was caused to fly so swiftly that as soon as the
prayer had left the prophet's lips, Gabriel stood there with the reply
to it. So, brethren and sisters, whenever your times of trial come,
always betake yourselves to your knees. Whatever shape your
trouble may take, if, to you, it should even seem to be a faint
representation of your Lord's agony in Gethsemane, put yourselves

* Sermon No. 2,769. Preached at the Metropolitan Tabernacle on Sunday
evening, 6 March 1881.

into the same posture as that in which he sustained the great shock that came upon him. Kneel down, and cry to your Father who is in heaven, who is able to save you from death, who will prevent the trial from utterly destroying you, will give you strength that you may be able to endure it, and will bring you through it to the praise of the glory of his grace.

That is the first lesson for us to learn from our Lord's experience in Gethsemane – the blessing of prayer. He has bidden us pray, but he has done more than that, for he has set us the example of prayer; and if example be, as we are sure it is, far more powerful than precept, let us not fail to imitate our Saviour in the exercise of potent, prevalent, repeated supplication, whenever our spirits are cast down, and we are in sore distress of soul. Possibly, you have sometimes said, 'I feel so sorrowful that I cannot pray.' Nay, brother, that is the very time when you must pray. As the spices, when bruised, give forth all the more fragrance because of the bruising, so let the sorrow of your spirit cause it to send forth the more fervent prayer to the God who is both able and willing to deliver you. You must express your sorrow in one way or another; so let it not be expressed in murmuring, but in supplication. It is a vile temptation, on the part of Satan, to keep you away from the mercy-seat when you have most need to go there; but do not yield to that temptation. Pray till you can pray; and if you find that you are not filled with the Spirit of supplication, use whatever measure of the sacred bedewing you have; and so, by-and-by, you shall have the anointing of the Spirit, and prayer shall become to you a happier and more joyful exercise than it is at present. Our Saviour said to his disciples, 'My soul is exceeding sorrowful, even unto death'; yet then, above all times, he was in an agony of prayer; and, in proportion to the intensity of his sorrow was the intensity of his supplication.

In our text, there are two things to note. First, *our Lord's weakness*; and, secondly, *our Lord's strengthening*.

I. First, then, let us meditate for a little while upon OUR LORD'S WEAKNESS.

That he was exceedingly weak, is clear from the fact that an angel came from heaven to strengthen him, for the holy angels never do anything that is superfluous. They are the servants of an eminently practical God, who never does that which it is unnecessary for him to do. If Jesus had not needed strengthening, an angel would not have come from heaven to strengthen him. But how strange it sounds to our ears that the Lord of life and glory should be so weak that he should need to be strengthened by one of his own creatures! How extraordinary it seems that he, who is 'very God of very God', should nevertheless, when he appeared on earth as Immanuel, God with us, so completely take upon himself our nature that he should become so weak as to need to be sustained by angelic agency! This struck some of the older saints as being derogatory to his divine dignity; so some manuscripts of the New Testament omit this passage; it is supposed that the verse was struck out by some who claimed to be orthodox, lest, perhaps, the Arians should lay hold upon it, and use it to bolster up their heresies. I cannot be sure who did strike it out, and I am not altogether surprised that they should have done so. They had no right to do anything of the kind, for whatever is revealed in the Scriptures must be true. But they seemed to shudder at the thought that the Son of God should ever have been so weakened as to need the support of an angelic messenger to strengthen him.

Yet, brethren and sisters, *this incident proves the reality of our Saviour's manhood.* Here you can perceive how fully he shares the weakness of our humanity – not in spiritual weakness, so as to become guilty of any sin – but in mental weakness, so as to be capable of great depression of spirit; and in physical weakness, so as to he exhausted to the last degree by his terrible bloody sweat. What is extreme weakness? It is something different from pain, for sharp pain evidences at least some measure of strength; but perhaps some of you know what it is to feel as if you were scarcely alive; you were so weak that you could hardly realize that you were actually living. The blood flowed, if it flowed at all, but very slowly in the canals of your veins; everything seemed stagnant within you. You were very faint, you almost wished that you could become unconscious, for the consciousness you had was extremely painful; you were so weak and sick that you seemed almost ready to die. Our Master's words, 'My soul is exceeding sorrowful, even unto death', prove that the shadow of impending dissolution hung darkly over his spirit, soul, and body, so that he could truly quote the Twenty-Second Psalm, and say, 'Thou hast brought me into the dust of death.' I think, beloved, that you ought to be glad it was so with your Lord, for now you can see how completely he is made like unto his brethren, in their mental depression and physical weakness, as well as in other respects.

It will help you to get an idea of the true manhood of Christ if you remember that *this was not the only time when he was weak*. He, the Son of man, was once a babe; and, therefore, all the tender ministries that have to be exercised because of the helplessness of infancy were necessary also in his case. Wrapped in swaddling bands, and lying in a manger, that little child was, all the while, the mighty God, though he condescended to keep his omnipotence in abeyance in order that he might redeem his people from their sins. Doubt not his true humanity, and learn from it how tenderly he is able to sympathize with all the ills of childhood, and, all the griefs of boyhood, which are not so few or so small as some people imagine.

Besides being thus an infant, and gradually growing in stature just as other children do, our Lord Jesus was often very weary. How the angels must have wondered as they saw him, who sways the sceptre of universal sovereignty, and marshals all the starry hosts according to his will, as he, 'being wearied with his journey, sat thus on the well' at Sychar, waiting for the woman whose soul he had gone to win, and wiping the sweat from his brow, and resting himself after having travelled over the burning acres of the land. The prophet Isaiah truly said that 'the everlasting God, the Lord, the Creator of the ends of the earth, fainteth not, neither is weary.' That is the divine nature of his glorious person. 'Jesus, therefore, being wearied with his journey, sat thus on the well.' That was the human nature of his person. We read that 'he did eat nothing' during the forty days' temptation in the wilderness, and 'he afterwards hungered.' Have any of you ever known what it has been to suffer the bitterness of hunger? Then, remember that our Lord Jesus Christ also endured that pang. He, whom we rightly worship and adore as 'God blessed for ever', as the Son of man, the Mediator between God and men, hungered; and he also thirsted, for he said to the woman at the well, 'Give me to drink.'

In addition to this, our Saviour was often so weary that he slept, which is another proof of his true humanity. He was so tired, once, that he slept even when the ship was tossing to and fro in a storm, and was ready to sink. On one occasion, we read that the disciples 'took him even as he was in the ship', which seems to me to imply even more than it says, namely, that he was so worn out that he was scarcely able to get into the ship; but 'they took him even as he was', and there he fell asleep. We know, moreover, that 'Jesus wept' – not merely once, or twice, but many times; and we also know what completes the proof of his humanity – that he died. It was a strange phenomenon that he, to whom the Father has given 'to have life in himself', should have been called to pass through the gloomy shades of death, that he might in all points be made like unto his brethren, and so be able to fully sympathize with us. O ye weak ones, see how weak your Lord became that he might make you strong! We might read that familiar passage, 'though he was rich, yet for your sakes he became poor, that ye through his poverty might be rich'; in a slightly different way, 'though he was strong, yet for your sakes he became weak, that ye through his weakness might be strong.' Therefore, beloved, 'Be strong in the Lord, and in the power of his might.'

What was *the reason for the special weakness of our Saviour when in the garden of Gethsemane?* I cannot now go fully into that matter, but I want you to notice what it was that tried him so severely there. I suppose, first, it was contact with sin. Our Saviour had always seen the effects of sin upon others, but it had never come home to him so closely as it did when he entered that garden; for there, more than ever before, the iniquity of his people was made to meet upon him, and that contact aroused in him a holy horror. You and I are not perfectly pure, so we are not as horrified at sin as we ought to be; yet, sometimes, we can say, with the psalmist, 'Horror hath taken hold upon me because of the wicked that forsake thy law'; but for our gracious Saviour – hearken to the inspired words, they are none of mine – to be 'numbered with the transgressors', must have been an awful thing to his pure and holy soul. He seemed to shrink back from such a position, and it needed that he should be strengthened in order that he might be able to endure the contact with that terrible mass of iniquity.

But he had, in addition, to bear the burden of that sin. It was not sufficient for him to come into contact with it; but it is written, 'The Lord hath laid on him the iniquity of us all'; and as he began fully to realize all that was involved in his position as the great Sin-bearer, his spirit seemed to droop, and he became exceedingly weak. Ah, sir! if you have to bear the burden of your own sin when you appear before the judgment seat of God, it will sink you to the lowest hell; but what must Christ's agony have been when he was bearing the sin of all his people? As the mighty mass of their guilt came rolling upon him, his Father saw that the human soul and the human body both needed to be upheld, else they would have been utterly crushed before the atoning work had been accomplished.

Contact with sin, and the bearing of sin's penalty, were reason enough to produce the Saviour's excessive weakness in Gethsemane; but, in addition, he was conscious of the approach of death. I have heard some people say that we ought not to shrink from death; but I aver that, in proportion as a man is a good man, death will be distasteful to him. You and I have become, to a large extent, familiarized with the thought of death. We know that we must die – unless the Lord should come soon – for all who have gone before us have done so, and the seeds of death are sown in us, and, like some fell disease, they are beginning to work within our nature. It is natural that we should expect to die, for we know that we are mortal. If anybody were to tell us that we should be annihilated, any reasonable and sensible man would be horrified at the idea, for that is not natural to the soul of man. Well, now, death was as unnatural to Christ as annihilation would be to us. It had never come to be a part of his nature, his holy soul had none of the seeds of death in it; and his untainted body – which had never known any kind of disease or corruption, but was as pure as when, first of all, 'that holy thing' was created by the Spirit of God – that also shrank back from death. There were not in it any of the things, which make death natural; and, therefore, because of the very purity of his nature, he recoiled at the approach of death, and needed to be specially strengthened in order to meet 'the last enemy'.

Probably, however, it was the sense of utter desertion that was preying upon his mind, and so produced that extremity of weakness. All his disciples had failed him, and presently would forsake him. Judas had lifted up his heel against him, and there was not one of all his professed followers who would faithfully cleave to him. Kings, princes, scribes, and rulers were all united against him, and of the people, there were none with him. Worst of all, by the necessity of his expiatory sacrifice, and his substitution for his people, his Father himself withdrew from him the light of his countenance; and, even in the garden, he was beginning to feel that agony of soul which, on the cross, wrung from him that doleful cry, 'My God, my God, why hast thou forsaken me?' And that sense of utter loneliness and desertion, added to all that he had endured, made him so exceedingly weak that it was necessary that he should be specially strengthened for the ordeal through which he had still to pass.

II. Now, in the second place, let us meditate for a little while upon OUR LORD'S STRENGTHENING: 'There appeared an angel unto him from heaven, strengthening him.'

It is night, and there he kneels, under the olives, offering up, as the author of the Letter to the Hebrews says, 'prayers and supplications with strong crying and tears unto him that was able to save him from death.' While wrestling there, he is brought into such a state of agony that he sweats great drops of blood; and, suddenly, there flashes before him, like a meteor from the midnight sky, a bright spirit that had come straight from the throne of God to minister to him in his hour of need.

Think of *the condescension on Christ's part to allow an angel to come and strengthen him.* He is the Lord of angels as well as of men. At his bidding, they fly more swiftly than the lightning flash to do his will. Yet, in his extremity of weakness, he was succoured by one of them. It was a wondrous stoop for the infinitely great and ever-blessed Christ of God to consent that a spirit of his own creation should appear unto him, and strengthen him.

But while I admire the condescension which permitted one angel to come, I equally admire *the self-restraint which allowed only one to come*; for, if he had so pleased, he might have appealed to his Father, and he would at once have sent to him 'more than twelve legions of angels'. No, he did not make such a request; he rejoiced to have one to strengthen him, but he would not have any more. Oh, what matchless beauties are combined in our blessed Saviour! You may look on this side of the shield, and you will perceive that it is of pure gold. Then you may look on the other side of it, but you will not discover that it is brass, as in the fable, for it is gold all through. Our Lord Jesus is 'altogether lovely'. What he does, or what he refrains from doing, equally deserves the praises of his people.

How could the angel strengthen Christ? That is a very natural enquiry; but it is quite possible that, when we have answered that question as well as we can, we shall not have given a full and satisfactory reply to it. Yet I can conceive that, in some mysterious manner, an angel from heaven *may have actually infused fresh vigour into the physical constitution of Christ.* I cannot positively affirm that it was so, but it seems to me a very likely thing. We do know that God can suddenly communicate new strength to fainting spirits; and, certainly, if he willed it, he could thus lift up the drooping head of his Son, and make him feel strong and resolute again.

Perhaps it was so; but, in any case, it must have strengthened the Saviour *to feel that he was in pure company.* It is a great joy to a man, who is battling for the right against a crowd who love the wrong, to find a comrade by his side who loves the truth as he loves it himself. To a pure mind, obliged to listen to the ribald jests of the licentious, I know of nothing that is more strengthening than to get a whisper in the ear from one who says, 'I, too, love that which is chaste and pure, and hate the filthy conversation of the wicked.' So, perhaps, the mere fact of that shining angel standing by the Saviour's side, or reverently bowing before him, may in itself have strengthened him.

Next to that, was *the tender sympathy which this angelic ministration proved.* I can imagine that all the holy angels leant over the battlements of heaven to watch the Saviour's wondrous life; and now that they see him in the garden, and perceive, by his whole appearance, and his desperate agony, that death is drawing to him, they are so astonished that they crave permission that at least one of their number shall go down to see if he cannot carry succour to him from his Father's house above. I can imagine the angels saying,

'Did we not sing of him at Bethlehem when he was born! Did not some of us minister to him when he was in the desert, and amongst wild beasts, hungry after his long fast and terrible temptation? Has he not been seen of angels all the while he has been on earth! Oh, let some one of us go to his relief!' And I can readily suppose that God said to Gabriel, 'Thy name means, "The strength of God"; Go and strengthen your Lord in Gethsemane'; 'and there appeared an angel unto him from heaven strengthening him'. And I think that he was strengthened, at least in part, by observing the sympathy of all the heavenly host with him in his season of secret sorrow. He might seem to be alone as man; but, as Lord and King, he had on his side an innumerable company of angels who waited to do his will; and here was one of them, come to assure him that he was not alone, after all.

Next, no doubt, our Saviour was comforted by *the angel's willing service*. You know, dear brothers and sisters, how a little act of kindness will cheer us when we are very low in spirit. If we are despised and rejected of men, if we are deserted and defamed by those who ought to have dealt differently with us, even a tender look from a child will help to remove our depression. In times of loneliness, it is something even to have a dog with you, to lick your hand, and show you such kindness as is possible from him. And our blessed Master, who always appreciated, and still appreciates, the least service rendered to him – for not a cup of cold water, given to a disciple, in Christ's name, shall lose its reward – was cheered by the devotion and homage of the ministering spirit that came from heaven to strengthen him. I wonder if the angel worshipped him – I think that he could do no less; and it must have been something to worship the blood-red Son of God. Oh, that any one of us could have paid him such homage as that! The time for such special ministry as that is over now; yet my faith seems to bring him back here, at this moment, just as if we were in Gethsemane. I adore thee, thou blessed eternal God – never more God-like than when thou didst prove thy perfect manhood by sweating great drops of blood in the awful weakness of thy depression in the garden of sorrow!

Perhaps, too, the angel's presence comforted and strengthened the Saviour *as being a sort of foretaste of his final victory*. What was this angel but the pioneer of all the heavenly host that would come to meet him when the fight was over? He was one who, in full confidence of his Lord's victory, had flown before the rest, to pay homage to the conquering Son of God, who would tread the old dragon beneath his feet. You remember how, when Jesus was born, first there came one angel who began to speak of him to the shepherds, 'and suddenly there was with the angel a multitude of the heavenly host praising God, and saying, Glory to God in the highest, and on earth peace, good will toward men.' The first angel had, as it were, stolen march upon his brethren, and got before them; but, no sooner was the wondrous news sounded through heaven's streets, than every angel resolved to overtake him before his message was completed. So, here again is one that had come as an outrider, to remind his Lord of his ultimate victory, and there were many more afterwards to come with the same glad tidings; but, to the Saviour's heart, that angel's coming was a token that he would lead captivity captive; and that myriads of other bright spirits would crowd around him, and cry, 'Lift up your heads, O ye gates; and be ye lifted up, ye everlasting doors; that the King of glory, fresh from his blood-red shame, may enter into his heavenly and eternal inheritance!'

Yet once more, *is it not very likely that this angel brought the Saviour a message from heaven?* The angels are generally God's messengers, so they have something to communicate from him; and, perhaps, this angel, bending over the Saviour's prostrate form, whispered in his ear, 'Be of good cheer; thou must pass through all this agony, but thou wilt thereby save an innumerable multitude of the sons and daughters of men, who will love and worship thee and thy Father for ever and for ever. He is with thee even at this moment. Though he must hide his face from thee, because of the requirements of justice that the atonement may be complete, his heart is with thee, and he loves thee ever.' Oh, how our Lord Jesus must have been cheered if some such words as these were whispered into his ears!

Now, in closing, let us try to learn the lessons of this incident. Beloved brothers and sisters, you and I may have to pass through great griefs – certainly, ours will never be so great as those of our Divine Master – but we may have to follow through the same waters. Well, at such times, as I have already said, let us resort to prayer, and *let us be content to receive comfort from the humblest instrumentality*. 'That is too simple an observation', say you. It is a very simple one, but it is one that some people have need to remember. You remember how Naaman the Syrian was healed through the remark of a little captive girl; and, sometimes, great saints have been cheered by the words of very little people. You recollect how Dr Guthrie, when he was dying, wanted 'a bairn's hymn'. It was just like him, great, glorious, simple-minded child-man that he was. He said what you and I must sometimes have felt that we wanted – a bairn's hymn – a child's joyful song to cheer us up in our hour of depression and sorrow.

There are some people, who seem as if they would not be converted unless they can see some eminent minister. Even that will not suit some of them; they want a special revelation from heaven. They will not take a text from the Bible – though I cannot conceive of anything better than that – but they think that, if they could dream something, or if they could hear words spoken, in the cool of the evening, by some strange voice in the sky, then they might be converted. Well, brothers and sisters, if you will not eat the apples that grow on trees, you must not expect angels to come and bring them to you. We have a more sure word of testimony in the Bible than we can have anywhere else. If you will not be converted by that Word, it is a great pity; and it is much more than a pity, it is a great sin. If your Lord and Master condescended to receive consolation from an angel whom he had himself created, you ought to be willing to gather comfort from the feeblest speech of the poorest person – from the least of the people of God when they try to cheer you.

I have known an old Christian say of a young minister, 'It is no use for me to hear him, for he has not had the experience that I have had, so how can he instruct or help me?' O sirs, I have known many old saints get more comfort out of godly boys than they did from those of their own age! God knows how, out of the mouths of babes and sucklings, to perfect praise; and I have never heard that he has done that out of the mouths of old men. Why is that? Because they know too much; but the children do not know anything; and, therefore, out of their mouths the praise of God is perfect. So let us never despise God's messengers, however humble they may be.

The next lesson is, while you should be thankful for the least comforter; yet, *in your times of deepest need, you may expect the greatest comforters to come to you.* Let me remind you that an angel appeared to Joseph when Herod was seeking Christ's life. Then, later, angels appeared to Christ when the devil had been tempting him. And now, at Gethsemane, when there was a peculiar manifestation of diabolical malice, for it was the hour of the powers of darkness; then, when the devil was loose, and doing his utmost against Christ, an angel came from heaven to strengthen him. So, when you are in your heaviest trials, you shall have your greatest strength. Perhaps you will have little to do with angels till you get into deep trouble, and then shall the promise be fulfilled, 'He shall give his angels charge over thee, to keep thee in all thy ways. They shall bear thee up in their hands, lest thou dash thy foot against a stone.' They are always ready to be your keepers; but, in the matter of spiritual strengthening, these holy spirits may have little to do with some of you until you stand foot to foot with Apollyon, and have to fight stern battles with the evil one himself. It is worthwhile to go through rough places to have angels to bear you up. It is worthwhile to go to Gethsemane, if there we may have angels from heaven to strengthen us. So, be of good comfort, brethren, whatever lies before you. The darker your experience is, the brighter will be that which comes out of it. The disciples feared as they entered the cloud on the Mount of Transfiguration; but when they had passed right into it, they saw Jesus, Moses, and Elijah in glory. O ye who are the true followers of Christ, fear not the clouds that lower darkly over you, for you shall see the brightness behind them, and the Christ in them; and blessed shall your spirits be.

But if you are not believing in Christ, I am indeed grieved for you, for you shall have the sorrow without the solace – the cup of bitterness without the angel – the agony, and that for ever, without the messenger from heaven to console you. Oh, that ye would all believe in Jesus! God help you so to do, for Christ's sake! Amen.

11

GETHSEMANE [1]

'And being in an agony he prayed more earnestly:
and his sweat was as it were great drops of
blood falling down to the ground.'
LUKE 22:44

FEW HAD FELLOWSHIP with the sorrows of Gethsemane. The
majority of the disciples were not there. They were not sufficiently
advanced in grace to be admitted to behold the mysteries of 'the
agony'. Occupied with the Passover feast at their own houses, they
represent the many who live upon the letter, but are mere babes
and sucklings as to the spirit of the gospel. The walls of Gethsemane
fitly typify that weakness in grace which effectually shuts in the
deeper marvels of communion from the gaze of ordinary believers.
To twelve, nay, to eleven only was the privilege given to enter
Gethsemane and see this great sight. Out of the eleven, eight were
left at some distance; they had fellowship, but not of that intimate
sort to which the men greatly beloved are admitted. Only three
highly favoured ones, who had been with him on the mount of
transfiguration, and had witnessed the life-giving miracle in the
house of Jairus – only these three could approach the veil of his
mysterious sorrow: within that veil even these must not intrude; a
stone's-throw distance must be left between. He must tread the
wine-press alone, and of the people there must be none with him.
Peter and the two sons of Zebedee, represent the few eminent,
experienced, grace-taught saints, who may be written down as
'Fathers'; these having done business on great waters, can in some

[1] Sermon No. 493. Preached at the Metropolitan Tabernacle on Sunday morning,
8 February 1863.

degree, measure the huge Atlantic waves of their Redeemer's passion; having been much alone with him, they can read his heart far better than those who merely see him amid the crowd. To some selected spirits it is given, for the good of others, and to strengthen them for some future, special, and tremendous conflict, to enter the inner circle and hear the pleadings of the suffering High Priest; they have fellowship with him in his sufferings, and are made conformable unto his death. Yet I say, even these, the elect out of the elect, these choice and peculiar favourites among the kings courtiers, even these cannot penetrate the secret places of the Saviour's woe, so as to comprehend all his agonies. 'Thine unknown sufferings' is the remarkable expression of the Greek liturgy; for there is an inner chamber in his grief, shut out from human knowledge and fellowship. Was it not here that Christ was more than ever an 'unspeakable gift' to us? Is not Watts right when he sings:

> And all the unknown joys he gives,
> Were bought with agonies unknown?

Since it would not be possible for any believer, however experienced, to know for himself all that our Lord endured in the place of the olive press, when he was crushed beneath the upper and the nether mill-stone of mental suffering and hellish malice, it is clearly far beyond the preacher's capacity to set it forth to you. Jesus himself must give you access to the wonders of Gethsemane: as for me, I can but invite you to enter the garden, bidding you put your shoes from off your feet, for the place whereon we stand is holy ground. I am neither Peter, nor James, nor John, but one who would gladly like them drink of the Master's cup, and be baptized with his baptism. I have hitherto advanced only so far as yonder band of eight, but there I have listened to the deep groanings of the Man of Sorrows. Some of you, my venerable friends, may have learned far more than I; but you will not refuse to hear again the roarings of the many waters which strove to quench the love of the Great Husband of our souls.

Several matters will require our brief consideration. Come Holy Spirit, breathe light into our thoughts, life into our words.

I. Come hither and behold the SAVIOUR'S UNUTTERABLE WOE.

The emotions of that dolorous night are expressed by several words in Scripture. John describes him as saying four days before his passion, 'Now is my soul troubled', as he marked the gathering clouds he hardly knew where to turn himself, and cried out 'What shall I say?' Matthew writes of him, 'he began to be sorrowful and very heavy.' Upon the word *adhmonein*, translated 'very heavy', Goodwin remarks that there was a distraction in the Saviour's agony since the root of the word signifies 'separated from the people – men in distraction, being separated from mankind'. What a thought, my brethren, that our blessed Lord should be driven to the very verge of distraction by the intensity of his anguish. Matthew represents the Saviour himself as saying, 'My soul is *exceeding sorrowful*, even unto death.' Here the word *perilupoV* means encompassed, encircled, overwhelmed with grief. 'He was plunged head and ears in sorrow and had no breathing-hole', is the strong expression of Goodwin. Sin leaves no cranny for comfort to enter, and therefore the Sin-bearer must be entirely immersed in woe. Mark records that he began to be *sore amazed*, and to be very heavy. In this case *qambeisqai* , with the prefix *ek*, shows extremity of amazement like that of Moses when he did exceedingly fear and quake. O blessed Saviour, how can we bear to think of thee as a man astonished and alarmed! Yet was it even so when the terrors of God set themselves in array against thee. Luke uses the strong language of my text – 'being in an agony'. These expressions, each of them worthy to be the theme of a discourse, are quite sufficient to show that the grief of the Saviour was of the most extraordinary character; well justifying the prophetic exclamation, 'Behold and see if there be any sorrow like unto my sorrow which was done unto me.' He stands before us peerless in misery. None are molested by the powers of evil as he was; as if the powers of hell had given commandment to their legions, 'Fight neither with small nor great, save only with the king himself.'

Should we profess to understand all the sources of our Lord's agony, wisdom would rebuke us with the question, 'Hast thou entered into the springs of the sea? or hast thou walked in search of the depths?' We cannot do more than look at the revealed causes of grief. It partly arose from the horror of his soul *when fully comprehending the meaning of sin.* Brethren, when you were first convinced of sin and saw it as a thing exceeding sinful, though your perception of its sinfulness was but faint compared with its real heinousness, yet horror took hold upon you. Do you remember those sleepless nights? Like the Psalmist, you said, 'My bones waxed old through my roaring all the day long, for day and night thy hand was heavy upon me; my moisture is turned into the drought of summer.' Some of us can remember when our souls chose strangling rather than life; when if the shadows of death could have covered us from the wrath of God we would have been too glad to sleep in the grave that we might not make our bed in hell. Our blessed Lord saw sin in its natural blackness. He had a most distinct perception of its treasonable assault upon his God, its murderous hatred to himself, and its destructive influence upon mankind. Well might horror take hold upon him, for a sight of sin must be far more hideous than a sight of hell, which is but its offspring.

Another deep fountain of grief was found in the fact that Christ now *assumed more fully his official position with regard to sin.* He was now made sin. Hear the word! He, who knew no sin, was made sin for us, that we might be made the righteousness of God in him. In that night the words of Isaiah were fulfilled – 'The Lord hath laid on him the iniquity of us all.' Now he stood as the Sin-bearer, the Substitute accepted by divine justice to bear that we might never bear the whole of wrath divine. At that hour heaven looked on him as standing in the sinner's stead, and treated as sinful man had richly deserved to be treated. Oh! dear friends, when the immaculate Lamb of God found himself in the place of the guilty, when he could not repudiate that place because he had voluntarily accepted it in order to save his chosen, what must his soul have felt, how must his perfect nature have been shocked at such close association with iniquity?

We believe that at this time, *our Lord had a very clear view of all the shame and suffering of his crucifixion.* The agony was but one of the first drops of the tremendous shower which discharged itself upon his head. He foresaw the speedy coming of the traitor-disciple, the seizure by the officers, the mock-trials before the Sanhedrim, and Pilate, and Herod, the scourging and buffeting, the crown of thorns, the shame, the spitting. All these rose up before his mind, and, as it is a general law of our nature that the foresight of trial is more grievous than trial itself, we can conceive how it was that he who answered not a word when in the midst of the conflict, could not restrain himself from strong crying and tears in the prospect of it. Beloved friends, if you can revive before your mind's eye the terrible incidents of his death the hounding through the streets of Jerusalem, the nailing to the cross, the fever, the thirst, and, above all, forsaking of his God, you cannot marvel that he began to be very heavy, and was sore amazed.

But possibly a yet more fruitful tree of bitterness was this – *that now his Father began to withdraw his presence from him.* The shadow of that great eclipse began to fall upon his spirit when he knelt in that cold midnight amidst the olives of Gethsemane. The sensible comforts which had cheered his spirit were taken away; that blessed application of promises which Christ Jesus needed as a man, was removed, all that we understand by the term 'consolations of God' were hidden from his eyes. He was left single-handed in his weakness to contend for the deliverance of man. The Lord stood by as if he were an indifferent spectator, or rather, as if he were an adversary, he wounded him 'with the wound of an enemy, with the chastisement of a cruel one'.

But in our judgment the fiercest heat of the Saviour's suffering in the garden lay in *the temptations of Satan.* That hour above any time in his life, even beyond the forty days' conflict in the wilderness, was the time of his temptation. 'This is your hour and the power of darkness.' Now could he emphatically say, 'The prince of this world cometh.' This was his last hand-to-hand fight with all the hosts of hell, and here must he sweat great drops of blood before the victory can be achieved.

We have glanced at the fountains of the great deep which were broken up when the floods of grief deluged the Redeemer's soul. Brethren, this one lesson before we pass from the contemplation. 'We have not an high priest which cannot be touched with the feeling of our infirmities; but was in all points tempted like as we are, yet without sin. Let us therefore come boldly unto the throne of grace, that we may obtain mercy, and find grace to help in time of need.' Let us reflect that no suffering can be unknown to him. We do but run with footmen – he had to contend with horsemen; we do but wade up to our ankles in shallow streams of sorrow – he had to buffet with the swellings of Jordan. He will never fail to succour his people when tempted; even as it was said of old, 'In all their affliction he was afflicted, and the angel of his presence saved them.'

II. Turn we next to contemplate THE TEMPTATION OF OUR LORD.

At the outset of his career, the serpent began to nibble at the heel of the promised Deliverer; and now as the time approached when the Seed of the woman should bruise the serpent's head, that old dragon made a desperate attempt upon his great Destroyer. It is not possible for us to lift the veil where revelation has permitted it to fall, but we can form some faint idea of the suggestions with which Satan tempted our Lord. Let us, however, remark by way of caution, before we attempt to paint this picture, that whatever Satan may have suggested to our Lord, his perfect nature did not in any degree whatever submit to it so as to sin. The temptations were, doubtless, of the very foulest character, but they left no speck or flaw upon him, who remained still the fairest among ten thousand. The prince of this world came, but he had nothing in Christ. He struck the sparks, but they did not fall, as in our case, upon dry tinder; they fell as into the sea, and were quenched at once. He hurled the fiery arrows, but they could not even scar the flesh of Christ; they smote upon the buckler of his perfectly righteous nature, and they fell off with their points broken, to the discomfiture of the adversary.

But what, think you, were these temptations? It strikes me, from some hints given, that they were somewhat as follows – there was, first, *a temptation to leave the work unfinished*; we may gather this from the prayer – 'If it be possible, let this cup pass from me.' 'Son of God', the tempter said, 'is it so? Art thou really called to bear the sin of man? Hath God said, "I have laid help upon one that is mighty", and art thou he, the chosen of God, to bear all this load? Look at thy weakness! Thou sweatest, even now, great drops of blood; surely thou art not he whom the Father hath ordained to be mighty to save; or if thou be, what wilt thou win by it? What will it avail thee? Thou hast glory enough already. See what miscreants they are for whom thou art to offer up thyself a sacrifice. Thy best friends are asleep about thee when most thou needest their comfort; thy treasurer, Judas, is hastening to betray thee for the price of a common slave. The world for which thou sacrificest thyself will cast out thy name as evil, and thy church, for which thou dost pay the ransom-price, what is it worth? A company of mortals! Thy divinity could create the like any moment it pleaseth thee; why needest thou, then, pour out thy soul unto death?' Such arguments would Satan use; the hellish craft of one who had then been thousands of years tempting men, would know how to invent all manner of mischief. He would pour the hottest coals of hell upon the Saviour. It was in struggling with this temptation, among others, that, being in an agony, our Saviour prayed more earnestly.

Scripture implies that our Lord was assailed by *the fear that his strength would not be sufficient*. He was heard in that he feared. How, then, was he heard? An angel was sent unto him strengthening him. His fear, then, was probably produced by a sense of weakness. I imagine that the foul fiend would whisper in his ear – 'Thou! thou endure to be smitten of God and abhorred of men! Reproach hath broken thy heart already; how wilt thou bear to be publicly put to shame and driven without the city as an unclean thing? How wilt thou bear to see thy weeping kinsfolk and thy broken-hearted mother standing at the foot of thy cross? Thy tender and sensitive spirit will quail under it. As for thy body, it is already emaciated; thy long fastings have brought thee very low; thou wilt become a prey to death long before thy work is done. Thou wilt surely fail. God hath forsaken thee. Now will they persecute and take thee; they will give up thy soul to the lion, and thy darling to the power of the dog.' Then would he picture all the sufferings of crucifixion, and say, 'Can thine heart endure, or can thine hands be strong in the day when the Lord shall deal with thee?' The temptation of Satan was not directed against the Godhead, but the manhood of Christ, and therefore the fiend would probably dwell upon the feebleness of man. 'Didst thou not say thyself, "I am a worm and no man, the reproach of men and the despised of the people?" How wilt thou bear it when the wrath-clouds of God gather about thee? The tempest will surely shipwreck all thy hopes. It cannot be; thou canst not drink of this cup, nor be baptized with this baptism.' In this manner, we think, was our Master tried. But see he yields not to it. Being in an agony, which word means in a wrestling, he struggles with the tempter like Jacob with the angel. 'Nay', saith he, 'I will not be subdued by taunts of my weakness; I am strong in the strength of my Godhead, I will overcome thee yet.' Yet was the temptation so awful, that, in order to master it, his mental depression caused him to 'sweat as it were great drops of blood falling down to the ground.'

Possibly, also, the temptation may have arisen from a suggestion *that he was utterly forsaken*. I do not know – there may be sterner trials than this, but surely this is one of the worst, to be utterly forsaken. 'See', said Satan, as he hissed it out between his teeth – 'see, thou hast a friend nowhere! Look up to heaven, thy Father hath shut up the bowels of his compassion against thee. Not an angel in thy Father's courts will stretch out his hand to help thee. Look thou yonder, not one of those spirits who honoured thy birth will interfere to protect thy life. All heaven is false to thee; thou art left alone. And as for earth, do not all men thirst for thy blood? Will not the Jew be gratified to see thy flesh torn with nails, and will not the Roman gloat himself when thou, the King of the Jews, art fastened to the cross? Thou hast no friend among the nations; the high and mighty scoff at thee, and the poor thrust out their tongues in derision. Thou hadst nowhere to lay thy head when thou wast in thy best estate; thou hast no place now where shelter will be given thee. See the companions with whom thou hast taken sweet counsel, what are they worth? Son of Mary, see there thy brother James, see there thy beloved disciple John, and thy bold apostle Peter – they sleep, they sleep; and yonder eight, how the cowards sleep when thou art in thy sufferings! And where are the four hundred others? They have forgotten thee; they will be at their farms and their merchandize by morning. Lo! thou hast no friend left in heaven or earth. All hell is against thee. I have stirred up mine infernal den. I have sent my missives throughout all regions summoning every prince of darkness to set upon thee this night, and we will spare no arrows, we will use all our infernal might to overwhelm thee; and what wilt thou do, thou solitary one?' It may be, this was the temptation; I think it was, because the appearance of an angel unto him strengthening him removed that fear. He was heard in that he feared; he was no more alone, but heaven was with him. It may be that this is the reason of his coming three times to his disciples – as Hart puts it –

> Backwards and forwards thrice he ran
> As if he sought some help from man.

He would see for himself whether it was really true that all men had forsaken him; he found them all asleep; but perhaps he gained some faint comfort from the thought that they were sleeping, not from treachery, but from sorrow, the spirit indeed was willing, but the flesh was weak.

We think Satan also assaulted our Lord with a bitter taunt indeed. You know in what guise the tempter can dress it, and how bitterly sarcastic he can make the insinuation – '*Ah! thou wilt not be able to achieve the redemption of thy people.* Thy grand benevolence will prove a mockery, and thy beloved ones will perish. Thou shalt not prevail to save them from my grasp. Thy scattered sheep shall surely be my prey. Son of David, I am a match for thee; thou canst not deliver out of my hand. Many of thy chosen have entered heaven on the strength of thine atonement, but I will drag them thence, and quench the stars of glory; I will thin the courts of heaven of the choristers of God, for thou wilt not fulfil thy suretyship; thou canst not do it. Thou art not able to bring up all this great people; they will perish yet. See, are not the sheep scattered now that the Shepherd is smitten? They will all forget thee. Thou wilt never see of the travail of thy soul. Thy desired end will never be reached. Thou wilt be for ever the man that began to build but was not able to finish.' Perhaps this is more truly the reason why Christ went three times to look at his disciples. You have seen a mother; she is very faint, weary with a heavy sickness, but she labours under a sore dread that her child will die. She has started from her couch, upon which disease had thrown her, to snatch a moment's rest. She gazes anxiously upon her child. She marks the faintest sign of recovery. But she is sore sick herself, and cannot remain more than an instant from her own bed. She cannot sleep, she tosses painfully, for her thoughts wander; she rises to gaze again – 'How art thou, my child, how art thou? Are those palpitations of thy heart less violent? Is thy pulse more gentle?' But, alas! she is faint, and she must go to her bed again, yet she can get no rest. She will return again and again to watch the loved one. So, I think, Christ looked upon Peter, and James, and John, as much as to say, 'No, they are not all lost yet; there are three left', and, looking upon them as the type of all the church, he seemed to say – 'No, no; I will overcome; I will get the mastery; I will struggle even unto blood; I will pay the ransom-price, and deliver my darlings from their foe.'

Now these, I think, were his temptations. If you can form a fuller idea of what they were than this, then right happy shall I be. With this one lesson I leave the point – *'Pray that ye enter not into temptation.'* This is Christ's own expression; his own deduction from his trial. You have all read, dear friends, John Bunyan's picture of Christian fighting with Apollyon. That master-painter has sketched it to the very life. He says, though 'this sore combat lasted for above half a day, even till Christian was almost quite spent, I never saw him all the while give so much as one pleasant look, till he perceived he had wounded Apollyon with his two-edged sword; then indeed, he did smile and look upward! But it was the dreadfullest sight I ever saw.' That is the meaning of that prayer, 'Lead us not into temptation.' Oh you that go recklessly where you are tempted, you that pray for afflictions – and I have known some silly enough to do that – you that put yourselves where you tempt the devil to tempt you, take heed from the Master's own example. He sweats great drops of blood when he is tempted. Oh! pray God to spare you such trial. Pray this morning and every day, 'Lead me not into temptation.'

III. Behold, dear brethren, THE BLOODY SWEAT.

We read, that 'he sweat as it were great drops of blood.' Hence a few writers have supposed that the sweat was not actually blood, but had the appearance of it. That interpretation, however, has been rejected by most commentators, from Augustine downward, and it is generally held that the words 'as it were' do not only set forth likeness to blood, but signify that it was actually and literally blood. We find the same idiom used in the text – 'We beheld his glory, the glory as of the only-begotten of the Father.' Now, clearly, this does not mean that Christ was like the only-begotten of the Father, since he is really so. So that generally this expression of Holy Scripture sets forth, not a mere likeness to a thing, but the very thing itself.

We believe, then, that Christ did really sweat blood. This phenomenon, though somewhat unusual, has been witnessed in other persons. There are several cases on record, some in the old medicine books of Galen, and others of more recent date, of persons who after long weakness, under fear of death have sweat blood. But this case is altogether one by itself for several reasons. If you will notice, he not only sweat blood, but it was in great drops; the blood coagulated, and formed large masses. I cannot better express what is meant than by the word 'gouts' – big, heavy drops. This has not been seen in any case. Some slight effusions of blood have been known in cases of persons who were previously enfeebled, but great drops never. When it is said 'falling to the ground' – it shows their copiousness, so that they not only stood upon the surface and were sucked up by his garments till he became like the red heifer which was slaughtered on that very spot, but the drops fell to the ground. Here he stands unrivalled. He was a man in good health, only about thirty years of age, and was labouring under no fear of death; but the mental pressure arising from his struggle with temptation, and the straining of all his strength, in order to baffle the temptation of Satan, so forced his frame to an unnatural excitement, that his pores sent forth great drops of blood which fell down to the ground. This proves how tremendous must have been the weight of sin when it was able so to crush the Saviour that he distilled drops of blood!

This proves too, my brethren, the mighty power of his love. It is a very pretty observation of old Isaac Ambrose that the gum which exudes from the tree without cutting is always the best. This precious camphire-tree yielded most sweet spices when it was wounded under the knotty whips, and when it was pierced by the nails on the cross; but see, it giveth forth its best spice when there is no whip, no nail, no wound. This sets forth the voluntariness of Christ's sufferings, since without a lance the blood flowed freely. No need to put on the leech, or apply the knife; it flows spontaneously. No need for the rulers to cry, 'Spring up, O well'; of itself it flows in crimson torrents. Dearly beloved friends, if men suffer some frightful pain of mind – I am not acquainted with the medical matter – apparently the blood rushes to the heart. The cheeks are pale; a fainting fit comes on; the blood has gone inward, as if to nourish the inner man while passing through its trial. But see our Saviour in his agony; he is so utterly oblivious of self, that instead of his agony driving his blood to the heart to nourish himself, it drives it outward to bedew the earth. The agony of Christ, inasmuch as it pours him out upon the ground, pictures the fullness of the offering which he made for men.

Do you not perceive, my brethren, how intense must have been the wrestling through which he passed, and will you not hear its voice to you? – 'Ye have not yet resisted unto blood, striving against sin.' It has been the lot of some of us to have sore temptations – else we did not know how to teach others – so sore that in wrestling against them the cold, clammy sweat has stood upon our brow. The place will never be forgotten by me – a lonely spot; where, musing upon my God, an awful rush of blasphemy went over my soul, till I would have preferred death to the trial; and I fell on my knees there and then, for the agony was awful, while my hand was at my mouth to keep the blasphemies from being spoken. Once let Satan be permitted really to try you with a temptation to blasphemy, and you will never forget it, though you live till your hairs are blanched; or let him attack you with some lust, and though you hate and loathe the very thought of it, and would lose your right arm sooner than indulge in it, yet it will come, and hunt, and persecute, and torment you. Wrestle against it even unto sweat, my brethren, yea, even unto blood. None of you should say, 'I could not help it; I was tempted.' Resist till you sweat blood rather than sin. Do not say, 'I was so pressed with it; and it so suited my natural temperament, that I could not help falling into it.' Look at the great Apostle and High Priest of your profession, and sweat even to blood rather than yield to the great tempter of your souls. Pray that ye enter not into temptation, so that when ye enter into it ye may with confidence say, 'Lord, I did not seek this, therefore help me through with it, for thy name's sake.'

IV. I want you, in the fourth place, to notice THE SAVIOUR'S PRAYER.

Dear friends, when we are tempted and desire to overcome, the best weapon is prayer. When you cannot use the sword and the shield, take to yourself the famous weapon of All-prayer. So your Saviour did. Let us notice his prayer. *It was lonely prayer*. He withdrew even from his three best friends about a stone's throw. Believer, especially in temptation, be much in solitary prayer. As private prayer is the key to open heaven, so is it the key to shut the gates of hell. As it is a shield to prevent, so is it the sword with which to fight against temptation. Family-prayer, social prayer, prayer in the church, will not suffice, these are very precious, but the best beaten spice will smoke in your censer in your private devotions, where no ear hears but God. Betake yourselves to solitude if you would overcome.

Mark, too, *it was humble prayer*. Luke says he knelt, but another evangelist says he fell on his face. What! does the King fall on his face? Where, then, must be thy place, thou humble servant of the great Master? Doth the Prince fall flat to the ground? Where, then, wilt thou lie? What dust and ashes shall cover thy head? What sackcloth shall gird thy loins? Humility gives us good foot-hold in prayer. There is no hope of any real prevalence with God, who casteth down the proud, unless we abase ourselves that he may exalt us in due time.

Further, *it was filial prayer*. Matthew describes him as saying, 'O my Father', and Mark puts it, '*Abba*, Father'. You will find this always a stronghold in the day of trial to plead your adoption. Hence that prayer, in which it is written, 'Lead us not into temptation, but deliver us from evil', begins with 'Our Father which art in heaven.' Plead as a child. You have no rights as a subject; you have forfeited them by your treason, but nothing can forfeit a child's right to a father's protection. Be not then ashamed to say, 'My Father, hear my cry.'

Again, observe that *it was persevering prayer*. He prayed three times, using the same words. Be not content until you prevail. Be as the importunate widow, whose continual coming earned what her first supplication could not win. Continue in prayer, and watch in the same with thanksgiving.

Further, see how it glowed to a red-hot heat – *it was earnest prayer.* 'He prayed more earnestly.' What groans were those which were uttered by Christ! What tears, which welled up from the deep fountains of his nature! Make earnest supplication if you would prevail against the adversary.

And last, *it was the prayer of resignation.* 'Nevertheless, not as I will, but as thou wilt.' Yield, and God yields. Let it be as God wills, and God will will it that it shall be for the best. Be thou perfectly content to leave the result of thy prayer in his hands, who knows when to give, and how to give, and what to give, and what to withhold. So pleading, earnestly, importunately, yet mingling with it humility and resignation, thou shalt yet prevail.

Dear friends, we must conclude, turn to the last point with this as a practical lesson – '*Rise and pray.*' When the disciples were lying down they slept; sitting was the posture that was congenial to sleep. Rise; shake yourselves; stand up in the name of God; rise and pray. And if you are in temptation, be you more than ever you were in your life before, instant, passionate, importunate with God that he would deliver you in the day of your conflict.

V. As time has failed us we close with the last point, which is, THE SAVIOUR'S PREVALENCE.

The cloud has passed away. Christ has knelt, and the prayer is over. 'But', says one, 'did Christ prevail in prayer?' Beloved, could we have any hope that he would prevail in heaven if he had not prevailed on earth? Should we not have had a suspicion that if his strong crying and tears had not been heard then, he would fail now? His prayers did speed, and therefore he is a good intercessor for us. 'How was he heard?' The answer shall be given very briefly indeed. He was heard, I think, in three respects. The first gracious answer that was given him was, *that his mind was suddenly rendered calm.* What a difference there is between 'My soul is exceeding sorrowful' – his hurrying too and fro, his repetition of the prayer three times, the singular agitation that was upon him – what a contrast between all these and his going forth to meet the traitor with 'Betrayest thou the Son of Man with a kiss?' Like a troubled sea before, and now as calm as when he himself said, 'Peace be still', and the waves were quiet. You cannot know a profounder peace than that which reigned in the Saviour when before Pilate he answered him not a word. He is calm to the last, as calm as though it were his day of triumph rather than his day of trouble. Now I think this was guaranteed to him in answer to his prayer. He had sufferings perhaps more intense, but his mind was now quieted so as to meet them with greater deliberation. Like some men, who when they first hear the firing of the shots in a battle are all trepidation, but as the fight grows hotter and they are in greater danger, they are cool and collected; they are wounded, they are bleeding, they are dying; yet are they quiet as a summer's eve; the first young flush of trouble is gone, and they can meet the foe with peace – so the Father heard the Saviour's cry, and breathed such a profound peace into his soul, that it was like a river, and his righteousness like the waves of the sea.

Next, we believe that he was answered *by God strengthening him through an angel*. How that was done we do not know. Probably it was by what the angel said, and equally likely is it that it was by what he did. The angel may have whispered the promises; pictured before his mind's eye the glory of his success; sketched his resurrection; portrayed the scene when his angels would bring his chariots from on high to bear him to his throne; revived before him the recollection of the time of his advent, the prospect when he should reign from sea to sea, and from the river even to the ends of the earth; and so have made him strong. Or, perhaps, by some unknown method God sent such power to our Christ, who had been like Samson with his locks shorn, that he suddenly received all the might and majestic energy that were needed for the terrific struggle. Then he walked out of the garden no more a worm and no man, but made strong with an invisible might that made him a match for all the armies that were round about him. A troop had overcome him, like Gad of old, but he overcame at last. Now he can dash through a troop; now he can leap over a wall. God has sent by his angel force from on high, and made the man Christ strong for battle and for victory.

And I think we may conclude with saying, that God heard him in granting him now, not simply strength, *but a real victory over*

Satan. I do not know whether what Adam Clarke supposes is correct, that in the garden Christ did pay more of the price than he did even on the cross; but I am quite convinced that they are very foolish who get to such refinement that they think the atonement was made on the cross, and nowhere else at all. We believe that it was made in the garden as well as on the cross; and it strikes me that in the garden one part of Christ's work was finished, wholly finished, and that was his conflict with Satan. I conceive that Christ had now rather to bear the absence of his Father's presence and the revilings of the people and the sons of men, than the temptations of the devil. I do think that these were over when he rose from his knees in prayer, when he lifted himself from the ground where he marked his visage in the clay in drops of blood. The temptation of Satan was then over, and he might have said concerning that part of the work – 'It is finished; broken is the dragon's head; I have overcome him.' Perhaps in those few hours that Christ spent in the garden the whole energy of the agents of iniquity was concentrated and dissipated. Perhaps in that one conflict all that craft could invent, all that malice could devise, all that infernal practice could suggest, was tried on Christ, the devil having his chain loosened for that purpose, having Christ given up to him, as Job was, that he might touch him in his bones and in his flesh, yea, touch him in his heart and his soul, and vex him in his spirit. It may be that every devil in hell and every fiend of the pit was summoned, each to vent his own spite and to pour their united energy and malice upon the head of Christ. And there he stood, and he could have said as he stood up to meet the next adversary – a devil in the form of man – Judas – 'I come this day from Bozrah, with garments dyed red from Edom; I have trampled on my enemies, and overcome them once for all; now go I to bear man's sin and my Father's wrath, and to finish the work which he has given me to do.' If this be so, Christ was then heard in that he feared; he feared the temptation of Satan, and he was delivered from it; he feared his own weakness, and he was strengthened; he feared his own trepidation of mind, and he was made calm.

What shall we say, then, in conclusion, but this lesson. Does it not say 'Whatsoever ye shall ask in prayer, believing, ye shall have.' Then if your temptations reach the most tremendous height and force, still lay hold of God in prayer and you shall prevail. Convinced sinner! that is a comfort for you. Troubled saint! that is a joy for you. To one and all of us is this lesson of this morning – 'Pray that ye enter not into temptation.' If in temptation let us ask that Christ may pray for us that our faith fail not, and when we have passed through the trouble let us try to strengthen our brethren, even as Christ has strengthened us this day.

12

THE AGONY IN GETHSEMANE [1]

'And being in an agony, he prayed more earnestly:
and his sweat was as it were great drops of
blood falling down to the ground.'
LUKE 22:44

OUR LORD, after having eaten the Passover and celebrated the
supper with his disciples, went with them to the Mount of Olives,
and entered the garden of Gethsemane. What induced him to select
that place to be the scene of his terrible agony? Why there in
preference to anywhere else would he be arrested by his enemies?
May we not conceive that as in a garden Adam's self-indulgence
ruined us, so in another garden the agonies of the second Adam
should restore us. Gethsemane supplies the medicine for the ills
which followed upon the forbidden fruit of Eden. No flowers which
bloomed upon the banks of the four-fold river were ever so precious
to our race as the bitter herbs which grew hard by the black and
sullen stream of Kedron.

May not our Lord also have thought of David, when on that
memorable occasion he fled out of the city from his rebellions son,
and it is written, 'The king also himself passed over the brook
Kedron', and he and his people went up bare-footed and bare-
headed, weeping as they went? Behold, the greater David leaves
the temple to become desolate, and forsakes the city which had
rejected his admonitions, and with a sorrowful heart crosses the
foul brook, to find in solitude a solace for his woes. Our Lord
Jesus, moreover, meant us to see that our sin changed everything

[1] Sermon No. 1,199. Preached at the Metropolitan Tabernacle on Sunday
morning, 18 October 1874.

about him into sorrow, it turned his riches into poverty, his peace into travail, his glory into shame, and so the place of his peaceful retirement, where in hallowed devotion he had been nearest heaven in communion with God, our sin transformed into the focus of his sorrow, the centre of his woe. Where he had enjoyed most, there he must be called to suffer most.

Our Lord may also have chosen the garden, because needing every remembrance that could sustain him in the conflict, he felt refreshed by the memory of former hours which there had passed away so quietly. He had there prayed, and gained strength and comfort. Those gnarled and twisted olives knew him well; there was scarce a blade of grass in the garden which he had not knelt upon; he had consecrated the spot to fellowship with God. What wonder then that he preferred this favoured soil? Just as a man would choose in sickness to lie in his own bed, so Jesus chose to endure his agony in his own oratory, where the recollections of former communings with his Father would come vividly before him.

But, probably, the chief reason for his resort to Gethsemane was, that it was his well-known haunt, and John tells us, 'Judas also knew the place.' Our Lord did not wish to conceal himself, he did not need to be hunted down like a thief, or searched out by spies. He went boldly to the place where his enemies knew that he was accustomed to pray, for he was willing to be taken to suffering and to death. They did not drag him off to Pilate's hall against his will, but he went with them voluntarily. When the hour was come for him to be betrayed there was he in a place where the traitor could readily find him, and when Judas would betray him with a kiss his cheek was ready to receive the traitorous salutation. The blessed Saviour delighted to do the will of the Lord, though it involved obedience unto death.

We have thus come to the gate of the garden of Gethsemane, let us now enter; but first let us put off our shoe from our foot, as Moses did, when he also saw the bush which burned with fire, and was not consumed. Surely we may say with Jacob, 'How dreadful is this place!' I tremble at the task which lies before me, for how shall my feeble speech describe those agonies, for which strong crying and tears were scarcely an adequate expression? I desire with you to survey the sufferings of our Redeemer, but oh, may the Spirit of God prevent our mind from thinking aught amiss, or our tongue from speaking even one word which would be derogatory to him either in his immaculate manhood or his glorious Godhead. It is not easy when you are speaking of One who is both God and man to observe the exact line of correct speech; it is so easy to describe the divine side in such a manner as to trench upon the human, or to depict the human at the cost of the divine. Make me not an offender for a word if I should err. A man had need himself to be inspired, or to confine himself to the very words of inspiration, fitly to speak at all times upon the great 'mystery of godliness', God manifest in the flesh, and especially when he has to dwell most upon God so manifest in suffering flesh that the weakest traits in manhood become the most conspicuous. O Lord, open thou my lips that my tongue may utter right words.

Meditating upon the agonizing scene in Gethsemane we are compelled to observe that our Saviour there endured a grief unknown to any previous period of his life, and therefore we will commence our discourse by raising the question, WHAT WAS THE CAUSE OF THE PECULIAR GRIEF OF GETHSEMANE? Our Lord was the 'man of sorrows and acquainted with grief' throughout his whole life, and yet, though it may sound paradoxical, I scarcely think there existed on the face of the earth a happier man than Jesus of Nazareth, for the griefs which he endured were counterbalanced by the peace of purity, the calm of fellowship with God, and the joy of benevolence. This last every good man knows to be very sweet, and all the sweeter in proportion to the pain which is voluntarily endured for the carrying out of its kind designs. It is always joy to do good, cost what it may. Moreover Jesus dwelt at perfect peace with God at all times; we know that he did so, for he regarded that peace as a choice legacy which he could bequeath to his disciples, and ere he died he said to them, 'Peace I leave with you, my peace I give unto you.' He was meek and lowly of heart, and therefore his soul had rest; he was one of the meek who inherit the earth; one of the peacemakers who are and must be blessed. I think I mistake not when I say that our Lord was far from being an unhappy man. But in Gethsemane all seems changed, his peace is gone, his calm is turned to tempest.

After supper our Lord had sung a hymn, but there was no singing in Gethsemane. Adown the steep bank which led from Jerusalem to the Kedron he talked very cheerfully, saying, 'I am the vine and ye are the branches', and that wondrous prayer which he prayed with his disciples after that discourse, is very full of majesty: 'Father, I will that they also whom thou hast given me be with me where I am', is a very different prayer from that inside Gethsemane's walls, where he cries, 'If it be possible, let this cup pass from me.' Notice that all his life long you scarcely find him uttering an expression of grief, and yet here he says, not only by his sighs and by his bloody sweat, but in so many words, 'My soul is exceeding sorrowful even unto death.' In the garden the sufferer could not conceal his grief, and does not appear to have wished to do so. Backward and forward thrice he ran to his disciples, he let them see his sorrow and appealed to them for sympathy; his exclamations were very piteous, and his sighs and groans were, I doubt not, very terrible to hear. Chiefly did that sorrow reveal itself in bloody sweat, which is a very unusual phenomenon, although I suppose we must believe those writers who record instances somewhat similar. The old physician Galen gives an instance in which, through extremity of horror, an individual poured forth a discoloured sweat, so nearly crimson as at any rate to appear to have been blood. Other cases are given by medical authorities. We do not, however, on any previous occasion observe anything like this in our Lord's life; it was only in the last grim struggle among the olive trees that our Champion resisted unto blood, agonizing against sin. What ailed Thee, O Lord, that thou shouldst be so sorely troubled just then?

We are clear that his deep sorrow and distress were not occasioned by any bodily pain. Our Saviour had doubtless been familiar with weakness and pain, for he took our sicknesses, but he never in any previous instance complained of physical suffering. Neither at the time when he entered Gethsemane had he been grieved by any bereavement. We know why it is written 'Jesus wept', it was because his friend Lazarus was dead; but here there was no funeral, nor sick bed, nor particular cause of grief in that direction. Nor was it the revived remembrance of any past reproaches which had lain dormant in his mind. Long before this 'reproach had broken his heart', and he had known to the full the vexations of contumely and scorn. They had called him a 'drunken man and a wine bibber', they had charged him with casting out devils by the prince of the devils; they could not say more and yet he had bravely faced it all: it could not be possible that he was now sorrowful unto death for such a cause. There must have been a something sharper than pain, more cutting than reproach, more terrible than bereavement, which now at this time grappled with the Saviour and made him 'exceeding sorrowful, and very heavy'.

Do you suppose it was the fear of coming scorn, or the dread of crucifixion? Was it terror at the thought of death? Is not such a supposition impossible? Every man dreads death, and as man Jesus could not but shrink from it. When we were originally made we were created for immortality, and therefore to die is strange and uncongenial work to us, and the instincts of self-preservation cause us to start back from it; but surely in our Lord's case that natural cause could not have produced such specially painful results. It does not make even such poor cowards as we are sweat great drops of blood, why then should it work such terror in him? It is dishonouring to our Lord to imagine him less brave than his own disciples, yet we have seen some of the very feeblest of his saints triumphant in the prospect of departing. Read the stories of the martyrs, and you will frequently find them exultant in the near approach of the most cruel sufferings. The joy of the Lord has given such strength to them, that no coward thought has alarmed them for a single moment, but they have gone to the stake, or to the block, with psalms of victory upon their lips. Our Master must not be thought of as inferior to his boldest servants, it cannot be that he should tremble where they were brave. Oh, no; the noblest spirit among yon martyr-band is the Leader himself, who in suffering and heroism surpassed them all; none could so defy the pangs of death as the Lord Jesus, who, for the joy which was set before him, endured the cross, despising the shame.

I cannot conceive that the pangs of Gethsemane were occasioned by any extraordinary attack from Satan. It is possible that Satan was there, and that his presence may have darkened the shade, but he was not the most prominent cause of that hour of darkness. Thus much is quite clear, that our Lord at the commencement of his ministry engaged in a very severe duel with the prince of darkness, and yet we do not read concerning that temptation in the wilderness a single syllable as to his soul's being exceeding sorrowful, neither do we find that he 'was sore amazed and was very heavy', nor is there a solitary hint at anything approaching to bloody sweat. When the Lord of angels condescended to stand foot to foot with the prince of the power of the air, he had no such dread of him as to utter strong cries and tears and fall prostrate on the ground with threefold appeals to the Great Father. Comparatively speaking, to put his foot on the old serpent was an easy task for Christ, and did but cost him a bruised heel, but this Gethsemane agony wounded his very soul even unto death.

What is it then, think you, that so peculiarly marks off Gethsemane and the griefs thereof? We believe that now the Father put him to grief for us. It was now that our Lord had to take a certain cup *from the Father's hand*. Not from the Jews, not from the traitor Judas, not from the sleeping disciples, not from the devil came the trial now, but it was a cup filled by One whom he knew to be his Father, but who nevertheless he understood to have appointed him a very bitter potion, a cup not to be drunk by his body and to spend its gall upon his flesh, but a cup which specially amazed his soul and troubled his inmost heart. He shrunk from it, and therefore be ye sure that it was a draught more dreadful than physical pain, since from that he did not shrink; it was a potion more dreadful than reproach, from that he had not turned aside; more dreadful than Satanic temptation – *that* he had overcome: it was a something inconceivably terrible, amazingly full of dread, which came from the Father's hand. This removes all doubt as to what it was, for we read 'It pleased the Lord to bruise him, he hath put him to grief: when thou shalt make his soul an offering for sin'. 'The Lord hath made to meet on him the iniquity of us all.' He hath made him to be sin for us though he knew no sin. This, then, is that which caused the Saviour such extraordinary depression. He was now about to 'taste death for every man', to bear the curse which was due to sinners, because be stood in the sinner's place and must suffer in the sinner's stead. Here is the secret of those agonies which it is not possible for me to set forth in order before you, so true is it that –

'Tis to God, and God alone,
That his griefs are fully known.

Yet would I exhort you to consider these griefs awhile, that you may love the Sufferer. He now realized, perhaps for the first time, what it was to be a sin bearer. As God he was perfectly holy and incapable of sin, and as man he was without original taint and spotlessly pure; yet he had to bear sin, to be led forth as the scape goat bearing the iniquity of Israel upon his head, to be taken and made a sin offering, and as a loathsome thing (for nothing was more loathsome than the sin offering) to be taken without the camp and utterly consumed with the fire of divine wrath. Do you wonder that his infinite purity started back from that? Would he have been what he was if it had not been a very solemn thing for him to stand before God in the position of a sinner? yea, and as Luther would have said it, to be looked upon by God as if he were all the sinners in the world, and as if he had committed all the sin that ever had been committed by his people, for it was all laid on him, and on him must the vengeance due for it all be poured; he must be the centre of all the vengeance and bear away upon himself what ought to have fallen upon the guilty sons of men. To stand in such a position when once it was realized must have been very terrible to the Redeemer's holy soul. Now also the Saviour's mind was intently fixed upon the dreadful nature of sin. Sin had always been abhorrent to him, but now his thoughts were engrossed with it, he saw its worse than deadly nature, its heinous character, and horrible aim. Probably at this time beyond any former period he had, as man, a view of the wide range and all-pervading evil of sin, and a sense of the blackness of its darkness, and the desperateness of its guilt as being a direct attack upon the throne, yea, and upon the very being of God. He saw in his own person to what lengths sinners would go, how they would sell their Lord like Judas, and seek to destroy him as did the Jews. The cruel and ungenerous treatment he had himself received displayed man's hate of God, and, as he saw it, horror took hold upon him, and his soul was heavy to think that he must bear such an evil and be numbered with such transgressors, to be wounded for their transgressions, and bruised for their iniquities. Not the wounding, nor the bruising

distressed him so much as the sin itself, and that utterly overwhelmed his soul.

Then, too, no doubt the penalty of sin began to be realised by
him in the garden – first the sin which had put him in the position
of a suffering substitute, and then the penalty which must be borne,
because he was in that position. I dread to the last degree that
kind of theology which is so common nowadays, which seeks to
depreciate and diminish our estimate of the sufferings of our Lord
Jesus Christ. Brethren, that was no trifling suffering which made
recompense to the justice of God for the sins of men. I am never
afraid of exaggeration, when I speak of what my Lord endured.
All hell was distilled into that cup, of which our God and Saviour
Jesus Christ was made to drink. It was not eternal suffering, but
since he was divine he could in a short time offer unto God a
vindication of his justice which sinners in hell could not have
offered had they been left to suffer in their own persons for ever.
The woe that broke over the Saviour's spirit, the great and
fathomless ocean of inexpressible anguish which dashed over the
Saviour's soul when he died, is so inconceivable, that I must not
venture far, lest I be accused of a vain attempt to express the
unutterable; but this I will say, the very spray from that great
tempestuous deep, as it fell on Christ, baptized him in a bloody
sweat. He had not yet come to the raging billows of the penalty
itself, but even standing on the shore, as he heard the awful surf
breaking at his feet, his soul was sore amazed and very heavy. It
was the shadow of the coming tempest, it was the prelude of the
dread desertion which he had to endure, when he stood where we
ought to have stood, and paid to his Father's justice the debt which
was due from us; it was this which laid him low. To be treated as a
sinner, to be smitten as a sinner, though in him was no sin – this it
was which caused him the agony of which our text speaks.

Having thus spoken of the cause of his peculiar grief, I think we
shall be able to support our view of the matter, while we lead you
to consider, WHAT WAS THE CHARACTER OF THE GRIEF
ITSELF? I shall trouble you, as little as possible, with the Greek
words used by the evangelists; I have studied each one of them, to
try and find out the shades of their meaning, but it will suffice if I

give you the results of my careful investigation. What was the grief itself? How was it described? This great sorrow assailed our Lord some four days before he suffered. If you turn to John 12:27, you find that remarkable utterance, 'How is my soul troubled.' We never knew him say that before. This was a foretaste of the great depression of spirit which was so soon to lay him prostrate in Gethsemane. 'Now is my soul troubled; and what shall I say? Father, save me from this hour; but for this cause came I unto this hour.' After that we read of him in Matthew 26:37, that 'he began to be sorrowful and very heavy.' The depression had come over him again. It was not pain, it was not a palpitation of the heart, or an aching of the brow, it was worse than these. Trouble of spirit is worse than pain of body; pain may bring trouble and be the incidental cause of sorrow, but if the mind is perfectly untroubled, how well a man can bear pain, and when the soul is exhilarated and lifted up with inward joy pain of body is almost forgotten, the soul conquering the body. On the other hand the soul's sorrow will create bodily pain, the lower nature sympathizing with the higher. Our Lord's main suffering lay in his soul – his soul-sufferings were the soul of his sufferings. 'A wounded spirit who can bear?' Pain of spirit is the worst of pain, sorrow of heart is the climax of griefs. Let those who have ever known sinking spirits, despondency, and mental gloom, attest the truth of what I say!

This sorrow of heart appears to have led to a very deep depression of our Lord's spirit. In Matthew 26:37 you find it recorded that he was '*very heavy*', and that expression is full of meaning – of more meaning, indeed, than it would be easy to explain. The word in the original is a very difficult one to translate. It may signify the abstraction of the mind, and its complete occupation by sorrow, to the exclusion of every thought which might have alleviated the distress. One burning thought consumed his whole soul, and burned up all that might have yielded comfort. For awhile his mind refused to dwell upon the result of his death, the consequent joy which was set before him. His position as a sinbearer, and the desertion by his Father which was necessitated thereby, engrossed his contemplations and hurried his soul away from all else. Some have seen in the word a measure of distraction, and though I will not go far in that direction, yet it does seem as if our Saviour's mind underwent perturbations and convulsions widely different from his usual calm, collected spirit. He was tossed to and fro as upon a mighty sea of trouble, which was wrought to tempest, and carried him away in its fury. 'We did esteem him stricken, smitten of God and afflicted.' As the psalmist said, innumerable evils compassed him about so that his heart failed him. His heart was melted like wax in the midst of his bowels with sheer dismay. He was 'very heavy'. Some consider the word to signify at its root, 'separated from the people', as if he had become unlike other men, even as one whose mind is staggered by a sudden blow, or pressed with some astounding calamity, is no more as ordinary men are. Mere onlookers would have thought our Lord to be a man distraught, burdened beyond the wont of men, and borne down by a sorrow unparalleled among men. The learned Thomas Goodwin says, 'The word denotes a failing, deficiency, and sinking of spirit, such as happens to men in sickness and swounding.' Epaphroditus' sickness, whereby he was brought near to death, is called by the same word; so that, we see, that Christ's soul was sick and fainted; was not his sweat produced by exhaustion? The cold, clammy sweat of dying men comes through faintness of body, but the bloody sweat of Jesus came from an utter faintness and prostration of soul. He was in an awful soul-swoon, and suffered an inward death, whose accompaniment was not watery tears from the eyes, but a weeping of blood from the entire man. Many of you, however, know in your measure what it is to be very heavy without my multiplying words in explanation, and if you do not know by personal experience all explanations must be vain. When deep despondency comes on, when you forget everything that would sustain you, and your spirit sinks down, down, down, then can you sympathise with your Lord. Others think you foolish, call you nervous, and bid you rally yourself, but they know not your case. Did they understand it they would not mock you with such admonitions, impossible to those who are sinking beneath inward woe. Our Lord was 'very heavy', very sinking, very despondent, overwhelmed with grief.

Mark 14:33 tells us next that our Lord was '*sore amazed*'. The Greek word does not merely import that he was astonished and surprised, but that his amazement went to an extremity of horror, such as men fall into when their hair stands on end and their flesh trembles. As the delivery of the law made Moses exceedingly fear and quake, and as David said, 'My flesh trembleth because of thy judgments', so our Lord was stricken with horror at the sight of the sin which was laid upon him and the vengeance which was due on account of it. The Saviour was first 'sorrowful', then depressed and 'heavy', and lastly, 'sore amazed' and filled with amazement; for even he as a man could scarce have known, what it was that he had undertaken to bear. He had looked at it calmly and quietly, and felt that whatever it was he would bear it for our sake; but when it actually came to the bearing of sin he was utterly astonished and taken aback at the dreadful position of standing in the sinner's place before God, of having his holy Father look upon him as the sinner's representative, and of being forsaken by that Father with whom he had lived on terms of amity and delight from old eternity. It staggered his holy, tender, loving nature, and he was 'sore amazed' and was 'very heavy'.

We are further taught that there surrounded, encompassed, and overwhelmed him an ocean of sorrow, for Matthew 26:38 contains the word *perilupos*, which signifies an encompassing around with sorrows. In all ordinary miseries there is generally some loophole of escape, some breathing place for hope. We can generally remind our friends in trouble that their case might be worse, but in our Lord's griefs worse could not be imagined; for he could say with David, 'The pains of hell gat hold upon me.' All God's waves and billows went over him. Above him, beneath him, around him, without him, and within, all, all was anguish, neither was there one alleviation or source of consolation. His disciples could not help him – they were all but one sleeping, and he who was awake was on the road to betray him. His spirit cried out in the presence of the Almighty God beneath the crushing burden and unbearable load of his miseries. No griefs could have gone further than Christ's, and he himself said, 'My soul is *exceeding sorrowful*', or surrounded with sorrow 'even unto death.' He did not die in the garden, but he suffered as much as if he had died. He endured death intensively, though not extensively. It did not extend to the making his body a corpse, but it went as far in pain as if it had been so. His pangs and anguish went up to the mortal agony, and only paused on the verge of death.

Luke, to crown all, tells us in our text, that our Lord was *in an agony*. The expression 'agony' signifies a conflict, a contest, a wrestling. With whom was the agony? With whom did he wrestle? I believe it was with himself; the contest here intended was not with his God; no, 'not as I will but as thou wilt' does not look like wrestling with God; it was not a contest with Satan, for, as we have already seen, he would not have been so sore amazed had that been the conflict, but it was a terrible combat within himself, an agony within his own soul. Remember that he could have escaped from all this grief with one resolve of his will, and naturally the manhood in him said, 'Do not bear it!' and the purity of his heart said, 'Oh do not bear it, do not stand in the place of the sinner'; and the delicate sensitiveness of his mysterious nature shrank altogether from any form of connection with sin; yet infinite love said, 'Bear it, stoop beneath the load'; and so there was agony between the attributes of his nature, a battle on an awful scale in the arena of his soul. The purity which cannot bear to come into contact with sin must have been very mighty in Christ, while the love which would not let his people perish was very mighty too. It was a struggle on a Titanic scale, as if a Hercules had met another Hercules; two tremendous forces strove and fought and agonised within the bleeding heart of Jesus. Nothing causes a man more torture than to be dragged hither and thither with contending emotions; as civil war is the worst and most cruel kind of war, so a war within a man's soul when two great passions in him struggle for the mastery, and both noble passions too, causes a trouble and distress which none but he that feels it can understand. I marvel not that our Lord's sweat was as it were great drops of blood, when such an inward pressure made him like a cluster trodden in the winepress. I hope I have not presumptuously looked into the ark, or gazed within the veiled holy of holies; God forbid that curiosity or pride should urge me to intrude where the Lord has set a barrier. I have brought you as far as I can, and must again drop the curtain with the words I used just now,

> 'Tis to God, and God alone,
> That his griefs are fully known.

Our third question shall be, WHAT WAS OUR LORD'S SOLACE IN ALL THIS? He sought help in human companionship, and very natural it was that he should do so. God has created in our human nature a craving for sympathy. We do not amiss when we expect our brethren to watch with us in our hour of trial; but our Lord did not find that men were able to assist him; however willing their spirit might be, their flesh was weak. What, then, did he do? He resorted to prayer, and especially to prayer to God under the character of Father. I have learned by experience that we never know the sweetness of the Fatherhood of God so much as when we are in very bitter anguish; I can understand why the Saviour said 'Abba, Father', it was anguish that brought him down as a chastened child to appeal plaintively to a Father's love. In the bitterness of my soul I have cried, 'If, indeed, thou be my Father, by the bowels of thy fatherhood have pity on thy child'; and here Jesus pleads with his Father as we have done, and finds comfort in that pleading. Prayer was the channel of the Redeemer's comfort, earnest, intense, reverent, repeated prayer, and after each time of prayer he seems to have grown quiet, and to have gone to his disciples with a measure of restored peace of mind. The sight of their sleeping helped to bring back his griefs, and therefore he returned to pray again, and each time he was comforted, so that when he had prayed for the third time he was prepared to meet Judas and the soldiers and to go with silent patience to judgment and to death. His great comfort was prayer and submission to the divine will, for when he had laid his own will down at his Father's feet the feebleness of his flesh spoke no more complainingly, but in sweet silence, like a sheep dumb before her shearers, he contained his soul in patience and rest. Dear brothers and sisters, if any of you shall have your Gethsemane and your heavy griefs, imitate your Master by resorting to prayer, by crying to your Father, and by learning submission to his will.

I shall conclude by drawing two or three inferences from the whole subject. May the Holy Spirit instruct us.

The first is this – Learn, dear brethren, *the real humanity of our Lord Jesus Christ*. Do not think of him as God merely, though he is assuredly divine, but feel him to be near of kin to you, bone of your bone, flesh of your flesh. How thoroughly can he sympathize with you! He has been burdened with all your burdens and grieved with all your griefs. Are the waters very deep through which you are passing? Yet they are not deep compared with the torrents with which he was buffeted. Never a pang penetrates your spirit to which your covenant Head was a stranger. Jesus can sympathize with you in all your sorrows, for he has suffered far more than you have ever suffered, and is able therefore to succour you in your temptations. Lay hold on Jesus as your familiar friend, your brother born for adversity, and you will have obtained a consolation which will bear you through the uttermost deeps.

Next *see here the intolerable evil of sin*. You are a sinner, which Jesus never was, yet even to stand in the sinner's place was so dreadful to him that he was sorrowful even unto death, What will sin one day be to you if you should be found guilty at the last! Oh, could we tell the horror of sin there is not one among us that would be satisfied to remain in sin for a single moment; I believe there would go up from this house of prayer this morning a weeping and a wailing such as might be heard in the very streets, if men and women here who are living in sin could really know what sin is, and what the wrath of God is that rests upon them, and what the judgments of God will be that will shortly surround them and destroy them. Oh soul, sin must be an awful thing if it so crushed our Lord. If the very imputation of it fetched bloody sweat from the pure and holy Saviour, what must sin itself be? Avoid it, do not go near it, turn away from the very appearance of it, walk humbly and carefully with your God that sin may not harm you, for it is an exceeding plague, an infinite pest.

Learn next, but oh how few minutes have I in which to speak of such a lesson, *the matchless love of Jesus*, that for your sakes and mine he would not merely suffer in body, but consented even to bear the horror of being accounted a sinner, and coming under the wrath of God because of our sins: though it cost him suffering unto death and sore amazement, yet sooner than that we shall perish, the Lord smarted as our Surety. Can we not cheerfully endure persecution for his sake? Can we not labour earnestly for him? Are we so ungenerous that his cause shall know a lack while we have the means of helping it? Are we so base that his work shall flag while we have strength to carry it on? I charge you by Gethsemane, my brethren, if you have a part and lot in the passion of your Saviour, love him much who loved you so immeasurably, and spend and be spent for him.

Again looking at Jesus in the garden, we learn the *excellence and completeness of the atonement.* How black I am, how filthy, how loathsome in the sight of God – I feel myself only fit to be cast into the lowest hell, and I wonder that God has not long ago cast me there; but I go into Gethsemane, and I peer under those gnarled olive trees, and I see my Saviour. Yes, I see him wallowing on the ground in anguish, and hear such groans come from him as never came from human breast before. I look upon the earth and see it red with his blood, while his face is smeared with gory sweat, and I say to myself, 'My God, my Saviour, what aileth thee?' I hear him reply, 'I am suffering for thy sin', and then I take comfort, for while I gladly would have spared my Lord such an anguish, now that the anguish is over I can understand how Jehovah can spare me, because he smote his Son in my stead. Now I have hope of justification, for I bring before the justice of God and my own conscience the remembrance of my bleeding Saviour, and I say, 'Canst thou twice demand payment, first at the hand of thine agonising Son and then again at mine? Sinner as I am, I stand before the burning throne of the severity of God, and am not afraid of it. Canst thou scorch me, O consuming fire, when thou hast not only scorched but utterly consumed my Substitute?' Nay, by faith, my soul sees justice satisfied, the law honoured, the moral government of God established, and yet my once guilty soul absolved and set free. The fire of avenging justice has spent itself, and the law has exhausted its most rigorous demands upon the person of him who was made a curse for us, that we might be made the righteousness of God in him. Oh the sweetness of the comfort which flows from the atoning blood! Obtain that comfort, my brethren, and never leave it. Cling to your Lord's bleeding heart, and drink in abundant consolation.

Last of all, *what must be the terror of the punishment which will fall upon those men who reject the atoning blood,* and who will have to stand before God in their own proper persons to suffer for their sins. I will tell you, sirs, with pain in my heart as I tell you it, what will happen to those of you who reject my Lord. Jesus Christ my Lord and Master is a sign and prophecy to you of what will happen to you. Not in a garden, but on that bed of yours where you have so often been refreshed, you will be surprised and overtaken, and the pains of death will get hold upon you. With an exceeding sorrow and remorse for your misspent life and for a rejected Saviour you will be made very heavy. Then will your darling sin, your favourite lust, like another Judas, betray you with a kiss. While yet your soul lingers on your lip you will be seized and taken off by a body of evil ones, and carried away to the bar of God, just as Jesus was taken to the judgment seat of Caiaphas. There shall be a speedy, personal, and somewhat private judgment, by which you shall be committed to prison where, in darkness and weeping, and wailing, you shall spend the night before the great assize of the judgment morning. Then shall the day break and the resurrection morning come, and as our Lord then appeared before Pilate, so will you appear before the highest tribunal, not that of Pilate, but the dread judgment seat of the Son of God, whom you have despised and rejected. Then will witnesses come against you, not false witnesses, but true, and you will stand speechless, even as Jesus said not a word before his accusers. Then will conscience and despair buffet you, you will become such a monument of misery, such a spectacle of contempt, as to be fitly noted by another *Ecce Homo*, and men shall look at you and say, 'Behold the man and the suffering which has come upon him, because he despised his God and found pleasure in sin.' Then shall you be condemned. 'Depart, ye cursed', shall be your sentence, even as 'Let him be crucified' was the doom of Jesus. You shall be taken away by the officers of justice to your doom. Then like the sinner's Substitute you will cry, 'I thirst', but not a drop of water shall be given you; you shall taste nothing but the gall of bitterness. You shall be executed publicly with your crimes written over your head that all may read and understand that you are justly condemned; and then will you be mocked as Jesus was, especially if you have been a professor of religion and a false one; all that pass by will say, 'He saved others, he preached to others, but himself he cannot save.' God himself will mock you. Nay, think not I dream, has he not said it: 'I also will laugh at your calamity, I will mock when your fear cometh'? Cry unto your gods, that you once trusted in! Get comfort out of the lusts ye once delighted in, O ye that are cast away for ever! To your shame, and to the confusion of your nakedness, shall you that have despised the Saviour be made a spectacle of the justice of God for ever. It is right it should be so, justice rightly demands it. Sin made the Saviour suffer an agony, shall it not make you suffer? Moreover, in addition to your sin, you have rejected the Saviour; you have said, 'He shall not be my trust and confidence.' Voluntarily, presumptuously, and against your own conscience you have refused eternal life; and if you die rejecting mercy what can come of it but that first your sin, and secondly your unbelief, shall condemn you to misery without limit or end. Let Gethsemane warn you, let its groans and tears and bloody sweat admonish you. Repent of sin, and believe in Jesus. May his Spirit enable you, for Jesus' sake. Amen.

13

'I WILL', YET 'NOT AS I WILL' [1]

'Father, I will'.
JOHN 17:24

'Not as I will'.
MATTHEW 26:39

WE HAVE HERE TWO PRAYERS uttered by the same person; yet there is the greatest possible contrast between them. How different men are at different times! Yet Jesus was always essentially the same: 'the same yesterday, and today, and for ever'. Still, his mood and state of mind varied from time to time. He seemed calmly happy when he prayed with his disciples, and said, 'Father, I will that they also, whom thou hast given me, be with me where I am; that they may behold my glory, which thou hast given me'; but he was in an agony when, in Gethsemane, having withdrawn from his disciples, and fallen on his face, he prayed, saying, 'O my Father, if it be possible, let this cup pass from me: nevertheless not as I will, but as thou wilt.' It is the same man, and an unchangeable Man, too, as to his essence, who uttered both prayers; yet see how different were his frames of mind, and how different the prayers he offered. Brother, you may be the same man, and quite as good a man, when you are groaning before God as when you are singing before him. There may be more grace even in the submissive 'Not as I will' than in the triumphant 'Father, I will.' Do not judge yourselves to have changed in your standing before God because you have undergone an alteration as to your feelings. If your Master prayed so differently at different times, you, who

[1] Sermon No. 2,376. Preached at the Metropolitan Tabernacle on Sunday evening, 1 July 1888.

have not the fullness of grace that he had, must not wonder if you have a great variety of inward experiences.

Notice, also, that it was not only the same person, but that he used these two expressions almost at the same time. I do not know how many minutes – I had better say minutes rather than hours – intervened between the last supper, and the wonderful high-priestly prayer, and the agonizing cries of Gethsemane. I suppose that it was only a short walk from Jerusalem to the olive garden, and that it would not occupy long to traverse the distance. At one end of the walk, Jesus prays, 'Father, I will'; and at the other end of it, he says, 'Not as I will.' In like manner, we may undergo great changes, and have to alter the tone of our prayers, in a few minutes. You prayed just now with holy confidence; you took firm hold of the covenant angel, and with wrestling Jacob you said, 'I will not let thee go, except thou bless me'; and yet it may be equally becoming on your part, within an hour, to lie in the very dust, and in an agony to cry unto the Lord, 'Pardon my prayers, forgive me that I was too bold, and hear me now as I cry to thee, and say, "Not as I will, but as thou wilt."'

> If but my fainting heart be blest
> With thy sweet Spirit for its guest,
> My God, to thee I leave the rest;
>   'Thy will be done'!

Never be ashamed because you have to mend your prayers; be careful not to make a mistake if you can help it; but, if you make one, do not be ashamed to confess it, and to correct it as far as you can. One of our frequent mistakes is that we wonder that we make mistakes. Whenever a man says, 'I should never have thought that I could have done such a foolish thing as that', it shows that he did not really know himself, for had he known himself, he would rather have wondered that he did not do worse, and he would have marvelled that he acted as wisely as he did. Only the grace of God can teach us how to run our prayers down the scale from the high note of 'Father, hear me, for thou hast said, "Ask what thou wilt"', right down to the deep, deep bass of 'Father, not as I will, but as thou wilt.'

I must further remark that these two prayers were equally characteristic of Christ. I think that I should know my Lord by his voice in either of them. Who but the eternal Son of God may dare to say, 'Father, I will'? There speaks Incarnate Deity; that is the sublime utterance of the well-beloved Son. And yet who could say as he said it, 'If it be possible, let this cup pass from me: nevertheless not as I will, but as thou wilt'? Perhaps you have uttered those words, dear friend; but in your case they were not concerning such a cup of woe as Christ emptied. There were but a few drops of gall in your cup. His was all bitterness, from the froth to the dregs; all bitterness, and such bitterness as, thank God, you and I can never taste! That cup he has drained to the dregs, and we shall not have to drink one drop from it; but it was of that cup that he said – and I detect the voice of the Son of God, the Son of man, in that brief utterance – 'Not as I will, but as thou wilt.'

My two texts make up a strange piece of music. Blessed are the lips that know how to express the confidence that rises to the height as far as we can go with Christ, and descends even to the deeps as far as we can go with him in full submission to the will of God. Does anybody say that he cannot understand the contrast between these two prayers? Dear friend, it is to be explained thus. There was a difference of position in the Suppliant on these two occasions. The first prayer, 'Father, I will,' is the prayer of our great High Priest, with all his heavenly garments on, the blue, and purple, and fine twined linen, and the pomegranates, and the golden bells, and the breastplate, with the twelve precious stones bearing the names of his chosen people. It is our great High Priest, in the glory of his majestic office and power, who says to God, 'Father, I will'. The second Suppliant is not so much the Priest as the Victim. Our Lord is there seen bound to the altar, about to feel the sacrificial knife, about to be consumed with the sacrificial fire; and you hear him as though it were a lamb bleating, and the utterance is, 'Not as I will, but as thou wilt.' The first petition is the language of Christ in power pleading for us; the second is the utterance of Christ made sin for us, that we might be made the righteousness of God in him. That is the difference of position that explains the contrast in the prayers.

Let me tell you also that there is a difference in the subject of his supplication, which is full of instruction. In the first prayer, where our Lord says so majestically, 'Father, I will', he is pleading for his people, he is praying for what he knows to be the Father's will, he is officiating there before God as the very mouthpiece of God, and speaking of something about which he is perfectly clear and certain. When you are praying for God's people, you may pray very boldly. When you are pleading for God's cause, you may speak very positively. When you know you are asking what is definitely promised in the Scriptures as part of the covenant ordered in all things and sure, you may ask without hesitation, as our Lord did. But, in the second case, Jesus was praying for himself: 'If it be possible, let this cup pass from me.' He was praying about a matter, concerning which he did not, as man, know the Father's will, for he says, 'If it be possible.' There is an 'if' in it: 'If it be possible, let this cup pass from me.' Whenever you go upstairs in an agony of distress, and begin to pray about yourself, and about a possible escape from suffering, always say, under such circumstances, 'Nevertheless not as I will, but as thou wilt.' It may be given you sometimes to pray very boldly even in such a case as that; but, if it is not given you, take care that you do not presume. I may pray for healing for my body, but not with such confidence as I pray for the prosperity of Zion and the glory of God. That which has to do with myself I may ask as a child of God asks of his Father; but I must ask submissively, leaving the decision wholly in his hands, feeling that, because it is for myself rather than for him, I must say, 'Nevertheless not as I will, but as thou wilt.' I think that there is a plain lesson here for Christians to take heed that, while they are very confident on one subject for which they pray, they are equally submissive on another, for there is a heavenly blending in the Christian character, as there was in Christ's character, a firm confidence and yet an absolute yielding to the will of God, let that will be what it may.

> Lord, my times are in thy hand;
> All my sanguine hopes have plann'd
> To thy wisdom I resign,
> And would make thy purpose mine.

Now all this while you may say that I have only been going round the text. Very well; but, sometimes, there is a good deal of instruction to be picked up round a text. The manna fell round about the camp of Israel; peradventure there is some manna round about this text. May the Lord help every one of us to gather his portion!

I want you now, for a few minutes, to view this great Suppliant in the two moods in which he prayed, 'Father, I will'; and, 'Not as I will', and then to combine the two. We will, first, view *Jesus in the power of his intercession*; next, we will talk of *Jesus in the power of his submission*; and in the third place, we will try to *combine the two prayers*, 'I will'; yet, 'Not as I will'.

I. First, let us view Jesus IN THE POWER OF HIS INTER-CESSION, saying, 'Father, I will'.

Whence did he derive that power? Who enabled him thus to speak with God, and say, 'Father, I will?' First, *Jesus prayed in the power of his Sonship.* Sons may say to a father what strangers may not dare to say; and such a Son as Jesus was – so near to his Father's heart, one who could say, 'The Father hath not left me alone; for I do always those things that please him'; one of whom the Father had said, 'This is my beloved Son, in whom I am well pleased' – well might he have power with God so as to be able to say, 'Father, I will'.

Next, he derived this power from *the Father's eternal love to him.* Did you notice how, in the very verse from which our text is taken, Jesus says to his Father, 'Thou lovedst me before the foundation of the world?' We cannot conceive what the love of the Father is to Christ Jesus his Son. Remember, they are one in essence. God is one – Father, Son, and Holy Spirit; and, as the Incarnate God, Christ is unspeakably dear to the Father's heart. There is nothing about him of which the Father disapproves; there is nothing lacking in him, which the Father would desire to see there. He is God's ideal of himself: 'In him dwelleth all the fullness of the Godhead bodily.' Well may one who is the subject of his Father's eternal love be able to say, 'Father, I will'.

But *our Lord Jesus also based this prayer upon his finished work.* I grant you that he had not yet actually died, but in the certain prospect of his doing so, he had said to his Father, 'I have glorified thee on the earth: I have finished the work which thou gavest me to do.' Now, he has actually finished it; he has been able in the fullest sense to say, 'It is finished', and he has gone up to take his place in glory at his Father's side. You remember the argument with which Paul begins his Epistle to the Hebrews: 'God, who at sundry times and in divers manners spake in time past unto the fathers by the prophets, hath in these last days spoken unto us by his Son, whom he hath appointed heir of all things, by whom also he made the worlds; who being the brightness of his glory, and the express image of his person, and upholding all things by the word of his power, when he had by himself purged our sins, sat down on the right hand of the Majesty on high; being made so much better than the angels, as he hath by inheritance obtained a more excellent name than they. For unto which of the angels said he at any time, Thou art my Son, this day have I begotten thee? And again, I will be to him a Father, and he shall be to me a Son?' When the Father looks at Christ, he sees in him atonement accomplished, satisfaction presented, sin annihilated, the elect redeemed, the covenant ratified, the everlasting purpose settled on eternal foundations. O beloved, since Christ has magnified God's law, and made it honourable, and since he has poured out his soul unto death, he may well possess the power to say, 'Father, I will'.

Remember, too, that *Jesus still possesses this power*, and possesses it for you and for me. O my dear hearers, you may well go to Christ, and accept him as your Mediator and Intercessor, since all this power to say, 'Father, I will', is laid up in him on purpose for poor believing sinners, who come and take him to be their Saviour! You say that you cannot pray. Well, he can; ask him to plead for you; and I thank God that, sometimes, when we do not ask him to plead for us, he does it all the same, as he did for Peter, when Satan had desired to have him, but Christ had prayed for him. Peter did not know his danger, but the Saviour did, and he pleaded for him at once. What a blessing it is to think of Christ, clothed with divine authority and power, using it all for us! Well does Toplady sing –

> With cries and tears he offer'd up
> His humble suit below;
> But with authority he asks,
> Enthroned in glory now.

> For all that come to God by him,
>   Salvation he demands
> Points to their names upon his breast
>   And spreads his wounded hands.
>
> His covenant and sacrifice
>   Give sanction to his claim;
> 'Father, I will that all my saints
>   Be with me where I am.'

Further, *that power of Christ will land every believer in heaven.* Notice how Christ turns all his pleading with God that way; he says, 'Father, I will, that they also, whom thou hast given me, be with me where I am; that they may behold my glory.' The devil says that we shall never get to heaven; but we remember that declaration of Moses, 'thine enemies shall be found liars unto thee', and the arch-enemy will be found to be the arch-liar, for the Lord's prayer will be heard, and as he pleads that those whom the Father gave him should be brought up to be with him where he is, you may depend upon it that they will all arrive safely in heaven; and you, if you are among those who are given to Christ – and you may know that by your faith in him – shall be among that blessed company.

I shall have finished with this first point when I have said this, *that power which Christ had may, in a measure, be gained by all his people.* I dare not say, and I would not say, that any one of us will ever be able to utter our Saviour's words, 'Father, I will'; but I do say this, if you abide in Christ, and his words abide in you, you may attain to such power in prayer, that you shall ask what you will, and it shall be done unto you. This is not a promise to all of you; no, not even to all of you who are God's people; but only to those of you who live wholly unto God, and serve him with all your heart. You can, by habitual intercourse with God, attain to such power with the Most High that men shall say of you what they used to say of Luther, 'There goes a man who can ask what he likes of God, and have it.' You may attain to that glorious altitude. Oh, I would that every one of us would seek to reach this height of power and blessing! It is not the feeble Christian, it is not the worldly Christian, who has just enough grace to make him miserable, the man who has only about enough grace to keep him from being absolutely immoral; that is not the man who will prevail with God. You paddlers in Christianity, who scarcely wet your toes; you who never go in beyond your ankles, or your knees; God will never give you this privilege unless you go in for it. Get where the waters are deep enough to swim in, and plunge in. Be perfectly consecrated to God; yield your whole lives to his glory without reserve; then may you obtain something of your Master's power in prayer when he said, 'Father, I will'.

II. Now I ask you kindly to accompany me, in the second place, to notice JESUS IN THE POWER OF HIS SUBMISSION. Our second text is all submission: 'Not as I will.'

This utterance, 'Not as I will', proved that *the shrinkings of Christ's nature from that dreadful cup were all overcome*. I do not believe that Christ was afraid to die; do you believe that? Oh, no; many of his servants have laughed at death; I am sure that he was not afraid to die; what was it, then, that made that cup so awfully terrible? Jesus was to be made sin for us, he was to come under the curse for us, he was to feel the Father's wrath on account of human guilt; and his whole nature, not alone his flesh, but his whole being, shrank from that fearful ordeal. It was not actual defilement that was to come upon him; but it looked like it; and, as man, he could not tell what that cup of wrath must contain.

> Immanuel, sunk with dreadful woe,
> Unfelt, unknown to all below –
>   Except the Son of God –
> In agonizing pangs of soul
> Drinks deep of wormwood's bitterest bowl,
>   And sweats great drops of blood.

After dwelling in the love of God from all eternity, he was in a few hours to bear the punishment of man's sin; yet he must bear it, and therefore he said, 'Not as I will, but as thou wilt.' Do you wonder that he prayed, 'If it be possible, let this cup pass from me'? Is Christ to be blamed for these shrinkings of nature? My dear friends, if it had been a pleasure to him, and he had had no shrinkings, where would have been his holy courage? If it had not been a horrible and dreadful thing to him, where would have been his submission, where would have been the virtue that made atonement of it? If it had been a thing that he could not, or must not, shrink from, where would have been the pain, the wormwood, and the gall of it? The cup must be, in the nature of things, something from which he that beareth it must shrink, or else it could not have been sufficient for the redemption of his people, and the vindication of the broken law of God. It was necessary, then, that Christ should, by such a prayer as this, prove that he had overcome all the shrinkings of his nature.

'Not as I will', is also an evidence of *Christ's complete submission to the will of his Father.* 'He is brought as a lamb to the slaughter, and as a sheep before her shearers is dumb, so he openeth not his mouth.' There is no resistance, no struggling, he gives himself up completely. 'There,' he seems to say to the Lord, 'do what thou wilt with me; I yield myself absolutely to thy will.' There was on Christ's part no reserve, no wish even to make any reserve; I go further, and say that Jesus willed as God willed, and even prayed that the will of God, from which his human nature at first shrank, might be fulfilled. 'Nevertheless not as I will, but as thou wilt.'

O brothers and sisters – for you both need this grace – pray God to help you to learn how to *copy your Lord in this submission!* Have you submitted to the Lord's will? Are you submitting now? Are not some of you like bullocks unaccustomed to the yoke? There is a text, you know, in the One Hundred and Thirty-First Psalm, 'My soul is even as a weaned child.' I have sometimes thought that, for some of the Lord's children, the passage would have to be read, 'My soul is even as a weaning child', and there are many of God's people who are very long in the weaning. You cannot get satisfaction, and quiet, and content, can you? Can you give yourself up entirely to God, that he may do whatever he likes with you? Have you some fear of a tumour, or a cancer? Is there before you the prospect of a painful and dangerous operation? Is business going badly with you, so that you will probably lose everything? Is a dear child sickening? Is the mother likely to be taken away? Will you have to lose your position and reputation if you are faithful to the Lord? Will you be exposed to cruel slanders? Will you probably be cast out of your situation if you do what is right? Come now, whatever you dread or expect, can you give yourself up wholly to God, and say, 'It is the Lord, let him do what seemeth him good'? Your Lord and Master did so; he said, 'Not as I will.' Oh, that he might teach you this divine art of absolute resignation to the purpose and ordinance of God, till you also should be able to say, 'Not as I will'! Thus you will sing –

> I bow me to thy will, O God,
> And all thy ways adore;
> And every day I live I'll seek
> To please thee more and more.

III. I have finished my discourse when I have just twisted these two sayings together a little; so, thirdly, let us COMBINE THE TWO PRAYERS: 'I will'; yet, 'Not as I will.'

First, let me say, *Number One will help you very much to Number Two*. If you learn to pray with Christ, with the holy boldness that almost says, 'Father, I will', you are the man who will know how to say, 'Not as I will'. Is it not strange that it should be so? It looks like a contradiction; but I am sure that it is not so. The man who can have his will with God is the very man who does not want his own way with God. He who may have what he likes, is the man who wishes to have what God likes. You remember the good old woman, who lay near to death, and one said to her, 'Do you not expect soon to die?' She answered, 'I do not know whether I shall live or die; and what is more, I have no concern which way it is.' Then the friend asked, 'But if you had your choice whether you should live or die, which would you choose?' She replied, 'I would rather that the Lord's will should be done.' 'But suppose the Lord's will were to leave it entirely to you to choose whichever you liked?' 'Then,' she said, 'I would kneel down, and pray the Lord to choose for me.' And I do think that is the best way to live; not to have any choice at all, but to ask the Lord to choose for you. You can always have your way, you know, when your way is God's way. The sure way to carry out self-will is when self-will is nothing else but God's will. Oh, that the Lord would teach us this mighty power with him in prayer! It will not be given without much close fellowship with him. Then, when we know that we can have what we will of him, we shall be in the right state to say, 'Not as I will.'

The next remark that I would make is, that *Number Two is needful for Number One;* that is to say, until you can say, 'Not as I will', you never will be able to say, 'Father, I will'. I believe that one reason why people cannot prevail in prayer, is because they will not yield to God; and they cannot expect God to yield to them. God does this and that with you, and you quarrel with him; and then you go upstairs, and begin to pray. Go down on your knees, and make your peace with him first; for if you must not come to the altar till you have become reconciled unto your brother, how can you come to the throne of grace till you have given up your quarrel with God?

But some people are never at peace with God. I have heard of a good friend who lost a child, and he was wearing mourning several years afterwards, and he was always fretting about the dear child, till a Quakeress said to him, 'What! hast thou not forgiven God yet?' and there are some people who have not yet forgiven God for taking their loved ones. They ought always to have blessed him, for he never takes away any but those whom he lent to us, and we should bless his name as much for taking them again as for lending them to us. Dear friends, you must submit to the will of God, or else you cannot have power with him in prayer. 'Well,' say you, 'you will not let me have my own way at all.' Certainly, I will not let you have your own way; but when you just say, 'There, Lord, I have no quarrel with thee now; do what thou wilt with me', then he will say, 'Rise, my child, ask what thou wilt, and I will give it thee; open thy mouth wide, and I will fill it.'

Notice, also, dear friends, that *Jesus will help us to have Number One and Number Two.* He gives himself over to us to teach us the power of prevailing prayer; but he also gives himself over to teach us the art of blessed submission in prayer; and it is his will that these two should not be separated. 'Father, I will', is Christ's word on our behalf; and 'Not as I will', is equally Christ's word on our behalf. When you cannot pray either of these prayers as you would, fall back upon Christ's prayer, and claim it as your own.

Lastly, I think that *true sonship will embody both Number One and Number Two.* It is the true child of God, who knows that he is his Father's child, who says, 'Father, I will'. He is often very bold where another would be presumptuous. Oh, I have heard full often of somebody's prayers – I will not say who the somebody is – he seemed so familiar with God in his prayer. Oh, yes; I know! You love those very stately prayers, in which the bounds are set about the mount, and no man may dare to come near. You make the throne of grace to be like Sinai was of old, of which the Lord said, 'Whosoever toucheth the mount shall be surely put to death: there shall not an hand touch it, but he shall surely be stoned, or shot through; whether it be beast or man, it shall not live.' 'Oh, but', you say, 'so-and-so is so familiar at the mercy-seat!' Yes, I know; and you think that is a pity, do you not? Perhaps you are acquainted with a judge; look at him on the bench wearing his wig and robe of office; but you will not dare to speak to him there unless you address him as 'My lord', and behave very respectfully to him. By-and-by he goes home, and he has a little boy there, Master Johnny. Why, the child has seized hold of his father's whiskers, there he is up on his father's back! 'Why, Johnny, you are disrespectful!' 'Oh, but he is my father!' says the boy; and his father says, 'Yes, Johnny, that I am; and I do not want you to say, "My lord", and talk to me as they do in the court.' So, there are certain liberties which God's children may take with him, which he counts no liberties at all; but he loves so to be treated by them. He will let each one of them say, 'Father, I will', because they are his children.

Then, mark you, you are not God's child unless you can also say, 'Father, not as I will.' The true child bends before his father's will. 'Yes,' says he, 'I would like so-and-so.' His father forbids it. 'Then I do not want it, and I will not touch it'; or he says, 'I do not like to take that medicine, but my father says I am to take it', and he takes the cup, and he drinks the whole of its contents. The true child says, 'Not as I will', although, after his measure, he also says, 'Father, I will'.

I have only been talking to you who are the Lord's people. I hope you have learned something from this subject; I know you have if the Lord has taught you to pray after the fashion of these two prayers, as you humbly yet believingly may, copying your Lord.

But oh, what shall I say to those of you who are not the Lord's people? If you do not know how to pray at all, may the Lord teach you! If you do not yet know your needs, may the Lord instruct you! But let me tell you that, if ever there shall come a time when you feel your need of a Saviour, the Lord Jesus will be willing to receive you. If ever you should yearn after him, be you sure that he is also yearning after you. Even now –

> 'Kindled his relentings are',

and if you will but breathe the penitent's prayer, 'God be merciful to me, a sinner', and turn your eye Christ-ward, and cross-ward, there is salvation for you even now. God grant that you may have it, for Jesu's sake! Amen.

14

CHRISTIAN RESIGNATION [1]

'Not as I will, but as thou wilt.'
MATTHEW 26:39

THE APOSTLE PAUL, writing concerning our Lord Jesus Christ, says, 'Though he were a Son, yet learned he obedience by the things which he suffered.' He who, as God, knew all things, had to learn obedience, in the time of his humiliation. He, who is in himself Wisdom Incarnate, did himself condescend to enter the school of suffering: there we learn that important lesson of the Christian life, obedience to the will of God; and here, in Gethsemane's garden, you can see the Divine Scholar going forth to practise his lesson. He had been all his lifetime learning it, and now he has to learn it for the last time in his agony and bloody sweat, and in his terrible death upon the cross. Now is he to discover the utmost, depths of suffering, and to attain to the height of the knowledge of obedience. See how well he has learned his lesson; note how complete and ripe a scholar he is. He has attained to the very highest class in that school; and, in the immediate respect of death, can say to his Father, 'Not as I will, but as thou wilt.'

The object of this discourse is to commend to you the blessed example of our Lord Jesus Christ, and, as God the Holy Spirit shall help me, to urge you to be made like unto, your glorious Head, and yourselves to learn, by all the daily providences with which God is pleased to surround you, this lesson of resignation to the will of God, and of making an entire surrender to him.

---

[1] Sermon No. 2,715. Preached at New Park Street Chapel on a Thursday evening early in 1859.

I have been struck lately, in reading works by some writers who belong to the Romish Church, with the marvellous love which they have towards the Lord Jesus Christ. I did think, at one time, that it could not be possible for any to be saved in that Church; but, often, after I have risen from reading the books of those holy men, and have felt myself to be quite a dwarf by their side, I have said, 'Yes, despite their errors, these men must have been taught of the Holy Spirit. Notwithstanding all the evils of which they have drunk so deeply, I am quite certain that they must have had fellowship with Jesus, or else they could not have written as they did.' Such writers are few and far between; but, still, there is a remnant according to the election of grace even in the midst of that apostate Church. Looking at a book by one of them, the other day, I met with this remarkable expression, 'Shall that body, which has a thorn-crowned Head, have delicate, pain-fearing members? God forbid!' That remark went straight to my heart at once. I thought how often the children of God shun pain, reproach, and rebuke, and think it to be a strange thing when some fiery trial happens to them. If they would but recollect that their Head had to sweat as it were great drops of blood falling down to the ground, and that their Head was crowned with thorns, it would not seem strange to them that the members of his mystical body also have to suffer. If Christ had been some delicate person, if our glorious Head had been reposing upon the soft pillow of ease, then might we, who are the members of his church, have expected to go through this world with joy and comfort; but if he must be bathed in his own blood, if the thorns must pierce his temples, if his lips must be parched, and if his mouth must be dried up like a furnace, shall we escape suffering and agony? Is Christ to have a head of brass and hands of gold? Is his head to be as if it glowed in the furnace, and are not we to glow in the furnace, too? Must he pass through seas of suffering, and shall we–

> Be carried to the skies,
> On flowery beds of ease?

Ah! no! we must be conformed unto our Lord in his humiliation if we would be made like him also in his glory.

So, brethren and sisters, I have to discourse to you upon this lesson, which some of us have begun to learn, but of which as yet we know so little – this lesson of saying, 'Not as I will, but as thou wilt.' First, let me *explain the meaning of this prayer;* then, *urge you, by certain reasons, to make this your constant cry;* next, *show what will be the happy effect of its being the paramount desire of your spirits;* and we will conclude with a practical enquiry – *what can bring us to this blessed condition?*

I. First, then, WHAT IS THE MEANING OF THIS PRAYER? 'Not as I will, but as thou wilt.'

I shall not address myself to those Christians who are but as dwarfs, who know little about the things of the kingdom. I will speak rather to those who do business in the deep waters of communion, who know what it is to pillow their heads upon the bosom of Jesus, to walk with God as Enoch did, and to talk with him as Abraham did. My dear brethren, only such as you can understand this prayer in all its length and breadth. Your brother, who as yet scarcely knows the meaning of the word communion, may pray thus in some feeble measure; yet it is not to be expected that he should discern all the spiritual teaching that there is in these words of our Lord; but to you who are Christ-taught, you who have become ripe scholars in the school of Christ, to you I may speak as unto wise men – judge ye what I say.

If you and I mean this prayer, and do not use it as a mere form of words, but mean it in all its fullness, we must, be prepared for this kind of experience. Sometimes, when we are in the midst of the most active service, when we are diligently serving God both with our hands and our heart, and when success is crowning all our labours, *the Lord will lay us aside,* take us right away from the vineyard, and thrust us into the furnace. Just, at the very time when the church seems to need us most, and when the world's necessities are most of all appealing to us, and when our hearts are full of love towards Christ and towards our fellow-creatures, it will often happen that, just then, God will strike us down with sickness, or remove us from our sphere of activity. But if we really mean this prayer, we must be prepared to say: 'Not as I will, but as thou wilt.' This is not easy, for does not the Holy Spirit himself teach us to long after active service for our Saviour? Does he not, when he gives us love towards our fellow-men, constrain us, as it were, to make their salvation our meat and our drink? When he is actively at work within our hearts, do we not feel as if we could not live without serving God? Do we not then feel that, to labour for the Lord is our highest rest, and that toil for Jesus is our sweetest pleasure? Does it not then seem most trying to our ardent spirit to be compelled to drink the cup of sickness, and to be incapable of doing anything actively for God? The preacher is seeing men converted and his ministry successful; but, on a sudden, he, is compelled to cease from preaching; or the Sunday-school teacher has, by the grace of God, been the means of bringing his class into an interesting and hopeful condition; yet, just when the class needs his presence most, he is smitten down, so that he cannot, go on with his work. Ah! then it is that the spirit finds it hard to say, 'Not as I will, but as thou wilt.' But if we adopt this prayer, this is what it means; that we should be prepared to suffer instead of to serve, and should be as willing to lie in the trenches as to scale the walls, and as willing to be laid aside in the King's hospital as to be fighting in the midst of the rank and file of the King's army. This is hard to flesh and blood, but we must do it if we present this petition.

If we really mean this prayer, there will be a second trial for us. Sometimes, *God will demand of us that we labour in unpropitious fields;* he will set his children to plough the rock and to cast their bread upon the waters. He will send his Ezekiel to prophesy in a valley full of dry bones, and his Jonah to carry his message to Nineveh. He will give his servants strange work to do – work which seems as if it never could be successful, or bring honour either to God or to themselves. I doubt not that there are some ministers, who toil and labour with all their might, yet who see but little fruit. Far away in the dark places of heathendom, there are men who have been toiling for years with scarcely a convert to cheer them; and here, too, in England, there are men who are preaching, in all sincerity and faithfulness, the word of the Lord, yet they do not see souls converted. They know that they are unto God a sweet savour of Christ, both in them that perish, and in them that are saved. Our hearts are, I trust, so full of the Spirit prompting us to cry, like Rachel, 'Give me children, or I die,' that we cannot rest content without seeing the success of our labours. Yet the Master, in effect, says to us, 'No, I tell you to continue to toil for me, though I give you no fruit for your labour; you are to keep on ploughing this rock, simply because I tell you to do it.' Ah! then, brethren, it is hard to say, 'Not my will but thine be done.' But we must say it; we must feel that we are ready to forego even the joy of harvest, and the glory of success, if God wills it.

At other times, *God will remove his people, from positions of honourable service, to other offices that are far inferior in the minds of men.* I think that I should feel it hard if I had to be banished from my large congregation, and from my thousands of hearers, to a small village where I could only preach the gospel to a little company of people; yet I am sure that, if I entered fully into the spirit of our Lord's words – 'Not as I will, but as thou wilt' – I should be quite as ready to be there as to be here. I have heard that, among the Jesuits, such is the extraordinary obedience which they are compelled to pay to their superiors that, on one occasion, there was a president of one of their colleges, who had written some of the most learned books in any language, a man of the highest talents, and the superior of the order took a capricious thought into his head, for some reason, to send him straight away from the country where he was to Bath, to stand there in the street for a year, and sweep the crossing, and the man did it. He was compelled to do it; his vow obliged him to do anything that he was told to do.

Now, in a spiritual sense, this is hard to perform; but, nevertheless, it is a Christian's duty. We remember the saying of a good man that the angels in heaven are so completely given up to obedience to God that, if there should be two works to do, ruling an empire and sweeping a crossing, neither of the two angels, who might be selected to go on these two errands, would have any choice in the matter, they would just leave it with their Lord to decide which part they were to fulfil. You may perhaps, be called from the charge of the services in a place of worship, to become one of the humblest members in another church; you may be taken from a place of much honour, and put in the very lowest ranks of the army; are you willing to submit to that kind of treatment? Your flesh and blood say, 'Lord, if I may still serve in thine army, let me be a captain; or, at least, let me be a sergeant, or a corporal. If I may help to draw thy chariot, let me be the leading horse, let me run first in the team, let me wear the bright ribbons.' But, God may say to you, 'I have put thee there in the thick of the battle, now I will place thee behind; I have given thee vigour and strength to fight with great success, now I will make thee tarry by the stuff; I have done with thee in the prominent position, now I will use thee somewhere else.' But if we can only pray this prayer, 'Not as I will, but as thou wilt', we shall be ready to serve God anywhere and everywhere, so long as we know that we are doing his will.

But there is another trial which we shall all have to endure in our measure, which will prove whether we understand by this prayer what Christ meant by it. Sometimes, *in the service of Christ, we must be prepared to endure the loss of reputation, of honour, and even of character itself.* I remember, when I first, came to London to preach the word, I thought that I could bear anything for Christ; but I found myself shamefully slandered, all manner of falsehoods were uttered concerning me, and in agony I fell on my face before God, and cried unto him. I felt as though that was a thing I could not bear; my character was very dear to me, and I could not endure to have such false things said about me. Then this thought came to me, 'You must give up all to Christ, you must, surrender everything for him, character, reputation, and all that you have; and if it is the Lord's will, you shall be reckoned the vilest of the vile, so long as you can still continue to serve him, and your character is really pure, you need not fear. If it is your Master's will that you shall be trampled and spit upon by all the wicked men in the world, you must simply bear it, and say, "Not as I will, but; as thou wilt."' And I remember then how I rose from my knees, and sang to myself that verse –

> If on my face, for thy dear name,
>   Shame and reproaches be,
> All hail reproach, and welcome shame,
>   If thou remember me.

'But how hard it was', you say, 'for you to suffer the loss of character, and to have evil things spoken against you falsely for

Christ's name's sake!' And what was the reason why it was so hard? Why, it was just because I had not fully learnt how to pray this prayer of our Lord Jesus Christ – and I am afraid that I have not completely learnt it yet. It is a very delightful thing to have even our enemies speaking well of us, to go through this world with such holiness of character that men who pour scorn upon all religion cannot find fault with us; but it is an equally glorious thing for us to be set in the pillory of shame, to be pelted by every passer-by, to be the song of the drunkard, to be the by-word of the swearer, when we do not deserve it, and to endure all this for Christ's sake. This is true heroism; this is the meaning of the prayer of our text.

Again, some of you have at times thought, 'Oh, if the Master will only be pleased to open a door for me where I may be the means of doing good! *How glad I should be if I could have either more wealth, or more influence, or more knowledge, or more talents, with which I might serve him better.*' You have prayed about the matter, and thought about it, and you have said, 'If I could only get into such-and-such a position, how excellently should I be able to serve God!' You have seen your Master give to some of his servants ten talents, but he has given you only one; you have gone on your knees, and asked him to be good enough to trust you with two, and he has refused it. Or you have had two and you have asked him to let you have ten; and he has said, 'No, I will give you two talents and no more.' But you say, 'Is it not a laudable desire, that I should seek to do more good?' Certainly; trade with your talents, multiply them if you can. But suppose you have no power of utterance, suppose you have no opportunities of serving God, or even suppose the sphere of your influence is limited, what then? Why, you are to say 'Lord, I hoped it was thy will that I might have a wider sphere, but if it is not, although I long to serve thee on a larger scale, I will be quite content to glorify thee in my present narrower sphere, for I feel that here is an opportunity for the trial of my faith and resignation, and again I say, "Not as I will, but as thou wilt."'

Christian men, are you prepared heartily to pray this prayer? I fear there is not a single individual amongst us who could pray it in all its fullness of meaning. Perhaps you may go as far as I have already gone; but if God should take you at your word, and say,

'My will is that your wife should be smitten with a fatal illness, and, like a fading lily, droop and die before your eyes; that your children should be caught up to my loving bosom in heaven; that your house should be burned with fire; that you should be left penniless, a pauper dependent on the charity of others; it is my will that you should cross the sea; that you should go to distant lands, and endure unheard-of hardships; it is my will that, at last, your bones should lie bleaching on the desert sand in some foreign clime.' Are you willing to endure, all this for Christ? Remember that you have not attained unto the full meaning of this prayer until you have said 'Yes' to all that it means; and, until you can go to the uttermost lengths to which God's providence may go, you have not gone to the full extent of the resignation in this cry of our Lord. Many of the early Christians, I think, did know this prayer by heart; it is wonderful how willing they were to do anything and be anything for Christ. They had got this idea into their heads, that they were not to live to themselves; and they had it also in their hearts; and they believed that, to be martyred, was the highest honour they could possibly wish for. Consequently, if they were brought to the tribunals of the judges, they never ran away from their persecutors; they almost courted death, for they thought it was the highest privilege that they could possibly have if they might be torn in pieces by the lions in the arena, or be decapitated with the sword. Now, if we also could but get that idea into our hearts, with what courage would it gird us, how fully might we then serve God, and how patiently might we endure persecution if we had but learnt the meaning of this prayer, 'Not as I will, but as thou wilt.'

II. In the second place, I AM TO TRY AND GIVE YOU SOME REASONS WHY IT WILL BE BEST FOR US ALL TO SEEK TO HAVE THE HOLY SPIRIT WITHIN US, SO THAT WE MAY BE BROUGHT INTO THIS FRAME OF MIND AND HEART.

And the first reason is because it is simply *a matter of right*. God ought to have his way at all times, and I ought not to have mine whenever it is contrary to his. If ever my will is at cross purposes to the will of the Supreme, it is but right that mine should yield to his. If I could have my own way – if such a poor, feeble creature as

I am could thwart the Omnipotent Creator, it would be wrong for me to do it. What! hath he made me, and shall he not do as he wills with me? Is he like the potter, and am I but as the clay, and shall the thing formed say to him that formed it, 'Why hast thou made me thus?' No, my Lord, it is but right that thou shouldest do what thou pleasest with me, for I am thine – thine, for thou hast made me – thine, for thou hast bought me with thy blood. If I am a jewel purchased with the precious blood of Jesus, then he may cut me into what shape he pleases, he may polish me as he chooses, he may let me lie in the darkness of the casket, or let me glitter in his hand or in his diadem; in fact, he may do with me just as he wills, for I am his; and so long as I know that he does it, I must say, 'Whatever he does is right; my will shall not be in opposition to his will.'

But, again, this is not only a matter of right, it is *a matter of wisdom with us*. Depend upon it, dear brethren, if we could have our own will, it would often be the worst thing in the world for us; but to let God have his way with us, even if it were in our power to thwart him, would be an act of wisdom on our part. What do I desire when I wish to have my own will? I desire my own happiness; well, but I shall get it far more easily if I let God have his will, for the will of God is both for his own glory and my happiness; so, however much I may think that my own will would tend to my comfort and happiness, I may rest assured that God's will would be infinitely more profitable to me than my own; and that, although God's will may seem to make it dark and dreary for me at the time, yet from seeming evil he will bring forth good, such as never could have been produced from that supposed good after which my weak and feeble judgment is so apt to run.

But, again, suppose it were possible for us to have our own will, *would it not be an infringement of that loving reliance which Christ may well ask at our hands, that we should trust him?* Are we not saved by trusting our Lord Jesus Christ? Has not faith in Christ been the means of saving me from sin and hell? Then, surely I must not run away from this rule when I come into positions of trial and difficulty. If faith has been superior to sin, through the blood of Christ, it will certainly be superior to trial, through the almighty arm of Christ. Did I not tell him, when I first came to him, that I would trust no one but him? Did I not declare that all my other confidences were burst and broken, and scattered to the winds; and did I not ask that he would permit me to put my trust in him alone; and shall I, after that, play the traitor? Shall I now set up some other object in which to place my trust? Oh, no! my love to Jesus, my gratitude to him for his condescension in accepting my faith, binds me henceforth to trust to him, and to him alone.

We often lose the force of a truth by not making it palpable to our own mind; let us try to make this one so. Imagine the Lord Jesus to be visibly present in this pulpit; suppose that he looks down upon one of you, and says, 'My child, thy will and mine do not, just now, agree; thou desirest such-and-such a thing, but I say, "Nay, thou must not have it"; now, my child, which will is to prevail, mine or thine?' Suppose you were to reply, 'Lord, I must have my will', do you not think he would look at you with eyes of infinite sadness and pity, and say to you, 'What! did I give up my will for thee, and wilt thou not give up thy will for me? Did I surrender all I had, even my life, for thy sake, and dost thou say, thou self-willed child, "I must have these things according to my will, and contrary to thy wish and purpose, O my Saviour?"' Surely, you could not talk like that; rather, I think I see you instantly falling on your knees, and saying, 'Lord Jesus, forgive me for ever harbouring such evil thoughts; no, my Lord, even if thy will be hard, I will think it pleasant; if it be bitter, I will believe that the bitterest draught is sweet. Let me but see thee dying on the cross for me, let me only know that thou lovest me, and wherever thou shalt put me, I will be in heaven as long as I can feel that it is thy will that is being done with me. I will be perfectly content to be just wherever thou choosest me to be, and to suffer whatever thou choosest for me to endure.'

Yes, dear friends, it would show a sad want of that love which we owe to Christ, and of that gratitude which he deserves, if we were once to set our wills up in opposition to his. Therefore, again, beloved, for love's sake, for wisdom's sake, for right's sake, I beseech you ask the Holy Spirit to teach you this prayer of our Lord Jesus Christ, and to impart to you its blessed meaning.

III. I notice, in the next place, THE EFFECT OF TRULY SAYING AND FEELING, 'NOT AS I WILL, BUT AS THOU WILT.'

The first effect is *constant happiness*. If you would find out the cause of most of your sorrows, dig at the root of your self-will; for that is where it lies. When your heart is wholly sanctified unto God, and your will is entirely subdued to him, the bitter becomes sweet, pain is changed to pleasure, and suffering is turned into joy. It is not possible for that man's mind to be disturbed whose will is wholly resigned to the will of God. 'Well,' says one, 'that is a very startling statement' – and another says, 'I have really sought to have my will resigned to God's will, yet I am disturbed.' Yes, and that is simply because, though you have sought, like all the rest of us, you have not yet attained to full resignation to the will of the Lord. But when once you have attained to it – I fear you never will in this life – then shall you be free from everything that shall cause you sorrow or discomposure of mind.

Another blessed effect of this prayer, if it is truly presented, is that *it will give a man holy courage and bravery*. If my mind is wholly resigned to God's will what have I to fear in all the world? It is with me then as it was with Polycarp; when the Roman emperor threatened that he would banish him he said, 'Thou canst not, for the whole world is my Father's house, and thou canst not banish me from it.' 'But I will slay thee,' said the emperor. 'Nay, thou canst not, for my life is hid with Christ in God.' 'I will take away all thy treasures.' 'Nay, thou canst not; for I have nothing that thou knowest of; my treasure is in heaven, and my heart is there also.' 'But I will drive thee away from men, and thou shalt have no friend left.' 'Nay, that thou canst not do, for I have a Friend in heaven from whom thou canst not separate me; I defy thee, for there is nothing that thou canst do unto me.' And so can the Christian always say, if once his will agrees with God's will; he may defy all men, and defy hell itself, for he will be able to say, 'Nothing can happen to me that is contrary to the will of God; and if it be his will, it is my will, too; if it pleases God, it pleases me. God has been pleased to give me part of his will, so I am satisfied with whatever he sends.'

Man is, after all, only the second cause of our sorrows. A persecutor says, perhaps, to a child of God, 'I can afflict thee.' 'Nay, thou canst not, for thou art dependent on the first Great Cause, and he and I are agreed.' Ah! dear friends, there is nothing that makes men such cowards as having wills contrary to the will of God; but, when we resign ourselves wholly into the hands of God, what have we to fear? The thing that made Jacob a coward was that he was not resigned to God's will when Esau came to meet him. God had foretold that the elder of the two sons of Isaac should serve the younger; Jacob's business was to believe that, and to go boldly forward with his wives and children, and not to bow down before Esau, but to say, 'The promise is, the elder shall serve the younger; I am not going to bow down to you; it is your place to fall prostrate before me.' But poor Jacob said, 'Perhaps it is God's will that Esau should conquer me and smite the mothers and their children; but my will is that it shall not be so.' The contest is well pictured at the ford Jabbok; but if Jacob had not disbelieved God's promise, he would never have bowed himself to the earth seven times before his brother Esau. In the holy majesty of his faith, he would have said, 'Esau, my brother, thou canst do me no hurt; for thou canst do nothing contrary to the will of God. Thou canst do nothing contrary to his decree, and I will be pleased with what-soever it is.'

So, this resignation to God's will gives, first, joy in the heart, and then it gives fearless courage; and yet another thing follows from it. As soon as anyone truly says, 'Not as I will, but as thou wilt', this resolve *tends to make every duty light, every trial easy, every tribulation sweet.* We should never feel it to be a hard thing to serve God; yet there are many people, who, if they do a little thing for the Lord, think so much of it; and if there is ever a great thing to be done, you have, first, to plead very hard to get them to do it; and when they do it, very often it is done so badly that you are half sorry you ever asked them to do it. A great many people make very much out of what is really very little. They take one good action which they have performed, and they hammer it out till it becomes as thin as gold leaf, and then they think they may cover a whole week with that one good deed. The seven days shall all be glorified by an action which only takes five minutes to perform; it shall be quite enough, they even think, for all time to come. But the Christian, whose will is conformed to God's will, says, 'My Lord, is there anything else for me to do? Then, I will gladly do it. Does it involve want of rest? I will do it. Does it involve loss of time in my business? Does it involve me, sometimes, in toil and fatigue? Lord it shall be done, if it is thy will; for thy will and mine are in complete agreement. If it is possible, I will do it; and I will count all things but loss that I may win Christ, and be found in him, rejoicing in his righteousness, and not in mine own.'

IV. There are many other sweet and blessed effects which this resignation would produce; but I must close by observing that THE ONLY WAY IN WHICH THIS SPIRIT CAN BE ATTAINED IS BY THE UNCTION OF THE HOLY ONE, the outpouring and the indwelling of the Holy Spirit in our hearts. You may try to subdue your own self, but you will never do it alone. You may labour, by self-denial, to keep down your ambition; but you will find that it takes another shape, and grows by that wherewith you thought to poison it. You may seek to concentrate all the love of your soul on Christ, and in the very act, you will find self creeping in. I am sometimes astonished – and yet not astonished when I know the evil of my own heart – when I look within myself, and find how impure my motive is at the very moment when I thought it was most pure; and I expect it is the same with you, dear friends. You perform a good action – some almsgiving to the poor, perhaps. You say, 'I will do it very quietly.' Someone speaks of it, and you say at once, 'I wish you had not spoken of that; I do not like to hear anyone talk of what I have done; it hurts me.' Perhaps it is only your pride that makes you say that it hurts you; for some folk make their modesty to be their pride; it is, in fact, their secret pride that they are doing good, and that people do not know it. They glory in that supposed secrecy; and by its coming out they feel that their modesty is spoilt, and they are afraid that people will say, 'Ah, you see that it is known what they do; they do not really do their good deeds in secret.' So that even our modesty may be our pride; and what some people think their pride may happen to be the will of God, and may be real modesty. It is very hard work to give up our own will; but it is possible, and that is one of the lessons we should learn from this text, 'Not as I will, but as thou wilt.'

Again, if there is anybody of whom you are a little envious – perhaps a minister who takes a little of the gloss off you by preaching better than you do, or a Sunday-school teacher who is more successful in his work – make that particular person the object of your most constant prayer, and endeavour as much as lies in you to increase that person's popularity and success. Someone asks, 'But you cannot bring human nature up to that point, can you – to try and exalt one's own rival?' My dear friends, you will never know the full meaning of this prayer till you have tried to do this, and actually sought to honour your rival more than yourself; that is the true spirit of the gospel, 'in honour preferring one another'. I have sometimes found it hard work, I must confess; but I have schooled myself down to it. Can this be done? Yes, John the Baptist did it; he said of Jesus, 'He must increase, but I must decrease.' If you had asked John whether he wished to increase, he would have said, 'Well, I should like to have more disciples; still, if it is the Lord's will, I am quite content to go down, and that Christ should go up.'

How important, therefore, it is for us to learn how we may attain to this state of acquiescence with our heavenly Father's will! I have given you the reasons for it, but how can it be done? Only by the operation of the Spirit of God. As for flesh and blood, they will not help you in the least, they will go just the other way; and when you think that, surely, you have got flesh and blood under control, you will find that they have got the upper hand of you just when you thought you were conquering them. Pray the Holy Spirit to abide with you, to dwell in you, to baptize you, to immerse you in his sacred influence, to cover you, to bury you in his sublime power; and so, and only so, when you are completely immersed in the Spirit, and steeped, as it were, in the crimson sea of the Saviour's blood, shall you be made fully to realize the meaning of this great prayer, 'Not as I will, but as thou wilt.' 'Lord, not self, but Christ; not my own glory, but thy glory; not my aggrandisement, but thine; nay, not even my success, but thy success; not the prosperity of my own church, or my own self, but the prosperity of thy church, the increase of thy glory – let all that be done as thou wilt, not as I will.'

How different, this is from everything connected with the world! I have tried to take you up to a very high elevation; and if you have been able to get up there, or even to pant to get up there, how striking has the contrast been between this spirit and the spirit of the worldling! I shall not say anything to those of you who are unconverted, except this. Learn how contrary you are to what God would have you be, and what you must be, ere you can enter the kingdom of heaven. You know that you could not say, 'Let God have his will', and you know also that you could not humble yourself to become as a little child. This shows your deep depravity; so, may the Holy Spirit renew you, for you have need of renewing, that you may be made a new creature in Christ Jesus! May he sanctify you wholly, spirit, soul, and body, and at last present you faultless, before the throne of God, for his dear name's sake! Amen.

15

CHRIST'S CARE OF HIS DISCIPLES [1]

'If therefore ye seek me, let these go their way.'
JOHN 18:8

WE NEED BUT HINT at the circumstances under which these words were uttered. Our Saviour was in the Garden of Gethsemane with his disciples; a multitude came with the officers commissioned by the high priest to seize him; he went boldly towards them, and asked, 'Whom seek ye?' They answered, 'Jesus of Nazareth.' At his words, 'I am he', 'they went backward and fell to the ground', and then Jesus said to them, 'I have told you that I am he: if therefore ye seek me, let these go their way.'

Now, in a very simple manner, I shall try, first of all, *to draw a few lessons from this occurrence;* and then, secondly, *to bring out a great truth which I think is foreshadowed in this utterance of our Redeemer.*

I. First, let us CONSIDER THE LESSONS OF THE OCCURRENCE ITSELF. Our Saviour said to these people, 'If therefore ye seek me, let these go their way.'

In this incident, our Master proved *his own willingness to die.* This word of his was a mandate so powerful that none of the disciples were seized, much less put to death. There was Peter, who had drawn his sword, and cut off the ear of the high priest's servant. We should naturally have expected that he would have been

[1] Sermon No. 2,616. Preached at New Park Street Chapel on a Sunday evening, early in 1857.

arrested, or smitten to the earth; but so powerful was the command of Christ that not a finger was laid upon his hasty-tempered disciple. Peter and John went afterwards into the judgment hall – as it were, into the very teeth of our Lord's enemies – but, with the exception of a few jeers, they were suffered to go their way. John did even more than that, for he went within the range of the spears of the Roman soldiers, and stood at the foot of Christ's cross, and wept; yet not a finger was laid on him, nor on any one of Christ's disciples – not for want of will, for, you remember, they seized a young man who left his garment in their hands, and fled naked – evidently supposing him to have been a disciple of Christ. This shows, then, the power of Christ's mandate that, in that hour of darkness, not so much as one of his disciples was maltreated, but all were suffered to go their way. If Christ, then, by his simple word, delivered his disciples, how much more could he have delivered himself? And in his not doing so, you cannot fail to see how willing he was to die. One word threw them to the ground; another word would have hurled them into the arms of death; but our Saviour would not speak the word which might have saved himself, for he came to save others, not himself.

There is something very courageous in the Saviour's saying, 'If ye seek me'. You know that, when Adam sinned, God had to seek the culprit; but, in this case, when Christ stood as the Surety for his people, instead of being sought, he seemed to seek his executioners. 'If ye seek me', said he; and he put in an 'if' – as though it were not so much their seeking him as his seeking them – for he had come into their very midst to die. Our blessed Lord was well acquainted with the circumstances of his own death. He sat at the table, at the institution of the Lord's Supper, on that memorable evening; why could he not wait and be seized there? But no; dauntless, 'the Lion of the tribe of Judah' steps out, and boldly faces his enemy. He does not wait to be attacked; but goes forth to meet death, to give himself up for us. Scarcely any martyr has done such a deed as this. God has helped them to die, when they have been delivered into the hands of their enemies; but our Saviour goes to his enemies, and says, 'Here I am: if ye seek me, I have come to give myself up; I will put you to no trouble in searching for me; there is no necessity to hunt through the length and breadth of Jerusalem to find me out, here I am; if ye seek me, I am ready to die; take me, I have no opposition to make. If ye seek me, all I have to say is, Let these go their way; as for myself, I am willing enough to die!'

Learn, then, Christian, the readiness of thy Master to suffer for thee. He was no unwilling Saviour. Thou hast sometimes borrowed money of a friend; and when thou hast taken it of him, it was a grief to thee to accept it, for he looked upon thee as a beggar, or even as a robber who had demanded spoil of him. But when thou takest Christ's favours, there is this sweet consideration with them, that they are all given willingly. The blood that thou drinkest, and the flesh that thou eatest, spiritually, is no dole of a strained benevolence, but the voluntary, munificent gift from the heart of Jesus to thee and to thy brethren. Rejoice, then, in the willingness of Christ to suffer for thee.

In the second place, upon the very face of our text, we read *the care of Christ towards his people*. 'If therefore ye seek me, let these go their way.' Oh! the agony of the Saviour's heart at that moment. A friend in trouble is frequently forgetful; expect not a man in great grief to remember you; the heart is then so full of its own bitterness, it hath no time to think of others. I would pardon any man for not noticing me in the street, if he were ill; I would easily forgive anyone for forgetting anything when loaded with pain and sorrow; and surely, beloved, we might have thought it not hard of Jesus if he had forgotten his disciples in his hour of grief. But mark. how kind his heart is: 'If ye seek me' – I say nothing about how ye should treat me – but 'let these' – these disciples were the only ones he cared about; he cared not for himself – 'let these go their way.' Like the mother in the snowstorm, who takes off her own clothes to wrap around her cold shivering babe; what cares she though the blast should find out her inmost soul, and though her body be frozen like ice, if her babe but lives? Her first thought, after she is restored to consciousness, when she has been well-nigh benumbed to death, but chafed to life by kindness, is concerning that babe. It was even so with Jesus: 'Let these go their way.'

When justice, by our sins provoked,
Drew forth its dreadful sword,

He gave his soul up to the stroke
Without a murmuring word.

This was compassion like a God,
That when the Saviour knew
The price of pardon was his blood,
He pity ne'er withdrew.

Now though he reigns exalted high,
His love is still as great;
Well he remembers Calvary,
Nor let his saints forget.

They are all recollected, all borne upon his heart, and still cared for. Therefore thou art cared for, thou lamb of the flock; thou art cared for, poor Ready-to-halt; thou art remembered, Miss Despondency; thou art regarded with the eyes of love, timid Mr Fearing; though thou stumblest at every stone, yet thy Saviour's love faileth not; he remembereth thee, for he cared for his disciples in his hour of greatest sorrow.

In the next place, learn from this incident *our Saviour's wisdom.* When he said, 'Let these go their way,' there was wisdom in it. How? Because they were not prepared to suffer, and it would have been unwise to have allowed them to suffer then, if they had been prepared; for if they had suffered then, it would have been thought that at least they shared the honour of our redemption; therefore Christ would have none but thieves upon the mount of doom, lest any should suppose that he had a helper. He did tread the winepress alone, and of the people there were none with him. Besides, these disciples were but infants in grace; they had not received the plenitude of the Spirit; they were not fit to suffer. Therefore Christ said, 'If ye seek me, let these go their way.' These raw recruits must not yet bear the brunt of the battle; let them tarry until, by a longer experience, and by greater grace, they shall be made brave to die, and shall each of them in his turn wear the crown of martyrdom; but not now. Christ spared his people at that moment, since it would have been unwise to have suffered them to die then.

Learn also, Christians, from your Master's example, *the duty of putting yourselves in the way of suffering when you can save your brethren*. Oh! there is something glorious in the spirit Christ manifested in placing himself first. 'If ye seek me, let these go their way.' That is the spirit all Christians ought to catch – the spirit of heroic self-sacrifice for the disciples' sake. The mere professor says, 'Let me go my way, seek another to be put to death'; but if we were what we should be, we should each one say, 'If ye seek me, let these go their way.' How many of us would be ready to escape martyrdom, and allow our brethren to be burned! But that would not be the spirit of our Master. How frequently you are ready to allow opprobrium and shame to fall upon the church if you can but be yourself screened! How very frequently you will allow a brother to perform a duty, at much inconvenience, which you could do without any trouble to yourself! Now, if you were like your Master, you would say, 'Let these go their way'; if there is sufficient ground for it, let me suffer; if there be a painful duty, let me do it; let others escape, let them go free; lo, I will give myself a willing substitute for them in this matter.' Oh! we want everywhere more of this spirit, to be able to say to the poor saint, 'Poverty is seeking thee, I will in some degree bear the inconvenience that thou mayest be screened. Thou art sick, I will watch thee; thou art naked, I will clothe thee; thou art hungry, I will feed thee; I will stand in thy stead as far as I am able, that thou mayest go thy way.'

These seem to me to be the lessons to be learned from our Saviour's words, 'If therefore ye seek me, let these go their way.'

II. Now I come to notice, secondly, THE GREAT DOCTRINE WHICH THIS INCIDENT SEEMS TO FORESHADOW.

Will you please observe the next verse to the text? 'That the saying might be fulfilled, which he spake, Of them which thou gavest me have I lost none.' If I had quoted this passage in such a connection, you would have told me it was a misquotation; you would have said, 'Why, my dear sir, that has nothing to do with the disciples going their way or not!' Ah! but you would be quite in error if you talked like that; God's Spirit knows how to quote, if we do not. Very often, we refer our hearers to a text which we think is exactly adapted and pertinent to the point before us, when it has really nothing to do with the matter; and, often, the Holy Spirit quotes a text which we think unsuitable; but, on closer examination, we find that the very gist of it bears directly upon the subject. This was the beginning of Christ's deliverances, which he would through eternity vouchsafe to all his children. Inasmuch as he then said, 'Let these go their way,' *it was the foreshadowing, the picturing, of the greet deed of substitution* whereby Christ would be able to say, 'If therefore ye seek me, let these go their way.' This point will appear clearly if we look at how Christ treats his people in Providence and at the bar of Justice.

It has always seemed to me as if *Christ had borne the brunt of Providence for his people,* so that now all things work together for their good. When Christ came into the world, he did, in spirit, say something like this, 'Ye wild beasts of the field, ye are against my people; come, now, be against me; and, then, let these go their way.' This was according to the ancient prophecy: 'I will make a covenant for them with the beasts of the field, and with the fowls of heaven, and with the creeping things of the ground.' Christ seemed to say, 'Stones, ye are enemies to my flock; now take me for their Substitute, and be at enmity against me; and then it shall be written, "The stones of the field shall be in league with them."' Christ, as it were, said to Providence, 'Thy black and bitter face shall look on me; thy quiver, full of fiery darts, shall be emptied, and they shall all find their target here in my bosom; thy dread aspect shall be seen by me'; but, 'Let these go their way.'

Providence has indicted its evils on Christ, and has now only good for God's people. 'What! sir, only good?' you say, 'why, I am poor, I am sick!' Yes, but it is only good; for that is good which worketh good. 'All things work together for good to them that love God.' Christ saith even to kings, 'Touch not mine anointed, and do my prophets no harm.' 'Let these go their way.' The kings of the earth have been seeking Christ's church, to destroy and to devour it; so Christ lets them find him, and put him to death; and before he dies, he turns round to the kings, and says, 'Touch not mine anointed, and do my prophets no harm.' He speaks to trouble, to trial, to grief, to accident, and to peril, and he says: 'Ye have sought me; now let my people go their way.' We should never have known the sweetness of the Psalm –

> He that hath made his refuge God,
> Shall find a most secure abode,

– if Christ had not died. The only way that you and I can have a refuge is by Christ bearing the brunt of our trouble. How does a shield save me? It saves me by bearing the blows itself. The shield doth, as it were, say to the swords of the enemy, 'If ye seek me, let this warrior go his way.' So Christ, our Shield and God's Anointed, beareth the brunt of Providence, the evil and the woe thereof; and he saith now to the mysterious dispensations of God, concerning all the children of the Lord, '"Let these go their way." Never, never work ill to them, but let them have only good.'

The other thought is, *Christ hath said this of his people even to Justice*. Before the throne of God, fiery Justice once drew his sword, and went out after sinners, to find full many, and to cast them into the pit. His sword thirsted for the blood of all that had sinned; but there stood a chosen multitude, reserved by love and chosen by grace; and Justice said, 'They are sinners; I will have them, I will sheathe this sword in their hearts, for they are sinners, and they must perish.' Then Christ came forward, and asked him, 'Whom seekest thou?' 'Sinners', answered Justice. Then said Jesus, 'They are not sinners; they were sinners once, but they are righteous now, clothed in my righteousness; if thou seekest the sinner, here am I.' 'What!' said Justice, 'art thou the sinner?' 'Nay, not the sinner, but I am the sinner's Substitute; all the sinner's guilt was imputed to me; all his unrighteousness is mine, and all my righteousness is his; I, the Saviour, am the sinner's Substitute; take me.' And Justice accepted the substitution; took the Saviour, crucified him, nailed him to that cross whose agonies we commemorate at the communion table. In that hour Jesus cried, 'If ye seek me, let these go their way.' Who are they that are to go their way? Why, the very men whose former way was one of iniquity, and whose end would have been destruction, if the curse had not been made to fall upon the head of Jesus!

'Let these go their way.' Oh, that wonderful sentence! I never knew its sweetness till I found the Lord; but I did know something of its power. Do you ask, 'How was that?' Why, long before you know the Lord, you have some of the power of the blood of Christ resting upon you. 'How so?' do you enquire. Why, do you not know it to be a fact that

> Determined to save, he watched o'er our path,
> When, Satan's blind slaves, we sported with death?

And so, some of the benefits of Christ's death were ours before we knew him, and before we loved him. The reason why I was not damned before I knew the Saviour was that he had said, 'Let him go his way; I have died for him.' You would have been in hell these twenty years, saint, for you were then unregenerate; but Christ said, 'Let him go his way; if ye seek me, he shall go his way, sinner though he be'; and now, when gloomy fears arise, and dark thoughts roll over our mind, let this be our comfort. Sinners we are still, guilty and vile; but the same voice says, 'Let these go their way.' It is the 'let' of command; and who can hinder when God letteth in this sense? 'Let these go their way.' You are going up Bunyan's Hill Difficulty, and there are lions at the top. Christians, remember this message, 'Let these go their way.' You will, perhaps, get into Giant Despair's dungeon; here is a key that will fit the lock: 'Let these go their way.' You will be tumbling about in the Slough of Despond; here is a stone to put your foot on to help you to get out: 'Let these go their way.' What for? Because they pray? No. Because they serve God? No; the mandate was given before they did either the one or the other. 'Let these go their way', because Christ died in their stead.

The day is coming, and shall soon be here, when you and I shall stretch our wings, and fly away to the land that is very far off. I think I might picture in my imagination the soul when it has left the body. The believer speeds his way up to his native city, Jerusalem, 'the mother of us all'. But at the gate one standeth; and he saith, 'Hast thou a right to admission here? It is written, "He that walketh righteously, and speaketh uprightly; he that despiseth the gain of oppressions, that shaketh his hands from holding of bribes, that stoppeth his ears from hearing of blood, and shutteth his eyes from seeing evil; he shall dwell on high." Art thou such an one?' 'Ah!' saith the soul, 'I hope by grace I have been made so; but I cannot claim to have always been so, for "I the chief of sinners am.'" 'Then how camest thou here? This gate gives no admission to those who are sinners.' While the angel is thus parleying, I hear a voice crying, 'Let these go their way'; and, forthwith, the gates of heaven are opened, and every soul for whom Christ died doth enter into Paradise.

Come, saint, close up this simple meditation by looking yonder. See Christ, with justice, vengeance, wrath, all seeking him. Lo, they have found him; they have slain him; he is buried; he hath risen again. Oh! see them seeking him; and as you sit down at his table, think, 'When they sought him, they let me go my way.' And what a sweet way it is! I am allowed to come to his table of communion. Why? Because they sought him. I am invited to hold fellowship with Jesus. Why? Because they sought him. I am permitted to have a good hope through grace; and, more than that, 'I know that when this earthly house of my tabernacle is dissolved, I have a building of God, a house not made with hands, eternal in the heavens.' Why am I to go that way? Why? Because they sought him, and found him. Else, where had I been now? My place might have been on the alehouse bench, or, perhaps, in the seat of the scorner; and what would have been my prospect? Why, that, at the last, I should be in hell amongst the fiends and the lost spirits of the pit; but now I tread the paths of righteousness and the ways of grace. Oh, let me remember why I do so; it is because they sought thee, O thou precious Lord of mine! They sought thee, my dear Redeemer and my God; they sought thy heart, and broke it; they sought thy head, and crowned it with thorns; they sought thy hands, and nailed them to the tree; they sought thy feet, and pierced them; they sought thy body, they slew and buried it. And now, though the roaring lion may seek me never so much, he cannot devour me; never can I be rent in pieces, never can I be destroyed, for I carry with me this sweet passport of the King of heaven, 'Let these go their way.' O child of God, take this with thee for thy safe conduct everywhere! When men travel abroad, they carry with them a permit to go to this town and the other. Take this little sentence, brother or sister in Jesus, and when unbelief stops thee, draw it out, and say, 'He hath said, "Let these go their way."' And when Satan stops thee, hold out to him this divine mandate, 'Let these go their way.' And when death shall stop thee, take out this sweet permit from thy Master, 'Let these go their way.' And when the throne of judgment shall be set, and thou standest before it, plead this sentence, plead it even before thy Maker, 'My Master said, "Let these go their way."' Oh, cheering words! I could weep them all out; but I will say no more. I hope many of you will enjoy the sweetness of them while we gather around the Lord's table, in obedience to his gracious command, 'This do in remembrance of me.'

16

THE LIVING CARE OF THE DYING CHRIST [1]

'Jesus answered, I have told you that I am he: if therefore
ye seek me, let these go their way: that the saying might
be fulfilled, which he spake, Of them which thou
gavest me have I lost none.'
JOHN 18:8–9

THE TWO REMARKABLE MIRACLES which our Lord wrought
in the Garden of Gethsemane ought not to be lightly passed over.
The first was the falling to the ground of the soldiers and the
servants of the priests. Jesus did but speak to them, and there was
such power and majesty about his presence and his voice that 'they
went backward, and fell to the ground.' They were quite unable
to seize him. Here was a display in some measure of Christ's divine
power. These men would have fallen into the grave, and into hell
itself, if Jesus had put forth the full force of his strength. He only
spake a word, and down they fell; they had no power whatever
against him. Beloved, take comfort from this miracle. When the
enemies and foes of Christ come against him, he can easily
overthrow them. Many times have there been crises in the church's
history when it seemed as if the truth would be destroyed. Then
has come the opportunity for divine interposition. A word from
Christ has vanquished his enemies. They that were waiting, like
lions ready to leap upon their prey, have been disappointed. Jesus
has but spoken, and they have fallen backward to the ground.
Wherefore, take heart, and be not dismayed even in the darkest

[1] Sermon No. 2,368. Preached at the Metropolitan Tabernacle on Sunday evening, 15 April 1888.

hour. Let Christ only utter a word, and the victory is certain to be with him.

The other miracle was this, that seeing the company that came together to take him, he should be able at pleasure to screen his disciples so that not one of them was injured. The ear of the high priest's servant was cut off; it was the opposite party that received the wound, but no ear of Peter or finger of John was smitten. The apostles escaped altogether unharmed; they were not able to protect themselves, being a very slender number as compared with the posse that had come forth from the high priest, yet their Master preserved them; from which learn that the Lord Jesus Christ is able to take care of his own. When they seem to be like so many lambs in the midst of wolves, he can keep them so that no wolf can devour them. He has done it, and he will continue to do it. 'Fear not, little flock; for it is your Father's good pleasure to give you the kingdom.' He will preserve you by his own miraculous power, and you need not be dismayed at any force that is arrayed against you. Think, then, of those two miracles. You may need to remember them; there may come a time when it shall be a great joy to you to think of Christ, all ruddy from the bloody sweat, yet driving back his adversaries with a word, and rescuing the little handful of his disciples from anything like harm.

But in my text I notice something which seems to me to be very remarkable. 'If therefore,' said Jesus, 'ye seek me, let these go their way: that the saying might be fulfilled.' After such an expression you naturally expect some Old Testament text, something said by David in the Psalms, or by one of the prophets, Isaiah, or Exekiel, but it is not so; it is, 'that the saying might be fulfilled, which he spake, Of them which thou gavest me have I lost none.' It is not an hour or two since Jesus uttered this sentence, but it is already among the inspired Scriptures, and it begins to take effect and to be fulfilled at once. It is not the age of God's word, but the verity of it, that constitutes its power. What Christ had said that very night in prayer was as true and as much the word of a King as that which God had spoken by his Spirit through holy men ages before.

Beloved, learn this lesson. The word of Christ is to be depended upon; you may hang your whole destiny upon it. What Christ has said is full of truth. He is Yea and Amen, and so are all his words;

they stand fast for ever and ever, like his own eternal Godhead. Wherefore, since this word of Christ, which had only just been spoken, must be fulfilled, believe that every word of his will be carried out to the utmost. Heaven and earth shall pass away; but not one word which was spoken by our Saviour shall ever fail, it shall not fail even the least of you in your worst hour of peril. I read this truth in the text with very great delight. We might have expected to find an Old Testament Scripture quoted here; but the New Testament Scripture is put upon the same level as the Old, and coming from the lips of Christ we are pleased to see it so soon fulfilled.

The soldiers and officers from the chief priests had come forth that night especially to arrest Christ. Peter, James, John, Bartholomew, Thomas, and the rest of the apostles, are all there; but Judas has come to betray, not the servants, but their Master; and they who are with the traitor have come to take, not the disciples, but their Lord. To me, there is something encouraging about this fact, although it is a dismal one. The fight of the great adversary is not so much against us as against our Master. Satan's emissaries are very furious sometimes with the faithful defenders of the truth, but their fury is not so much against them as against the truth and against the Christ who is the centre of that truth. In olden times, they hated Luther, and Calvin, and Zwingli, and the rest of the Reformers, but the main point of attack was the doctrine of justification by faith in the Lord Jesus Christ; and at this day the great fight is around the Cross. Did Jesus die as his people's Substitute? That is the question; and there are some, I grieve to say it, to whom that text is applicable, 'He that despised Moses' law died without mercy, under two or three witnesses: of how much sorer punishment, suppose ye, shall he be thought worthy, who hath trodden under foot the Son of God, and hath counted the blood of the covenant, wherewith he was sanctified an unholy thing, and hath done despite unto the Spirit of grace?' This is the chief aim of the enemy's assaults; to get rid of Christ, to get rid of the atonement, to get rid of his suffering in the room and place and stead of men. They say they can embrace the rest of the gospel; but what 'rest' is there? What is there left? A bloodless, Christless gospel is fit neither for the land nor for the dunghill; it neither honours God nor converts the sons of men.

This is our consolation, that the attack is, after all, against the Master himself. Our Lord Jesus Christ is still the great butt for the archer's arrows. Though his enemies do not always let his disciples go their way, yet they do seek him; it is against him that they rave most of all. As it is the quarrel of God's covenant, he will fight it out to the end; and so far as your part in the battle is concerned, as it is for his truth, and his eternal power and Godhead, and his great sacrifice, you may safely go through with it, for he who fights for this cause shall surely have God with him.

Now let us come to our text, and try to learn some lessons from it. I notice here, first, *Christ's dying care for his disciples*. Then, next, I see that *his care extends to their bodies*; and, thirdly, I observe that *his care offers himself instead of them*. He thrusts himself upon the edge of the adversaries' sword, and says, 'If therefore ye seek me, let these go their way.'

I. First, then, I call upon you to notice in our text CHRIST'S DYING CARE FOR HIS DISCIPLES. Let me correct what I have said, and put it, THE LIVING CARE OF THE DYING CHRIST; for you see he is occupied first of all with his disciples' safety. The soldiers have come to seize him, but he does not seek to escape. They bind him, but he does not burst his bonds. They will take him to prison, and to death; but he has not a word to say in his own defence, he utters no curse against his persecutors. His one thought is for his disciples, his ruling passion is strong in death, his love still masters him.

This was the more wonderful because he was *in the first brunt of the danger*. He had been betrayed by Judas, and the high priest's servants were gathering about him to capture him; yet he was calm and quiet, and his one thought was concerning the eleven who were with him. Usually, we become quieter when we get used to a trouble; it is in the first fluster of it that we are disconcerted, and thrown off our balance. I suppose it is so with you; I know it is so with me. We learn, after a little while, to look calmly around us; we gird up the loins of our mind, and we begin to think as we should think; but at first we are like birds driven out to sea by a rough wind, that have not learnt yet to manage their wings in the gale. It was not so with our Saviour. In that first moment of attack he still thought of his disciples. Oh, the splendour of that love which could not be disturbed! Many waters could not quench it even at their first breaking out; nor could the floods drown it when they were swollen to their height! Beloved, Jesus never forgets you who are his own. Never does anything happen in this world or in heaven that leads him to forget you. He has graven your names upon the palms of his hands, they are written upon his heart; so be it the first brunt of your battle or of his own, he still thinks of you, and cares for you.

But it is more remarkable still that Jesus thought of his disciples *in the faintness of his agony*. All crimson from the bloody sweat, he rose from under the olive trees, and came forward, and stood there in the torchlight before his persecutors; but the light that fell upon his brow revealed no care for anything but the safety of his followers. His whole soul had gone out to them. That crimson sweat meant a heart flowing out at every pore with love for those whom his Father had given him, and whom he had so long preserved. I doubt not that he was faint with the dreadful agony. He must have been brought to the very lowest point of endurance by it, yet he still thought of his disciples. Beloved, when you and I are sick and faint, other people do not expect us to think of them. We grow a little selfish when we are weak and ill; we want water to moisten our lips, we expect our friends to watch over us, and wipe the sweat from our brow. It was not so with our Master; he came, not to be ministered unto, but to minister; and he does so by saying to the rabble throng, 'If therefore ye seek me, let these go their way.'

And mark, dear friends, that our Lord Jesus was not only in the brunt of danger, and in the faintness of his agony, but he was *in full prospect of a cruel death*. He knew all that was to be done to him. When you and I have to suffer, we do not know what is before us; it is a happy circumstance that we do not. But Jesus knew that they would buffet him, that they would blindfold him, that they would spit in his face, that they would scourge him, he knew that the crown of thorns would tear his temples, he knew that he would be led forth like a malefactor, bearing the gibbet on his shoulder. He knew that they would nail his feet and hands to the cruel cross, he knew that he would cry, 'I thirst', he knew that his Father must forsake him on account of the sin of man that would be laid upon him. He knew all that; these huge Atlantic billows of grief cast their spray in his face already, his lips were salt with the brine of his coming grief; but he did not think of that, his one thought was for his beloved, those whom his Father had given him. Till he dies, he will keep his eye on his sheep, and he will grasp his Shepherd's crook with which to drive the foe from them. Oh, the all-absorbing, self-consuming love of Christ! Verily, it was like coals of juniper, which have a most vehement flame. Do you know that love, beloved? If so, let your hearts reciprocate it, loving him in return with all the strength of your life, and all the wealth of your being. Even then you can never love him as he has loved you.

I must add that it was all the more remarkable that Jesus should continue to think of his disciples at such a time when *he knew what they were*. They had been asleep, even while he was in the bloody sweat. Even the three whom he had chosen as his body-guard, and stationed within a stone's cast of his terrible agony, had slept. Jesus knew also that the eleven would all forsake him and flee, and that one of them would even deny him; yet he thought of them. O Lord, how canst thou think of such sinful creatures as we are? I feel glad that these apostles were not perfect. We must not rejoice in anything that is evil; but still it is some comfort to me that though they were such poor creatures as they were, Jesus cared for them, for now I can believe that he loves me. Though I sleep when I ought to wake and watch with him, yet he loves me. Although, under the brunt of a strong temptation, I may flee, still he loves me; ay, and even if I should deny him, yet I can understand that, as he loved Peter, he may still love me. O faulty saints, you who do love him, and yet often fail him, you who do trust him, and yet are oftentimes dismayed, gather strength, I pray you, from this wonderful love of Jesus! Is not the love of Christ a mass of miracles, all wonders packed together? It is not a subject for surprise that he should love, but that he should love such worms as we are, that he should love us when we were dead in trespasses and sins, that he should love us into life, should love us despite our faults, should love us to perfection, and should love us till he brings us to share his glory. Rejoice, then, in this wondrous care of Christ – the dying Christ with a living care for his disciples.

II. But now, secondly, HIS CARE EXTENDS TO THEIR BODIES.

I will not be long upon this point, but I want you to note some of the sweetness there is in it. When I was reading to you just now, you must have noticed that our Lord said, 'Those that thou gavest me I have kept, and none of them is lost.' Surely he meant that he kept them from wandering into sin, did he not? Did he not mean that he kept them unto eternal salvation? Undoubtedly he did; but the greater includes the less. He who keeps a man, keeps the whole man, spirit, soul, and body. So our Lord Jesus here interprets his own prayer, which dealt with the souls of his people. He mainly interprets it as to their bodies, for he bade those who came to seize him to let his disciples go, saying, 'If therefore ye seek me, let these go their way.'

You say to me, 'That is a small interpretation of a great utterance.' I know it is, and that is the comfort of it, that, if there be small meanings to the promises, you may quote them, and pray for them, as well as believe in and pray for the greater and immeasurable meaning of the promises. I like to believe that he who loves me as an immortal spirit, loves me as a mortal man. He who loves me as I shall be before his throne in glory, loved me as I was when I hung upon my mother's breast, and loves me as I now am, with many a weakness and infirmity clinging to me. He who takes care of the soul, takes care of the body, too.

Notice that *this care of our Lord was effectual*. Is it not singular that none of those soldiers and servants of the high priest touched one of the eleven? Is it not remarkable that Malchus, having lost his right ear, did not feel it his duty to thrust at Peter? But the Saviour interposes, and just touches the wounded ear, and it is healed, and Peter is suffered to go. That act of Peter was enough to bring on a battle royal all round, and we know that the whole eleven had only two swords between them. They could have made only a very feeble stand against a band of armed men; yet not one of them was injured. How well does Jesus protect his own!

What is more remarkable, the apostles were not harmed at the time of Christ's death. It would not at all have surprised me if the mob that cried, 'Crucify him, crucify him', had also said, 'Here are some of his disciples, let us put them also to death; let us increase the agonies of the dying Nazarene by the slaughter of his disciples before his eyes.' Yet not a dog moved his tongue against them. And when it was reported that Christ had risen from the dead, why did not his enemies pounce upon Mary Magdalene, and the rest of the women? Forty days was Jesus on the earth, and I do not find that in all that time there was any hindrance to the coming or going anywhere of any one of his disciples. After the Holy Spirit had been poured out, there came a time of persecution; but until then it was not in the Saviour's mind that the Jews should touch one of his disciples, and they could not do it. The devil cannot go any farther than his chain permits, and the worst enemies of Christ can do no more than Christ allows. What an effectual care was this of the Master, which held the broad shield of his divine protection not only over the eleven, but also over all the rest of the faithful! He was at his lowest when they took him, and bound him, and led him away, but even then, with his sovereign word, he protected his people from all harm, as to their bodies as well as their souls.

Notice also that *it was needful that they should have special protection*. Jesus meant them all to remain alive to see him after his death, that they might be witnesses of his resurrection. They were a little handful of seed-corn, and he would not have one grain wasted, because it was by that precious wheat that his church was to be fed, and the world was to be sown with spiritual life.

Besides, they were not ready yet to bear persecution. Afterwards they bore it manfully, joyfully; but just now they were poor feeble children, until the Spirit of God was poured out. Brethren, the Lord Jesus Christ can shelter us from sickness, and from every kind of bodily affliction, until we are fit to bear it; and he can also preserve us from death till our work is done. It is a good saying, though it is not a Scriptural one, 'We are immortal till our work is done.' If God has given thee aught to do, get thee to the doing of it; the time is short, but dream not that thou shalt be cut off too soon. Thou hast a work for thy time, and thou shalt have time for thy work. Believe it, and thou mayest go between the jaws of behemoth without a fear, while God has work for thee to accomplish for him; wherefore, be not afraid, for Jesus says, 'Let these go their way.'

Once more, *the care which the Lord took of his people was much better than their own care*. See, Peter is going to take care of his Master, and he makes a poor mess of it; but when his Master took care of him, that was a very different affair. Peter is going to fight for his brethren; out comes the sword, off goes the ear of Malchus, and Peter probably regretted that he had not cut off his head. But what good did Peter do? He only increased the danger they were in, and made the men feel the more furious against them. But Christ's word was ample; here was sufficient defence for all the apostles, 'Let these go their way', and go their way they did. Brothers and sisters, we should do a deal better in many things if we did not do anything at all. There is many a man who is drowning, and makes his drowning sure by his struggling. I am told that, if he could but lie still on his back, he would float; and I believe that, in many a trouble, we make the trouble ten times worse by our kicking and plunging. 'O rest in the Lord, and wait patiently for him.' Especially do so if it is a matter of scandal. If anybody speaks evil of you, do not answer him. I have had a great deal of experience of this kind – perhaps as much as anybody – and I have always found that, if I got a spot of mud anywhere on my coat, and I proceeded to brush it off, it was much worse than before. Let it alone till it is dry; then it will come off easily. Perhaps even then you had better leave somebody else to do your clothes-brushing and your boot-cleaning; you cannot do it nearly so well yourself as somebody else can do it for you. I say again, we should do better often if we did nothing. These eleven apostles did best when Peter had put up that ugly old sword of his, and left off fighting, and at his Master's word went away safe and sound from the armed men who had arrested his Lord.

Beloved, you are all right if you are in Jesus Christ's hands; right for your body, right for your estate, right for your character, right for little things as well as for great, if you just leave all in those dear hands that never fail, because they act for the dear heart that never ceases to beat with infinite affection towards all those whom the Father has given to him.

III. I have continued longer than I intended, so I am coming now to the third and last point, which is this, CHRIST'S CARE LED HIM TO OFFER HIMSELF INSTEAD OF HIS PEOPLE.

Jesus said, 'If therefore ye seek me, let these go their way.' This was as much as to say, *'You cannot hurt both myself and my people.'* This is a great truth, though I put it very simply to you. When the judgments of God are abroad, it is not possible that they should fall on both Christ and his people. Was Jesus Christ the Substitute for his people? Grant that; then, if the punishment of sin fell on Christ, it cannot fall on those for whom Christ died. It is not according to natural justice, much less divine justice, first that the Substitute should suffer, and then the person for whom he stood as Substitute should also suffer. That cannot be. Why have a Substitute at all, unless that Substitute by his suffering clears those for whom he was substituted? I will give you a very simple illustration; you will find it in the Book of Deuteronomy. There is the old divine ordinance that, when a man found a bird's nest, and there were young birds in the nest, if he took the young, he must let the mother-bird go free, he must not take both; that was contrary to the divine law. So, Christ may die, or his people may die; but not both of them. Justice will not have it that they shall both suffer, and the Lord Jesus Christ gives a tongue to that great law when he says, 'If ye seek me, here I am, but let these go their way; for you cannot take us both.' That were contrary to the sacred law, and to the divine equity which lies at the bottom of everything that is true. Did Christ, my ransom, die for me? Then I shall not die. Did he pay my debt? Then it is paid, and I shall not be called upon to pay it.

> If thou hast my discharge procured,
> And freely in my room endured
>   The whole of wrath divine.
> Payment God cannot twice demand,
> First at my bleeding Surety's hand,
>   And then again at mine.

Did Jesus suffer in my stead without the city-gate? Then, turn thou, my soul, unto thy rest, since he died for thee. Justice could not claim both the Surety and those for whom he stood as Substitute; but, beloved, *it was the Master who died.* They did seek him, they did take him, they did crucify him; he did bear it all as his people's Substitute. 'The Lord hath laid on him the iniquity of us all.' Do not be deceived about this matter, but grip it as a fact most sure that the Lord Jesus Christ did bear his people's sins in his own body on the tree. 'The chastisement of our peace was upon him; and with his stripes we are healed.' Men and brethren, I am not making this up, and telling you words of my own. These are the precious truths of Holy Writ, divinely inspired. Oh, that all would believe them!

Christ has suffered in the stead of his people. What then? As I have said to you before, both cannot suffer; therefore, as Jesus suffered, *you who are his people are clear*. Perhaps you will go down to the grave; unless the Lord should speedily come, we shall die; but, since Jesus died, death cannot hold us. The resurrection trumpet will ring out its silver note, and this will be the message to the dull cold ear of death, 'Since I died, let these go their way', and every sepulchre shall open wide, the caverns of death shall no longer enclose the bodies of the saints, but from beds of dust and silent clay, the whole of Christ's redeemed shall rise. Because he lives, they shall live also. Death sought him, and therefore death must let these who belong to him go their way; and as for justice, there comes the dread tremendous day, the day for which all other days were made, the day of judgment, and of condemnation of ungodly men. Shall I stand shivering before that eternal judgment-seat? Nay, not so. Shall I feel the earth quake beneath me, and see heaven splitting above me, and the stars falling like withered leaves in autumn? Doubtless it will be so. Will the avenging angel come, with his dread sword of fire, and sweep us poor sinful ones away? He will, unless we are in Christ; but if we are among the blood-redeemed ones, he must stay his fiery vengeance, for there shall come a voice from the risen and reigning Saviour, 'Thou hast smitten me, therefore let these go their way', and because he died for us, we shall go our way. Which way? Up yonder shining staircase, made of light; up where the angels come and go, we shall make our way, like children who run upstairs at home, up into the world of light, and to the home of glory, where our Saviour's face is the sun, and his presence makes heaven. Yes, and this shall be our permit for ascending there, Jesus hath loved us, and hath died to redeem us from our sins.

With this I close, dear hearers. When I come into this pulpit, and especially during the last two or three Sunday nights, when I have felt my head swim at the sight of you, I seem like one standing on a high cliff, half afraid to remain there, and I think to myself, 'Shall I long preach to these people?' Well, well, whether I do or do not, I would press home this question upon your consciences, as I shall meet you in that great day, *have you a share in Jesus Christ's love and care?* Did he bear your sins in his own body on the tree? Do you believe in him? That is, do you trust him? Have you put your soul into his hands, that he may save it? If so, you are justified by him, you are saved in him.

Say, dear friend, next; do you obey him? Is he your Master and Lord? Is his will the supreme law of your life? Or do you wish it to be so, and pray to make it so? Then again you may go your way, for Christ has stood in your stead. Do you suffer with him? Are you willing to suffer for him? There are some who will go with Christ if he will put on his silver slippers, and his purple mantle, and his jewelled crown. How good they are! How bravely will they say, 'I am a Christian', when everybody will throw primroses on their path, Ay, but when people sneer, and call you an old Puritan, a Methodist, a Presbyterian, or some other pretty name, and when those who preach to you are much abused, and ill things are said of them, can you take the side of a despised Christ? Can you stand at his cross? Can you own him when the blood is dripping from his wounds, when everybody thrusts out his tongue at him, and has ill words for the Crucified One? Can you say, 'I love him still? Remember the good Scotch woman, when Claverhouse had murdered her godly husband. 'Ah!' he said, 'What think you of your bonny husband now?' and she answered, 'I always thought my man was very beautiful; but I never saw him look as he does now that he has died for his Master.' Can you say the same of Christ? He was ever precious to me; I love him in every shape and form, but when I see him put on his crimson robe, and bleed at every pore for me, when the rubies are in his hands, and on his feet, and I see him still despised and rejected of men, I love him more than ever; and I love his cross, and take it up; I love his shame, and his reproach, and count it 'greater riches than the treasures in Egypt'. If it be so with you, if you are with him in his shame, I will warrant that you shall be with him in his glory. I count it to be a mean position to be only with a reigning Christ on earth, and to go with him only in fair weather. Oh, but this is the pledge and proof of love, if you are with him when the snow-flakes blow into your face, and the storm comes hurtling against you, and yet you can follow bravely where he leads the way! God make you such followers of the Crucified! May your feet know what it is to be pricked with thorns, or your head will never know what it is to feel the weight of the glory diadem! May you be willing to be despised and rejected; for if not, you have thrown away your crown! God bless you, dear friends, and blessed be his name for helping me again to speak to you tonight! Amen.

17

THE CAPTIVE SAVIOUR FREEING HIS PEOPLE [1]

'Jesus answered, I have told you that I am he: if therefore
ye seek me, let these go their way: that the saying might
be fulfilled, which he spake, Of them which thou
gavest me have I lost none.'
JOHN 18:8–9

THE WHOLE STORY of our Lord's passion is exceedingly rich
in meaning. One is tempted to linger over every separate sentence
of the narratives given by the evangelists. It were possible to preach
several series of sermons upon the whole story, and there is not a
single incident, though it may seem to be but accidental, which
might not furnish a wealth of holy thought to the careful student.
In looking through this chapter one was greatly tempted to speak
awhile upon the Master's selecting the place of his prayer as the
place of his agony and betrayal: the holy prudence and forethought
by which he had, as it were, cast up his entrenchments, and made
his defences upon the very spot where he knew he should meet the
shock of the evening's first onslaught; a lesson to us, Christians,
not to venture out into the day's battle without girding on our
armour, nor make a voyage upon the sea of life without having
seen to it that the vessel is well supplied against every possible
danger which may be encountered upon the storm-tossed sea. Jesus
prays before he fights, and so must we if we would overcome.

One was tempted also to dwell upon that remarkable expression,
'Judas also which betrayed him knew the place'; to show the futility

[1] Sermon No. 722. Preached at the Metropolitan Tabernacle on Sunday
morening, 25 November 1866.

of knowledge apart from sincerity, nay, the injuriousness of knowledge if it be not attended with corresponding grace. Had the traitor not known he could not have betrayed, and had he not been an intimate friend he could not have been so base a wretch. Strange, but strangely true is it, that the ability to become the child of perdition by betraying his Master was found in the fact of his having been the near acquaintance of the Saviour. He could never have been so sevenfold an inheritor of hell if he had not been so largely a receiver of the privilege of companionship with Christ. Direful truth, that to be educated to take the highest degree in hell it is almost necessary to enter hypocritically into the school of Christ. Terrible reflection, which should well check any of us who make high professions without a corresponding weight of sincerity. But as time does not allow us like the bee to gather honey from every flower we shall dwell upon the text. In this passage *there is much instruction, and we shall endeavour to draw it forth;* and then, *we shall take the liberty to spiritualize it,* to set the words in another sense in order that we may still be promoting our great object of setting forth our Lord Jesus Christ.

I. When we observe the words of the text, we notice upon the very surface a sure proof of THE WILLINGNESS OF OUR LORD JESUS CHRIST TO GIVE HIMSELF TO SUFFER FOR OUR SINS. The voluntary character of Christ's suffering makes it beam with a matchless splendour of love. He needed not to have died. If it had been his good pleasure he might have tarried gloriously amongst the songs of angels. He came not to earth to win a crown because he had none, for all honour and glory are his by right. It was not to earn a dominion, or because he was not Lord of principalities and powers, that he descended from the skies: 'Who though he was rich yet for our sakes he became poor, that we, through his poverty, might be made rich.' It was a disinterested mission upon which the Redeemer came to the abodes of sinful men. He had nothing to gain, rather he had everything to lose; and yet, let me say to correct myself, by that losing he did gain; for now, as our Mediator, he is clothed with a special glory of unrivalled grace, unequalled by any other manifestation of the divine perfections.

The proofs that the Master went voluntarily to his death are very abundant. He rose from supper when he knew that Judas had gone out to betray him, and he did not seek a hiding-place in the corners of Jerusalem, or retire to the calm retreat of Bethany. If he had chosen to parry his betrayer's thrust that night and to wait until the day, the fickle multitude would have gathered around him, and protected him from his foes, for they would soon have been won to his side, if he would have consented to become their king. Instead of retreating even for a moment, Jesus, attended by his disciples, boldly advanced to the spot where Judas had planned to betray him; he went as calmly as though he had made an appointment to meet a friend there, and would not be behindhand when he arrived. He entered upon his terrible sufferings with his whole heart, with the full concurrence of his whole being, having a baptism to be baptized with, and being straitened until it was accomplished. What true courage is there in those words, 'Arise, let us go hence'! when he knew that he was going to the cross. When the band came to take him, it appears that they did not know him. He said to them twice, 'Whom seek ye?' He had to reveal himself, or the lanterns and the torches would not have discovered him. He was not after all taken by Judas' kiss; the kiss was given, but in the confusion they may have missed the token. Jesus had to ask, 'Whom seek ye?' and to announce himself plainly twice with the words, 'I am he.' He yielded himself to his blood-thirsty foes, and went willingly with his tormentors. You are clear that he went willingly, for since a single word made the captors fall to the ground, what could he not have done? Another word and they would have descended into the tomb; another, and they would have been hurled into hell. He put forth just that little finger of his potency in order to let them feel what he could have done if he had chosen to lay bare the arm of his strength, and to utter but one word of wrath against them. You are sure that he went cheerfully, for how should he have gone at all if not with his own consent? There was no power on earth that could possibly have bound the Lord Jesus, had he been unwilling. He who said, 'Let these go their way', and by that word secured the safety of all his disciples, it is certain could have said the same of himself, and so have gone his way whither he would. Men might as well speak of loading the sun with chains, or holding the lightning flash in bondage, or like the foolish king of old, fettering the wild uproarious sea, as to suppose that they could constrain the Lord of Life and Glory, and lead him a captive against his will. He was led, and led bound too, but he could have snapped those bonds as Samson did the Philistines' bonds of old. There were other cords that bound him, invisible to carnal sense; the bonds of covenant engagements, the bonds of his own oath and promise, the bonds of his love to you and to me, my brethren, the mighty bonds of his marriage union to our souls, which constrained him, without a word, to yield himself as a lamb to the slaughter. The willingness of Jesus! let us see it clearly, and let us reverently adore him for it. Blessed Master! thou goest of thyself to die for us. No compulsion but that of thine own heart! Nothing brought thee to the tomb but thine almighty love to us.

I do not intend to dwell upon this thought, but having brought it before you, the practical use of it is just this: Let us take care that our service of Christ shall ever be most manifestly a cheerful and a willing one. Let us never come, for instance, up to the place of worship unwillingly, merely because of custom, or because it is the right thing to do, which we would gladly avoid doing if we dare. Let us never contribute of our substance to the Master's cause with a grudging hand, as though a tax-gatherer were wringing from us what we could ill afford. Let us never enter upon Christian exercises as a slave would enter upon his labour, hearing the crack of the whip behind him; but let love put wings to our feet, and inspire our souls with a sacred alacrity, that as the seraphs fly upon the high behests of heaven, we may run upon our Saviour's commands with as much swiftness as mortals can command. Let our duty be our delight. Let the service of Christ be a kingdom to us. Let us count it to be our highest gain to suffer loss for him, and our greatest ease to be fully immersed in abundant labours for his sake. His willing sacrifice ought to ensure our willing sacrifice. The Saviour bleeds freely like the camphor tree that needs no pressure; let us as freely from our very hearts pour forth our love, and all the kindred graces and deeds of virtue.

II. Turning from this thought, I beg you, secondly, to notice OUR LORD'S CARE FOR HIS PEOPLE IN THE HOURS OF HIS GREATEST DISTURBANCE OF MIND. 'If ye seek me, let these go their way.' That word was intended, in the first place, to be a preservation for his immediate attendants. It is singular that the Jews did not surround that little handful of disciples, put them in prison, and then execute them in due season. If they had done so, where would have been the Christian church? If they should have destroyed, as it seems easy for them to have done, the first nucleus of Christianity, where would have been the church of after ages? But that word, 'Let these go their way', very efficiently protected all the weak and trembling fugitives; why did not the soldiers capture John? He seems to have gone in and out of the palace without even a single word of challenge. Why did they not seize upon Peter? they were searching for witnesses, why did they not examine Peter under torture, as was the Roman custom, in order to have extorted from him some railing accusation against his Lord, whom he so readily denied? Where were the others? Timid, trembling folk, they had fled like harts and roes, when they first heard the baying of the dogs of persecution; why were they not hunted up? The Jews did not lack for will, for afterwards they were gratified when James was killed with the sword, and pleased when Peter was laid in prison – why were they suffered to go unharmed? Was it not because the Master had need of them? The Holy Ghost had not yet been poured out upon them, and they were not fit to be martyrs; they were like green wood that would not burn; they were as yet unbroken to the sacred yoke of suffering, and unendowed with that irresistible spiritual strength, which made them able to bear tribulation with rejoicing, and therefore that good Shepherd, who tempers the wind to shorn lambs, tempered the wind to these young beginners.

Those words, 'If ye seek me, let these go their way', were like coats of mail to them, or those fabled, invisible garments which concealed their wearers from their enemies. Under the more than brazen shield of their Lord's words, the disciples walked securely in the midst of the boisterous mob, and we find John and others of the disciples even standing at the foot of the cross while those who gnashed their teeth at Christ and laughed at him, and revealed their savage malice in a thousand ways, did not touch so much as a hair of their heads, or, as far as we know, utter one jest against them. The word of Jesus proved to be a right royal word; it was a divine word; and men were constrained to obey it. The Lord had said, 'Touch not mine anointed, and do my prophets no harm', and therefore for the time his disciples were safe.

It strikes me that the expression was not only a guard for the disciples for the time, but, as no Scripture is of private inter-pretation, I believe that such a royal passport has been given to all Christ's people in the way of *providence*. Fear not, thou servant of Christ, thou art immortal till thy work is done. When thou art fit to suffer, and if needs be even to die, Christ will not screen thee from so high an honour, but permit thee to drink of his cup, and to be baptized with his baptism; but until thine hour is come, thou mayest go and return secure from death. Though cruel men may desire thine ill, and devise mischief against thee, thou art safe enough until the Lord shall be pleased to let loose the lion, and even then thou shalt suffer no permanent injury. It is wonderful in the lives of some of God's ministers how strikingly they have been preserved from imminent peril. We cannot read the life of Calvin without being surprised that he should have been permitted to die peaceably in his bed, an honoured man, surrounded by the town councillors and the great ones of the very city from which he had been once expelled. It seems astounding that a poor weak man whose body was emaciated with diseases of all kinds, who had no arms to wield against the furious hosts of Rome, should yet live in usefulness and then die in circumstances of peace and comfort. It is not less remarkable that the brave hero of the cross, Martin Luther, should seem as if he had carried a safe conduct, which permitted him to go anywhere and everywhere. He stood up in the Diet of Worms expecting to die, but he came out unscathed. He passed, as it were, between the very jaws of death and yet re-mained unharmed. Though, as I have said before, Christ has suffered many of his people to die for him, and they have rejoiced so to do, yet, when he has willed to preserve any of his servants who were needed for a special work, as Calvin and Luther undoubtedly were, he had a way of taking care of them, and saying, 'Let these go their way.' Take, for instance, another illustration, the life of our remarkable reformer, John Wycliffe. Many times his life was not worth a week's purchase, and yet the old enemies of the saints were robbed of their prey, and could never touch a bone of him until years after he had been buried. When he was brought up for trial before the bishop, at St Paul's, it was a very singular circumstance that John of Gaunt should stand at his side fully armed, proudly covering the godly man with the prestige of his rank and the arm of his power. When Wycliffe was faint with standing, and begged to be allowed to sit, the bishop tells him that heretics shall have no seats, but John of Gaunt with rough, uncourtly words swears that he shall sit when he wills, and when the time comes the good man goes forth through the midst of the rabble protected by his friend. I know not that John of Gaunt knew the truth, but yet God touched the man's heart to protect his servant in the hour of peril. Vultures, when God has willed it, have protected doves, and eagles have covered with their wings defenceless children whom God would save. When the Lord wills it, if all hell should shoot such a shower of arrows as should put out the sun, and if all those arrows were aimed at one poor heart, yet not a single shaft should hit, but all be turned aside by an invisible but irresistible power from the man whom Jehovah ordained to save. We understand, then, that Jesus has issued a royal passport for all his servants, which enables them to live on in the midst of deaths innumerable.

Mystically understood the words have a far deeper meaning. The true seizure of Christ was not by Romans or by the envious Jews, but by our sins; and the true deliverance which Jesus gave to his disciples was not so much from Roman weapons as from the penalty of our sins. How anxiously do I desire that those here this morning whose sins have been tormenting them would hear the voice of Jesus, 'If ye seek me, let these go their way.' *The law of God* comes out to seek us who have violated it. It has many and just demands against us, but Jesus who stood in our place puts himself before the law, and he says, 'Dost thou seek me? Here I am; but when thou takest me a prisoner let these, for whom I stood, go their way.' So then, beloved, when the law met with the Lord Jesus and made him its servant, and constrained him to bear its penalty, all those for whom Christ stood were by his being bound, absolutely and for ever set free. Christ's suffering the penalty of the law was the means of removing his people for ever from under the legal yoke. Now let me try to apply that truth to your case. A poor soul under distress of mind has gone to the priest, and he says, 'If thou wouldst be pardoned do penance.' While he is flogging his back and laying on the stripes most earnestly I think I hear the Saviour saying to the whole tribe of priests, 'Let these poor souls go their way. My shoulders have borne all they ought to have borne; my heart has suffered all the griefs that they were condemned to know. The chastisement of their peace was upon me, and by my stripes they are healed. Let these go!' Put up your whip, cease from your bodily tortures, they are of no service. The law has taken the Redeemer, it does not want you. You need not suffer, Christ has suffered, and all your sufferings will now be useless and vain. Christ has paid the debt, no need for you to attempt it again. Another poor trembler has been sitting under a legal ministry, and he has been told that if he would he saved he must keep the commandments. He has therefore endeavoured to forego this sin and the other, and as far as possible to be perfect in holiness. But he has made no advance; his soul is as much in bondage as ever, unsaved with all his exertions, destitute still of true peace notwithstanding all his good works. This morning my Master cries to the preacher who talks after this fashion, 'Let these poor bondaged ones go their way. Do not preach to them salvation by their own doings. Do not tell them that they are to merit admittance to heaven. I have wrought out and finished their redemption; their salvation is complete in me. There is nothing for sinners to do to win forgiveness. All they have to do is to receive what I have done for them. All the righteousness they need to recommend them before God is my righteousness, which requires not that theirs be added to it, for why should their rags be joined to my cloth of gold? All the merit a sinner can plead is the merit of my passion. Wherefore should they seek after merit through their repentance and their good works? Why should such stagnant water be poured into the midst of the wine of my merit? Away with your fancied good works, away with your boastings, your religious doings, your weepings, and your prayings, for if they be used as a ground of confidence instead of the work of Jesus they are things of nought, mere rottenness and dung to be cast upon the dunghill. Since Jesus was accepted and punished by the law, sinners believing in him are free from the law's exactions, and may go their way. Perhaps there are here some in whose hearts the law of God is making terrible confusion. You feel that you have broken the law and that you cannot keep it, and now the law is flogging you; it has tied you up as they tie up soldiers in the army to the halberts, and it has been laying on the great cat of ten tails to your back, the ten commandments of the law, till you are smarting, smarting all over. Your whole conscience is troubled. Now the Lord Jesus Christ says to the Law, 'Put up, put up that whip! do not smite the sinner any more! Didst thou not smite me, why shouldst thou vex him.' But, sinner, the only way in which thou canst escape from the law's whip is this, hasten to Jesus Christ. Thou must flee to Christ, thou must trust in Jesus, and if thou shalt trust in Jesus he will cast his skirt over thee, he will lift up the broad buckler of his merit and protect thee from the shafts of the foe, so that thou canst say to the law, 'I am not under the curse of the law now, for I have fulfilled it in the person of my Surety, and I have suffered its penalty in the person of my Saviour.'

> The terrors of law and of God
> With me can have nothing to do;
> My Saviour's obedience and blood
> Hide all my transgressions from view.

Jesus Christ then, as he stands before the law and is bound by the law, and flogged by the law, and crucified by the law, and buried by the law, says to you who trust in him, 'Go your way, the law cannot touch you, for it has smitten me instead of you. I was your substitute, and you may go free.'

Why you all know that this is simple justice; if another person shall have paid your debts, you are not afraid of having those debts inflicted again upon you; and if you are drafted for the army and a substitute has taken your place, you are not afraid of being drawn a second time. So the Lord Jesus Christ is the substitute for all his people, and if he was a substitute for you, the law has no further penal claims upon you. Christ has obeyed it; Christ has suffered its penalty; you may rejoice in the law as being now to you a gracious rule of life, but it is not to you a yoke of bondage; you are not under it as a slave, you are free from its dominion; you are not under the law, but you are under grace. What a blessing is this!

Further, these words seem to me to bear such a meaning as this, that as we are delivered from legal exaction so are we also *delivered from all penal infliction.* I wish that some children of God were clearer on this point. When you suffer tribulation, affliction, and adversity, do not think that God is punishing you for your sins, for no child of God can be punished for sin penally. Let me not be misunderstood. A man is brought before God first of all as a criminal before a judge. You and I have stood there. Through Christ's blood and righteousness we have been absolved and acquitted as before God the Judge, and it is not possible for the law to lay so much as the weight of a feather upon us since we have been perfectly acquitted. In all the pains and sufferings which a Christian may endure, there is not so much as a single ounce of penal infliction. God cannot punish a man whom he has pardoned. But that criminal being pardoned, is then adopted into the family and becomes a child. Now, if he shall as a child offend against his father's rule, he will be chastened for it. Every one can see the distinction between the chastening of a father and the punishment of a judge. If your child were to steal you would not think of punishing that child in the light in which the judge would do it, who would commit him to imprisonment for having broken the law; but you chasten your child yourself, not so much to avenge the law as for the child's good, that he may not do this evil thing again. So our heavenly Father chastens his people with the rod of the covenant, but he never punishes them with the sword of vengeance. There is a difference between chastening and punishing. Punishing is from a judge; Christ has suffered all such punishment, so that no penal infliction can fall upon a soul that believes in him; but we may have chastisement which comes to us as the result of a father's love, and not as the result of a judge's anger; we have felt such chastisement, and have reason to bless God for it. Our Lord Jesus says with regard to all legal penalty, 'If ye seek me, I have borne it: let these go free.'

Once more, this text will have its grandest fulfilment *at the last.* When the destroying angel shall come forth with his sword of fire to smite the sinner, when the gulf of hell shall open and vomit forth its floods of flame, when the dread trumpet shall sound and shall make all ears to hear the voice of an avenging God, Christ shall stand forth in the front of all the blood-bought souls that came to trust under the shadow of the wings of his mercy, and he will say to Justice, 'Thou hast sought me once, and thou hast found all thou canst ask of me. Then let these go their way.' And up the glorious steeps of the celestial hills the happy throng shall stream, singing as they pass through the gate of pearl and tread the pavement of transparent gold, 'Unto him that loved us and washed us from our sins in his blood, unto him be glory for ever and ever.' Then shall the great manumission of the slave take place, because Christ was bound; then shall the deliverance of the captive come, because Christ slept in the prison-house of the tomb. 'If ye seek me, let these go their way.' I would to God that some here would perceive that the way of deliverance is for the Lord Jesus to be bound in their stead. Trust thou in Jesus, and it shall be so.

III. Thirdly, but very briefly, notice why our Lord exhibited this great care for his people; PONDER OVER HIS SAYING concerning them, 'That the saying might be fulfilled which he spake, Of them which thou gavest me I have lost none.' Here is much of matter for thought at your leisure. Do not you know that that text was a prayer? Now here it is made into a promise. What, then, is everything that Christ asks for guaranteed to his people, so that his prayer is God's promise? It is so.

Notice next that, verbally understood, this expression, which is quoted from the seventeenth of John, could only relate to the souls of God's people; but here it is taken as though it related to their bodies. From which I gather that we are never wrong in understanding promises in the largest possible sense. It is, I believe, a rule of law that if a man should get a privilege from the king that privilege is to be understood in the widest sense; whereas a punishment, or penalty, is always to be understood in the narrowest sense. In the olden times, when princes and kings used to grant monopolies, if a king had granted a monopoly upon all kinds of foreign fruits, if the words had so run, you may rest assured that the person obtaining that monopoly would have put everything down as foreign fruit that could possibly bear the name, and he would have been justified by the law for so doing. Now, when the great King gives a promise, you may encompass everything within its range, which can possibly come under the promise, and we may be sure that the Lord will not run back from his word. God's words are never to be taken with a rebate, or discount, but with such blessed interest as your faith is able to put thereto. The grant of eternal life includes such providential protections and provisions as shall be necessary on the road to heaven. The house is secured for the sake of the tenant, and the body because of the soul.

There is also one more remark I cannot help making, namely, that this text is not in the form of a promise at all. 'Of them which thou gavest me *have* I lost none.' It relates to the past, but here it is used as a reason why none should be lost of the present; from which I gather, that as Jesus has done in the past so will he act in the future, and that all he ever was to his people he will be to them for ever more. We may look upon every past act of grace as being a token and guarantee of future grace, and we may gather from all our experience of the Lord's goodness in the days that are gone that he will do yet again unto us as he has done, and still more abundantly until we see his face in heaven.

The gracious words before us read as follows: 'Of all them which thou hast given me I have lost none.' Then some are given. There is an elect nation. Oh that we may be found in that happy number! Then Jesus keeps those who are given; they cannot keep themselves, but he can keep them and will. He so well preserves them that not so much as one is lost. I have sometimes thought I might imagine such a scene as this at the gates of heaven, when the great Shepherd comes to give in his charge. 'Here am I,' saith he, 'and the children which thou hast given me.' 'But are they every one brought safely here?' 'Yes,' saith the great Shepherd, 'of all whom thou hast given me I have lost none.' 'But where is Peter? Did he not deny thee to thy face in the hall? Did he not three times say, "I know him not!"' 'Yes, but I made him go out and weep bitterly, and then I washed him in my precious blood, and here he is', and Peter sings as sweetly as any. Then perhaps the question may be asked, 'And where is such a one, the least of all saints?' Brother, you feel yourself to be the weakest, the meanest, the most useless, but an enquiry will be made for you, and the answer will be, 'He is here; of all whom thou hast given me I have lost none.' Oh, happy sheep in the care of such a Shepherd! Oh happy, happy hearts that can rely upon such a keeper! Dear hearer, is Jesus yours? Are you depending upon him? Say, have you cast yourself upon him? Then do not fear concerning your last days; it must be well at the last, if it is well now. If you are now in Christ, he never did cast away any and he never will. Oh if you have but come to him and are now depending on him:

> His honour is engaged to save
> The meanest of his sheep;
> All that his heavenly Father gave
> His hands securely keep.

He suffered for you and therefore you shall go your way, and the covenant shall be fulfilled. 'Of those whom thou hast given me I have lost none.'

I have thus used the text as briefly as I could. I shall want your patience a few minutes while I apply this text in a sort of SPIRITUAL SENSE.

The first remark in this department of the subject is – *many seek Jesus but do not know who he is.* So that Christ says to them, 'Whom seek ye?' Some here this morning are seeking rest, but they do not know that Jesus is the rest. You feel an aching void in your hearts. You are not happy; the theatre does not give you the pleasure it once did. Somehow life has grown insipid to you. There is a still small voice within your soul like the voice of wailing, like Rachel weeping for her children and refusing to be comforted. You are seeking you know not what. You have begun to read your Bible; you are eager to attend upon the preaching of the gospel, but you do not know what it is you want. Ah well, it is a good thing to be a seeker; though you cannot tell what it is you need, for if you do but desire and lift up your voice to God sincerely and earnestly, he will be found of you.

We now note the fact, namely, that *those who seek Christ will find him,* but they find him only because he reveals himself to them. These men sought Christ to kill him, yet he came and said. 'I am he.' There was a woman, if you remember, at the well of

Sychar, who sought him for a very different purpose. She said, 'I know that Messiah cometh, which is called Christ; when he is come he will tell us all things.' And Jesus said, 'I that speak unto thee am he.' Whoever seeks Jesus, Jesus will show himself to them. They came with lanterns and with torches, but they did not find Christ with lanterns and with torches. And you may come, my dear friend, with a great many of your own inventions, a great many fancies and imaginings, but you will not so find him. How could you expect to find the sun with a lantern? No. Christ must come and reveal himself to you, and if you seek him he will do so. Only continue to seek him. Let not past disappointments make you leave off seeking. Long as you have breath continue in prayer. I charge you before the living God if you have sought in vain, do not let Satan make thee give it up; but ask that Christ would lead thee in the right way, for if thou didst but know the right way thou needst not seek long for he is here now. Jesus can forgive this morning; before you leave that seat you shall have a full assurance of your interest in him, if you be led to understand the way of salvation. That way is simply to trust Christ, simply to believe that he can and will save you, and to trust yourself with him. I will never believe that he will let a sincere soul go hungering and thirsting after him, and let that soul die without him; but though he may be pleased for a while to let that spirit wander even in apparent blackness and darkness, yet he will at the last lift the veil from his blessed face, and ah! the sight of that face will well repay you for all the sighs and cries with which you sought him; and to hear him say, 'I have loved thee with an everlasting love, therefore with loving-kindness have I drawn thee', will so wake up the music of heaven within your soul that you will think of the months of weariness and the nights of waiting as all too little, and more than enough repaid.

One thing more, *when Jesus is found, there is always much to be given up*. 'If ye seek me, let these go their way.' There are always many things that you will have to let go if you have Christ, and this is very often the testing point. If a man keeps a public-house which he opens on Sunday, in which cursing and swearing abounds, if he has encouraged all sorts of vice, in order to increase his custom, can he continue in this and yet have Christ? Impossible.

Now that man would like to go to heaven, but if he would he must let go his evil occupation. Yonder is a woman who has tasted the pleasures of sin. She would fain have a Saviour, but if she will have a Saviour she must let her sins go. There is a young man over yonder, proud, vain, giddy; if he would have Christ, he must let all these evils go. Our sins must be abandoned, or we cannot receive a Saviour. Christ Jesus will pardon sin, but he will never dwell in the same heart with sin. Though you may have been as base as base could be, it can all be forgiven you now; but if you continue in it, there is no mercy for you. He that confesseth his sin and forsaketh it, shall find mercy; but not the man who with hypocritical lip bewails it, and then with vicious heart plunges into it again. 'If ye seek me, let these go.' What, cannot you give them up? Silly companions, idle habits, foolish songs, pleasure-seeking, so-called, are these too dear to be renounced? Really, some of the things which give pleasure to men nowadays are so absurd, so empty, so devoid of true wit, that I wonder the swine do not revolt against the mouldy husks which they are fed with nowadays. We cannot wonder that swine do eat husks, it is natural they should, and we would not deny them their native food. If I were a swine, I think I should like to have husks that have some sort of substance in them, but the world's pleasure grows more and more vapid and worthless, the pleasure of idiots rather than of men. Cannot you give these poor things up? Are they such dear attractions, such precious things, that you let heaven go, and Christ go, sooner than let them go? Nay, I hope it will be a voice of power to you, and that you will say, 'My Saviour, let them all go! what are they to thee? I shall find ten thousand times more pleasure and more profit too in following thee than in following the best of them. So let them go for ever, and may they never entice me more.' Have you any self-righteousness remaining? Are you in your own conceit better than other people? Do you secretly trust in your works? Now if you want Christ, you must let all that go. Christ will tread the wine-press alone, and of the people, there must be none with him; and if you seek to be saved by Christ it must not be by the works of the law, but by grace alone. Would to God that there might be a clean sweep made in some of your hearts, and that you would come to Jesus all empty-handed as you are, and say, 'Yes, Master, thy precious blood, thy triumphant resurrection, thine effectual plea; these are our hope and these our joy. We would serve thee in life, and bless thee in death. Thine we are, thou Son of God, and all that we have. Take us and keep us, and thine be the praise. Amen.

18

THE BETRAYAL [1]

'And while he yet spake, behold a multitude, and he that was
called Judas, one of the twelve, went before them, and drew
near unto Jesus to kiss him. But Jesus said unto him, Judas,
betrayest thou the Son of man with a kiss?'
LUKE 22:47–48

WHEN SATAN had been entirely worsted in his conflict with
Christ in the garden, the man-devil Judas came upon the scene.
As the Parthian in his flight turns round to shoot the fatal arrow,
so the arch-enemy aimed another shaft at the Redeemer, by
employing the traitor into whom he had entered. Judas became
the devil's deputy, and a most trusty and serviceable tool he was.
The Evil One had taken entire possession of the apostate's heart,
and, like the swine possessed of devils, he ran violently downwards
towards destruction. Well had infernal malice selected the Saviour's
trusted friend to be his treacherous betrayer, for thus he stabbed
at the very centre of his broken and bleeding heart. But, beloved,
as in all things God is wiser than Satan, and the Lord of goodness
outwitteth the Prince of Evil, so, in this dastardly betrayal of
Christ, prophecy was fulfilled, and Christ was the more surely
declared to be the promised Messiah. Was not Joseph a type? and,
lo! like that envied youth, Jesus was sold by his own brethren. Was
he not to be another Samson, by whose strength the gates of hell
should be torn from their posts? lo! like Samson, he is bound by
his countrymen, and delivered to the adversary. Know ye not that
he was the anti-type of David? and was not David deserted by

[1] Sermon No. 494. Preached at the Metropolitan Tabernacle on Sunday morning,
15 February 1863.

Ahithophel, his own familiar friend and counsellor? Nay, brethren, do not the words of the Psalmist receive a literal fulfilment in our Master's betrayal? What prophecy can be more exactly true than the language of the forty-first and fifty-fifth Psalms? In the first we read, 'Yea, mine own familiar friend, in whom I trusted, which did eat of my bread, hath lifted up his heel against me'; and in the fifty-fifth the Psalmist is yet more clear; 'For it was not an enemy that reproached me; then I could have borne it: neither was it he that hated me that did magnify himself against me; then I would have hid myself from him: but it was thou, a man mine equal, my guide, and mine acquaintance. We took sweet counsel together, and walked unto the house of God in company. He hath put forth his hands against such as be at peace with him: he hath broken his covenant. The words of his mouth were smoother than butter, but war was in his heart: his words were softer than oil, yet were they drawn swords.' Even an obscure passage in one of the lesser prophets, must have a literal fulfilment, and for thirty pieces of silver, the price of a base slave, must the Saviour be betrayed by his choice friend. Ah! thou foul fiend, thou shalt find at the last that thy wisdom is but intensified folly; as for the deep plots and plans of thy craft, the Lord shall laugh them to scorn; after all, thou art but the unconscious drudge of him whom thou abhorrest; in all the black work thou doest so greedily, thou art no better than a mean scullion in the royal kitchen of the King of kings.

Without further preface, let us advance to the subject of our Lord's betrayal. First, concentrate your thoughts upon *Jesus, the betrayed one;* and when ye have lingered awhile there, solemnly gaze into the villainous countenance of *Judas, the betrayer* – he may prove a beacon to warn us against the sin which gendereth apostasy.

I. LET US TARRY AWHILE, AND SEE OUR LORD UN-GRATEFULLY AND DASTARDLY BETRAYED.

It is appointed that he must die, but how shall he fall into the hands of his adversaries? Shall they capture him in conflict? It must not be, lest he appear an unwilling victim. Shall he flee before his foes until he can hide no longer? It is not meet that a sacrifice should be hunted to death. Shall he offer himself to the foe? That were to excuse his murderers, or be a party to their crime. Shall he be taken accidentally or unawares? That would withdraw from his cup the necessary bitterness which made it wormwood mingled with gall. No; he must be betrayed by his friend, that he may bear the utmost depths of suffering, and that in every separate circumstance there may be a well of grief. One reason for the appointment of the betrayal, lay in the fact *that it was ordained that man's sin should reach its culminating point in his death*. God, the great owner of the vineyard, had sent many servants, and the husbandmen had stoned one and cast out another; last of all, he said, 'I will send my Son; surely they will reverence my Son.' When they slew the heir to win the inheritance, their rebellion had reached its height. The murder of our blessed Lord was the extreme of human guilt; it developed the deadly hatred against God which lurks in the heart of man. When man became a deicide, sin had reached its fullness; and in the black deed of the man by whom the Lord was betrayed, that fullness was all displayed. If it had not been for a Judas, we had not known how black, how foul, human nature may become.

I scorn the men who try to apologize for the treachery of this devil in human form, this son of perdition, this foul apostate. I should think myself a villain if I tried to screen him, and I shudder for the men who dare extenuate his crimes. My brethren, we should feel a deep detestation of this master of infamy; he has gone to his own place, and the anathema of David, part of which was quoted by Peter, has come upon him, 'When he shall be judged, let him be condemned: and let his prayer become sin. Let his days be few; and let another take his office.' Surely, as the devil was allowed unusually to torment the bodies of men, even so was he let loose to get possession of Judas as he has seldom gained possession of any other man, that we might see how foul, how desperately evil is the human heart. Beyond a doubt, however, the main reason for this was *that Christ might offer a perfect atonement for sin*. We may usually read the sin in the punishment. Man betrayed his God. Man had the custody of the royal garden, and should have kept its green avenues sacred for communion with his God; but he betrayed the trust; the sentinel was false; he admitted evil into his own heart, and so into the paradise of God. He was false to the good name of the Creator, tolerating the insinuation which he should have repelled with scorn. Therefore must Jesus find man a traitor to him. There must be the counterpart of the sin in the suffering which he endured. You and I have often betrayed Christ. We have, when tempted, chosen the evil and forsaken the good; we have taken the bribes of hell, and have not followed closely with Jesus. It seemed most fitting, then, that he who bore the chastisement of sin should be reminded of its ingratitude and treachery by the things which he suffered. Besides, brethren, *that cup must be bitter to the last degree which is to be the equivalent for the wrath of God.* There must be nothing consolatory in it; pains must be taken to pour into it all that even Divine wisdom can invent of awful and unheard of woe, and this one point – 'He that eateth bread with me hath lifted up his heel against me' – was absolutely necessary to intensify the bitterness. Moreover, we feel persuaded that by thus suffering at the hand of a traitor *the Lord became a faithful High Priest,* able to sympathize with us when we fall under the like affliction. Since slander and ingratitude are common calamities, we can come to Jesus with full assurance of faith; he knows these sore temptations, for he has felt them in their very worst degree. We may cast every care, and every sorrow upon him, for he careth for us, having suffered with us. Thus, then, in our Lord's betrayal, Scripture was fulfilled, sin was developed, atonement was completed, and the great all-suffering High Priest became able to sympathize with us in every point.

Now let us *look at the treason itself.* You perceive how black it was. Judas was *Christ's servant,* what if I call him his confidential servant. He was a partaker in apostolic ministry and the honour of miraculous gifts. He had been most kindly and indulgently treated. He was a sharer in all the goods of his Master, in fact he fared far better than his Lord, for the Man of Sorrows always took the lion's share of all the pains of poverty and the reproach of slander. He had food and raiment given him out of the common stock, and the Master seems to have indulged him very greatly. The old tradition is, that next to the apostle Peter he was the one with whom the Saviour most commonly associated. We think there must be a mistake there, for surely John was the Saviour's greatest friend; but Judas, as a servant had been treated with the utmost confidence. Ye know, brethren, how sore is that blow which comes from a servant in whom we have put unlimited trust. But Judas was more than this: *he was a friend, a trusted friend.* That little bag into which generous women cast their small contributions had been put into his hands, and very wisely too, for he had the financial vein. His main virtue was economy, a very needful quality in a treasurer. As exercising a prudent foresight for the little company, and watching the expenses carefully, he was, as far as men could judge, the right man in the right place. He had been thoroughly trusted. I read not that there was any annual audit of his accounts; I do not discover that the Master took him to task as to the expenditure of his privy purse. Everything was given to him, and he gave, at the Master's direction, to the poor, but no account was asked. This is vile indeed, to be chosen to such a position, to be installed purse-bearer to the King of kings, Chancellor of God's exchequer, and then to turn aside and sell the Saviour; this is treason in its uttermost degree. Remember that the world looked upon Judas as colleague and partner with our Lord. To a great extent the name of Judas was associated with that of Christ. When Peter, James, or John had done anything amiss, reproachful tongues threw it all on their Master. The Twelve were part and parcel of Jesus of Nazareth. One old commentator says of Judas – 'He was Christ's alter ego' – to the people at large there was an identification of each apostle with the leader of the band. And oh! when such associations have been established, and then there is treachery, it is as though our arm should commit treason against our head, or as if our foot should desert the body. This was a stab indeed! Perhaps, dear brethren, our Lord saw in the person of Judas a representative man, the portraiture of the many thousands who in after ages imitated his crime. Did Jesus see in Iscariot all the Judases who betray truth, virtue, and the cross? Did he perceive the multitudes of whom we may say, that they were, spiritually, in the loins of Judas? Hymenaeus, Alexander, Hermogenes, Philetus, Demas, and others of that tribe, were all before him as he saw the man, his equal, his acquaintance, bartering him away for thirty pieces of silver.

Dear friends, the position of Judas must have tended greatly to aggravate his treason. Even the heathens have taught us that ingratitude is the worst of vices. When Caesar was stabbed by his friend Brutus, the world's poet writes –

> This was the most unkindest cut of all;
> For when the noble Caesar saw him stab,
> Ingratitude, more strong than traitor's arms,
> Quite vanquish'd him; then burst his mighty heart;
> And, in his mantle muffling up his face,
> Even at the base of Pompey's statue,
>   – Great Caesar fell.

Many ancient stories, both Greek and Roman, we might quote to show the abhorrence which the heathens entertain towards ingratitude and treachery. Certain, also, of their own poets, such, for instance, as Sophocles, have poured out burning words upon deceitful friends; but we have no time to prove what you will all admit, that nothing can be more cruel, nothing more full of anguish, than to be sold to destruction by one's bosom friend. The closer the foeman comes the deeper will be the stab he gives; if we admit him to our heart, and give him our closest intimacy, then can he wound us in the most vital part.

Let us notice, dear friends, while we look at the breaking heart of our agonizing Saviour, *the manner in which he met this affliction.* He had been much in prayer; prayer had overcome his dreadful agitation; he was very *calm;* and we need to be very calm when we are forsaken by a friend. Observe his gentleness. The first word he spake to Judas, when the traitor had polluted his cheek with a kiss, was this – 'FRIEND'! FRIEND!! Note that! Not 'Thou hateful miscreant', but 'Friend, wherefore art thou come?' not 'Wretch, wherefore dost thou dare to stain my cheek with thy foul and lying lips?' no, 'Friend, wherefore art thou come?' Ah! if there had been anything good left in Judas, this would have brought it out. If he had not been an unmitigated, incorrigible, thrice-dyed traitor, his avarice must have lost its power at that instant, and he would have cried – 'My master! I came to betray thee, but that generous word has won my soul; here, if thou must be bound, I will be bound with thee; I make a full confession of my infamy!' Our Lord added these words – there is reproof in them, but notice how kind they are still, how much too good for such a caitiff –

'Judas, betrayest thou the Son of Man with a kiss?' I can conceive that the tears gushed from his eyes, and that his voice faltered, when he thus addressed his own familiar friend and acquaintance – 'Betrayest thou', my Judas, my treasurer, 'betrayest thou the Son of man', thy suffering, sorrowing friend, whom thou hast seen naked and poor, and without a place whereon to lay his head. Betrayest thou the Son of man – and dost thou prostitute the fondest of all endearing signs – a kiss – that which should be a symbol of loyalty to the King, shall it be the badge of thy treachery – that which was reserved for affection as her best symbol – dost thou make it the instrument of my destruction? Betrayest thou the Son of man with a kiss?' Oh! if he had not been given up to hardness of heart, if the Holy Ghost had not utterly left him, surely this son of perdition would have fallen prostrate yet again, and weeping out his very soul, would have cried – 'No, I cannot betray thee, thou suffering Son of man; forgive, forgive; spare thyself; escape from this bloodthirsty crew, and pardon thy treacherous disciple!'

But no, no word of compunction, while the silver is at stake! Afterwards came the sorrow that worketh death, which drove him, like Ahithophel, his prototype, to court the gallows to escape remorse. This, also, must have aggravated the woe of our beloved Lord, when he saw the final impenitence of the traitor, and read the tearful doom of that man of whom he had once said, it would be better for him that he had never been born.

Beloved, I would have you fix your eyes on your Lord in your quiet meditations as being thus despised and rejected of men, a man of sorrows and acquainted with grief; and gird up the loins of your minds, counting it no strange thing if this fiery trial should come upon you, but being determined that though your Lord should be betrayed by his most eminent disciples, yet, through his grace you will cling to him in shame and in suffering, and will follow him, if needs be, even unto death. God give us grace to see the vision of his nailed hands and feet, and remembering that all this came from the treachery of a friend, let us be very jealous of ourselves, lest we crucify the Lord afresh and put him to an open shame by betraying him in our conduct, or in our words, or in our thoughts.

II. Grant me your attention while we make an estimate of the man by whom the Son of man was betrayed – JUDAS THE BETRAYER. I would call your attention, dear friends, *to his position and public character*. Judas was a preacher; nay, he was a foremost preacher, 'he obtained part of this ministry', said the Apostle Peter. He was not simply one of the Seventy; he had been selected by the Lord himself as one of the Twelve, an honourable member of the college of the apostles. Doubtless he had preached the gospel so that many had been gladdened by his voice, and miraculous powers had been vouchsafed to him, so that at his word the sick had been healed, deaf ears had been opened; and the blind had been made to see; nay, there is no doubt that he who could not keep the devil out of himself, had cast devils out of others. Yet how art thou fallen from heaven, O Lucifer, son of the morning! He that was as a prophet in the midst of the people, and spake with the tongue of the learned, whose word and wonders proved that he had been with Jesus and had learned of him – he betrays his Master. Understand, my brethren, that no gifts can ensure grace, and that no position of honour or usefulness in the church will necessarily prove our being true to our Lord and Master. Doubtless there are bishops in hell, and crowds of those who once occupied the pulpit are now condemned for ever to bewail their hypocrisy. You that are church-officers, do not conclude that because you enjoy the confidence of the church, that therefore of an absolute certainty the grace of God is in you. Perhaps it is the most dangerous of all positions for a man to become well known and much respected by the religious world, and yet to be rotten at the core. To be where others can observe our faults is a healthy thing though painful; but to live with beloved friends who would not believe it possible for us to do wrong, and who if they saw us err would make excuses for us – this is to be where it is next to impossible for us ever to be aroused if our hearts be not right with God. To have a fair reputation and a false heart is to stand upon the brink of hell.

Judas *took a very high degree officially*. He had the distinguished honour of being entrusted with the Master's financial concerns, and this, after all, was no small degree to which to attain. The Lord, who knows how to use all sorts of gifts, perceived what gift the man had. He knew that Peter's unthinking impetuosity would soon empty the bag and leave the company in great straits, and if he had entrusted it to John, his loving spirit might have been cajoled into unwise benevolence towards beggars of unctuous tongue; he might even have spent the little moneys in buying alabaster boxes whose precious ointments should anoint the Master's head. He gave the bag to Judas, and it was discreetly, prudently, and properly used; there is no doubt he was the most judicious person, and fitted to occupy the post. But oh! dear friends, if the Master shall choose any of us who are ministers or church-officers, and give us a very distinguished position; if our place in the ranks shall be that of commanding officers, so that even our brother ministers look up with esteem, and our fellow-elders or deacons regard us as being fathers in Israel – oh! if we turn, if we prove false, how damnable shall be our end at the last! What a blow shall we give to the heart of the church, and what derision will be made in hell!

You will observe that the character of Judas *was openly an admirable one.* I find not that he committed himself in any way. Not the slightest speck defiled his moral character so far as others could perceive. He was no boaster, like Peter; he was free enough from the rashness which cries, 'Though all men should forsake thee yet will not I.' He asks no place on the right hand of the throne, his ambition is of another sort. He does not ask idle questions. The Judas who asks questions is 'not Iscariot'. Thomas and Philip are often prying into deep matters, but not Judas. He receives truth as it is taught him, and when others are offended and walk no more with Jesus, he faithfully adheres to him, having golden reasons for so doing. He does not indulge in the lusts of the flesh or in the pride of life. None of the disciples suspected him of hypocrisy; they said at the table, 'Lord, is it I?' They never said, 'Lord, is it Judas?' It was true he had been filching for months, but then he did it by littles, and covered his defalcations so well by financial manipulations that he ran no risk of detection from the honest unsuspecting fishermen with whom he associated. Like some merchants and traders we have heard of – invaluable gentlemen as chairmen of speculating companies and general managers of swindling banks – he could abstract a decent percentage and yet make the accounts exactly tally. The gentlemen who have learned of Judas, manage to cook the accounts most admirably for the shareholders, so as to get a rich joint for their own table; over which they, no doubt, entreat the divine blessing. Judas was, in his known life, a most admirable person. He would have been an alderman ere long there is no doubt, and being very pious and richly-gifted, his advent at churches or chapels would have created intense satisfaction. 'What a discreet and influential person', say the deacons. 'Yes,' replies the minister; 'what an acquisition to our councils; if we could elect him to office he would be of eminent service to the church.' I believe that the Master chose him as apostle on purpose that we might not be at all surprised if we find such a man a minister in the pulpit, or a colleague of the minister, working as an officer in Christ's church. These are solemn things, my brethren; let us take them to heart, and if any of us wear a good character among men and stand high in office, let this question come home close to us – 'Lord, is it I? Lord, is it I?' Perhaps he who shall last ask the question is just the man who ought to have asked it first.

But, secondly, I call your attention *to his real nature and sin.* Judas was a man with a conscience. He could not afford to do without it. He was no Sadducee who could fling religion overboard; he had strong religious tendencies. He was no debauched person; he never spent a two-pence in vice on his life, not that he loved vice less, but that he loved the two-pence more. Occasionally he was generous, but then it was with other people's money. Well did he watch his lovely charge, the bag. He had a conscience, I say, and a ferocious conscience it was when it once broke the chain, for it was his conscience which made him hang himself. But then it was a conscience that did not sit regularly on the throne; it reigned by fits and starts. Conscience was not the leading element. Avarice predominated over conscience. He would get money, if honestly, he liked that best, but if he could not get it conscientiously, then anyhow in the world. He was but a small trader; his gains were no great things, or else he would not have sold Christ for so small a sum as that – ten pounds at the outside, of our money at its present value – some three or four pounds, as it was in those days. It was a poor price to take for the Master; but then a little money was a great thing to him. He had been poor; he had joined Christ with the idea that he would soon be proclaimed King of the Jews, and that then he should become a nobleman, and be rich. Finding Christ a long while in coming to his kingdom, he had taken little by little, enough to lay by in store; and now, fearing that he was to be disappointed in all his dreams, and never having had any care for Christ, but only for himself, he gets out of what he thinks to have been a gross mistake in the best way he can, and makes money by his treason against his Lord. Brethren, I do solemnly believe, that of all hypocrites, those are the persons of whom there is the least hope whose God is their money. You may reclaim a drunkard; thank God, we have seen many instances of that; and even a fallen Christian, who has given way to vice, may loathe his lust, and return from it; but I fear me that the cases in which a man who is cankered with covetousness has ever been saved, are so few, that they might be written on your finger-nail. This is a sin which the world does not rebuke; the most faithful minister can scarce smite its forehead. God knoweth what thunders I have launched out against men who are all for this world, and yet pretend to be Christ's followers; but yet they always say, 'It is not for me.' What I should call stark naked covetousness, they call prudence, discretion, economy, and so on; and actions which I would scorn to spit upon, they will do, and think their hands quite clean after they have done them, and still sit as God's people sit, and hear as God's people hear, and think that after they have sold Christ for paltry gain, they will go to heaven. O souls, souls, souls, beware, beware, beware, most of all of greed! It is not money, nor the lack of money, but the love of money which is the root of all evil. It is not getting it; it is not even keeping it; it is loving it; it is making it your god; it is looking at that as the main chance, and not considering the cause of Christ, nor the truth of Christ, nor the holy life of Christ, but being ready to sacrifice everything for gains' sake. Oh! such men make giants in sin; they shall be set up for ever as butts for infernal laughter; their damnation shall be sure and just.

The third point is, *the warning which Judas received, and the way in which he persevered.* Just think – the night before he sold his Master what do you think the Master did? Why, he washed his feet! And yet he sold him! Such condescension! Such love! Such familiarity! He took a towel, and girded himself, and washed Judas's feet! And yet those very feet brought Judas as a guide to them that took Jesus! And you remember what he said when he had washed his feet – 'Now ye are clean, but not all'; and he turned a tearful eye on Judas. What a warning for him! What could be more explicit? Then when the Supper came, and they began to eat and drink together, the Lord said – 'One of you shall betray me.' That was plain enough; and a little farther on he said explicitly – 'He that dippeth with me in the dish the same is he.' What opportunities for repentance! He cannot say he had not a faithful preacher. What could have been more personal? If he does not repent now, what is to be done? Moreover, Judas saw that which was enough to make a heart of adamant bleed; he saw Christ with agony on his face, for it was just after Christ had said 'Now is my soul troubled', that Judas left the feast and went out to sell his Master. That face, so full of grief, ought to have turned him, must have turned him, if he had not been, given up and left alone, to deliver over his soul unto his own devices. What language could have been more thundering than the words of Jesus Christ, when he said, 'Woe unto that man by whom the Son of man is betrayed; it had been good for that man if he had not been born.' He had said, 'Have not I chosen you twelve, and one of you is a devil.'

Now, if while these thunders rolled over his head, and the lightning flashes pointed at his person, if, then, this man was not aroused, what a hell of infernal pertinacity and guilt must have been within his soul! Oh! but if any of you, if any of you shall sell Christ for the sake of keeping the shop open on Sunday, if you shall sell Christ for the extra wages you may earn for falsehood – oh! if you shall sell Christ for the sake of the hundred pounds that you may lay hold of by a villainous contract – if you do that, you do not perish unwarned. I come into this pulpit to please no man among you. God knoweth if I knew more of your follies you should have them pointed out yet more plainly; if I knew more of the tricks of business, I would not flinch to speak of them! But, O sirs, I do conjure you by the blood of Judas, who hanged himself at last, turn you – if such there be – turn you from this evil, if haply your sin may be blotted out!

Let us for one minute *notice the act itself.* He sought out his own temptation. He did not wait for the devil to come to him; he went after the devil. He went to the chief priests and said, 'What will ye give me?' One of the old Puritan divines says, 'This is not the way people generally trade; they tell their own price.' Judas says 'What will ye give me? Anything you like. The Lord of life and glory sold at the buyer's own price. What will ye give me?' And another very prettily puts it, 'What could they give him? What did the man want? He did not want food and raiment; he fared as well as his Master and the other disciples; he had enough; he had all that his needs could crave, and yet he said, What will ye give me? What will ye give me? What will ye give me?' Alas! some people's religion is grounded on that one question – 'What will you give me?' Yes, they would go to church if there are any charities given away there, but if there were more to be got by not going they would do that. 'What will you give me?' Some of these people are not even so wise as Judas. Ah! there is a man over yonder who would sell the Lord for a crown, much more for ten pounds, as Judas did! Why, there are some who will sell Christ for the smallest piece of silver in our currency. They are tempted to deny their Lord, tempted to act in an unhallowed way, though the gains are so paltry that a year's worth of them would not come to much. No subject could be more dreadful than this, if we really would but look at it carefully. This temptation happeneth to each of us. Do not deny it. We all like to gain; it is but natural that we should; the propensity to acquire is in every mind, and under lawful restrictions it is not an improper propensity; but when it comes into conflict with our allegiance to our Master, and in a world like this it often will, we must overcome it or perish. There will arise occasions with some of you many times in a week in which it is 'God – or gain'; 'Christ, or the thirty pieces of silver'; and therefore I am the more urgent in pressing this on you. Do not, though the world should bid its highest, though it should heap its comforts upon one another, and add fame, and honour, and respect, do not, I pray you, forsake your Master. There have been such cases; cases of persons who used to come here, but they found they did not get on, because Sunday was the best day's trade in the week; they had some good feelings, some good impressions once, but they have lost them now. We have known others who have said, 'Well, you see, I did once think I loved the Lord, but my business went so badly when I came up to the house of God, that I left it; I renounced my profession.' Ah, Judas! ah, Judas! ah, Judas! let me call thee by thy name, for such thou art! This is the sin of the apostate over again; God help thee to repent of it, and go, not to any priest, but to Christ and make confession, if haply thou mayest be saved.

You perceive that in the act of selling Christ, Judas was faithful to his master. 'Faithful to his master?' you say. Yes, his master was the devil, and having made an agreement with him he carried it out honestly. Some people are always very honest with the devil. If they say they will do a wrong thing they say they ought to do it because they said they would; as if any oath could be binding on a man if it be an oath to do wrong? 'I will never go into that house again', some have said, and they have said afterwards, 'Well, I wish I had not said it.' Was it a wrong thing? What is your oath then? It was an oath given to the devil. What was that foolish promise but a promise to Satan, and will you be faithful to him? Ah! would God that you were faithful to Christ! Would that any of us were as true to Christ as Satan's servants are to their master!

Judas betrayed his Master with a kiss. That is how most apostates do it; it is always with a kiss. Did you ever read an infidel book in your life which did not begin with profound respect for truth? I never have. Even modern ones, when bishops write them, always begin like that. They betray the Son of man with a kiss. Did you ever read a book of bitter controversy which did not begin with such a sickly lot of humility, such sugar, such butter, such treacle, such everything sweet and soft, that you said, 'Ah! there is sure to be something bad here, for when people begin so softly and sweetly, so humbly and so smoothly, depend upon it they have rank hatred in their hearts.' The most devout looking people are often the most hypocritical in the world.

We conclude with the repentance of Judas. He did repent; he did repent, but it was the repentance that worketh death. He did make a confession, but there was no respect to the deed itself, but only to its consequences. He was very sorry that Christ was condemned. Some latent love that he had once had to a kind

Master, came up when he saw that he was condemned. He did not think, perhaps, it would come to that; he may have had a hope that he would escape out of their hands, and then he would keep his thirty pieces of silver and perhaps sell him over again. Perhaps he thought that he would rid himself from their hands by some miraculous display of power, or would proclaim the kingdom, and so he himself would only be hastening on that very blessed consummation. Friends, the man who repents of consequences does not repent. The ruffian repents of the gallows but not of the murder, and that is no repentance at all. Human law of course must measure sin by consequences, but God's law does not. There is a pointsman on a railway who neglects his duty; there is a collision on the line, and people are killed; well, it is manslaughter to this man through his carelessness. But that pointsman, perhaps, many times before had neglected his duty, but no accident came of it, and then he walked home and said, 'Well, I have done no wrong.' Now the wrong, mark you, is never to be measured by the accident, but by the thing itself, and if you have committed an offence and you have escaped undetected it is just as vile in God's eye; if you have done wrong and Providence has prevented the natural result of the wrong, the honour of that is with God, but you are as guilty as if your sin had been carried out to its fullest consequences, and the whole world set ablaze. Never measure sin by consequences, but repent of them as they are in themselves.

Though being sorry for consequences, since these are unalterable, this man was led to remorse. He sought a tree, adjusted the rope, and hanged himself, but in his haste he hanged himself so badly that the rope broke, he fell over a precipice, and there we read his bowels gushed out; he lay a mangled mass at the bottom of the cliff, the horror of every one who passed. Now you that make a gain of godliness – if there be such here – you may not come to a suicide's end, but take the lesson home. Mr Keach, my venerable predecessor, gives at the end of one of his volumes of sermons, the death of a Mr John Child. John Child had been a Dissenting minister, and for the sake of gain, to get a living, he joined the Episcopalians against his conscience; he sprinkled infants; and practiced all the other paraphernalia of the Church against his conscience. At last, at last, he was arrested with such terrors for having done what he had, that he renounced his living, took to a sick bed, and his dying oaths, and blasphemies, and curses, were something so dreadful, that his case was the wonder of that age. Mr Keach wrote a full account of it, and many went to try what they could do to comfort the man, but he would say, 'Get ye hence; get ye hence; it is of no use; I have sold Christ.' You know, also, the wonderful death of Francis Spira. In all literature, there is nothing so awful as the death of Spira. The man had known the truth; he stood well among Reformers; he was an honoured, and to a certain extent apparently a faithful man; but he went back to the Church of Rome; he apostatized; and then when conscience was aroused he did not fly to Christ, but he looked at the consequences instead of at the sin, and so, feeling that the consequences could not be altered, he forgot that the sin might be pardoned, and perished in agonies extreme. May it never be the unhappy lot of any of us to stand by such a death-bed; but the Lord have mercy upon us now, and make us search our hearts. Those of you who say, 'We do not want that sermon', are probably the persons who need it most. He who shall say, 'Well, we have no Judas amongst us', is probably a Judas himself. Oh! search yourselves; turn out every cranny; look in every corner of your soul, to see whether your religion be for Christ's sake, and for truth's sake, and for God's sake, or whether it be a profession which you take up because it is a respectable thing, a profession which you keep up because it keeps you up. The Lord search us and try us, and bring us to know our ways.

And now, in conclusion – there is a Saviour, and that Saviour is willing to receive us now. If I am not a saint, yet I am a sinner. Would it not be best for all of us to go again to the fountain, and wash and be clean. Let each of us go anew, and say, 'Master, thou knowest what I am; I know not myself; but, if I be wrong, make me right; if I be right, keep me so. My trust is in thee. Keep me now, for thine own sake, Jesus.' Amen.

19

JESUS DECLINING
THE LEGIONS [1]

'Thinkest thou that I cannot now pray to my Father, and
he shall presently give me more than twelve legions of
angels? but how then shall the scriptures be
fulfilled, that thus it must be?'
MATTHEW 26:53–54

IT IS THE GARDEN OF GETHSEMANE. Here stands our Lord,
and yonder is the betrayer. He is foremost of the multitude. You
know his face, the face of that son of perdition, even Judas Iscariot.
He comes forward, leaving the men with the staves, and the swords,
and the torches, and lanterns, and he proceeds to kiss his Master;
it is the token by which the officers are to know their victim. You
perceive at once that the disciples are excited: one of them cries,
'Lord, shall we smite with the sword?' Their love to their Master
has overcome their prudence. There are but eleven of them, a small
band to fight against the cohort sent by the authorities to arrest
their Master; but love makes no reckoning of odds. Before an
answer can be given, Peter has struck the first blow, and the servant
of the high-priest has narrowly escaped having his head cleft in
two; as it is, his ear is cut off.

One is not altogether surprised at Peter's act; for, in addition to
his headlong zeal, he had most likely misunderstood the saying of
his Lord at supper – 'He that hath no sword, let him sell his
garment, and buy one.' There was not time for our Lord to explain,
and they were so accustomed to his concrete style of speech, that

[1] Sermon No. 1,955. Preached at the Metropolitan Tabernacle on Sunday
morning, 27 March 1887.

they should not have misunderstood him; but they did so. He had simply told them that the days of peace, in which they could go in and out among the people, and be joyfully received by them, had now come to an end; for as he himself, who had once been in favour with all the people, would now be 'reckoned among the transgressors' (see *Luke* 22:35–38), so would they be counted among the offscouring of all things. Now they could no longer reckon on the hospitality of a friendly people, but must carry their own purse and scrip; and instead of feeling safe, wherever they went, they must understand that they were in an enemy's country, and must travel through the world like men armed for self-defence. They were now to use their own substance, and not to hope for cheerful entertainment among a grateful people; and they would need to be on their guard against those who in killing them would think that they were doing God service. They took his language literally, and therefore replied, 'Lord, behold, here are two swords.' Methinks he must have smiled sadly at their blunder as he answered, 'It is enough.' He could never have thought of their fighting that he might not be delivered unto the Jews, since for that purpose two swords were simply ridiculous. They had missed his meaning, which was simply to warn them of the changed circumstances of his cause: but they caught at the words which he had used, and exhibited their two swords. Possibly, as some have supposed, these were two long sacrificial knives with which they had killed the Paschal lamb; but, indeed, the wearing of weapons is much more general in the East than with us. Our Lord's disciples were largely Galileans, and as the Galileans were more of a fighting sort than other Jews, the wearing of swords was probably very general among them. However, two of the apostles had swords; not that they were fighting men, but probably because it was the fashion of their country, and they had thought it needful to wear them when passing through a dangerous district. At any rate, Peter had a sword, and instantly used it. He smites the first man he could reach. I wonder he had not smitten Judas, one might have excused him if he had; but it is a servant of the high-priest who bears the blow and loses his ear.

Then the Saviour comes forward in all his gentleness, as self-possessed as when he was at supper, as calm as if he had not already passed through an agony. Quietly he says, 'Suffer it to be so now'; he touches the ear, and heals it, and in the lull which followed, when even the men that came to seize him were spellbound by this wondrous miracle of mercy, he propounds the great truth, that they that take the sword shall perish with the sword, and bids Peter put up his weapon. Then he utters these memorable words: 'Thinkest thou that I cannot now pray to my Father, and he shall presently give me more than twelve legions of angels? But how then shall the scriptures be fulfilled, that thus it must be?' And he also said what John alone appears to have heard – 'The cup which my Father hath given me, shall I not drink it?' (*John* 18:11).

The wound of Malchus served a gracious purpose; for it enabled our Lord to work a new miracle, the like of which he had never wrought before, namely, the restoration of a member maimed or cut off by violence. The blunder of the apostles was also overruled to answer a very instructive purpose. You wonder that the Lord should, even in appearance, encourage his disciples to have swords, and then forbid them to use them. Follow me in a thought which is clear to my own mind. For a man to abstain from using force when he has none to use is no great virtue: it reminds one of the lines of Cowper's ballad: –

> Stooping down, as needs he must
> Who cannot sit upright.

But for a man to have force ready to his hand, and then to abstain from using it, is a case of self restraint, and possibly of self-sacrifice, of a far nobler kind. Our Saviour had his sword at his side that night, though he did not use it. 'What!' say you, 'how can that be true?' Our Lord says, 'Can I not now pray to my Father, and he will give me twelve legions of angels?' Our Lord had thus the means of self-defence; something far more powerful than a sword hung at his girdle; but he refused to employ the power within his reach. His servants could not bear this test; they had no self-restraint, the hand of Peter is on his sword at once. The failure of the servants in this matter seems to me to illustrate the grand self-possession of their Master. 'Alas,' he seems to say, 'you cannot be trusted even with swords, much less could you be entrusted with greater forces. If you had the angelic bands at your command, down they would come streaming from the sky to execute works of vengeance, and so mar my great life-work of love.' Brethren, we are better without swords and other forms of force than with them; for we have not yet learned, like our Lord, to control ourselves. Admire the glorious self-restraint of our Lord Jesus Christ, who, armed not with a sword but with the embattled hosts of 'helmed cherubim and sworded seraphim', yet refused even by a prayer to bring them down to his relief. Peter's passionate use of the sword illustrates the happy self-control of his Lord, and this is the use of the incident.

Let us now proceed to learn from the words of the Lord Jesus which we have selected as our text.

I. First, brethren, I would have you notice from the text OUR LORD'S GRAND RESOURCE. 'Thinkest thou that I cannot now pray to my Father?' Our Lord is surrounded by his adversaries, and there are none about him powerful enough to defend him from their malice; what can he do? He says, 'I can pray to my Father.' This is our Lord's continual resource in the time of danger; yea, even in that time of which he said, 'This is your hour and the power of darkness.' He can even now pray to his Father.

First, Jesus had no possessions on earth, but *he had a Father*. I rejoice in his saying, 'Thinkest thou that I cannot now pray to my Father?' He is a betrayed man; he is given up into the hands of those who thirst for his blood; but he has a Father almighty and divine. If our Lord had merely meant to say that God could deliver him, he might have said, 'Thinkest thou not that I can pray to Jehovah?' or, 'to God': but he uses the sweet expression 'my Father' both here and in that text in John, where he says, 'The cup which my Father hath given me, shall I not drink it?' O brethren, remember that we have a Father in heaven. When all is gone and spent, we can say, 'Our Father'. Relatives are dead, but our Father lives. Supposed friends have left us, even as the swallows quit in our wintry weather; but we are not alone, for the Father is with us. Cling to that blessed text, 'I will not leave you orphans; I will come unto you.' In every moment of distress, anxiety, perplexity, we have a Father in whose wisdom, truth, and power, we can rely. Your dear children do not trouble themselves much, do they? If they have a want, they go to father; if they are puzzled, they ask father; if they are ill-treated, they appeal to father. If but a thorn is in their finger, they run to mother for relief. Be it little or great, the child's sorrow is the parent's care. This makes a child's life easy: it would make ours easy if we would but act as children towards God. Let us imitate the Elder Brother, and when we, too, are in our Gethsemane, let us, as he did, continue to cry, 'My Father, My Father'. This is a better defence than shield or sword.

Our Lord's resource was to approach his Father with prevailing prayer. 'Can I not now pray to my Father?' Our Lord Jesus could use that marvellous weapon of All-prayer, which is shield, and sword, and spear, and helmet, and breast-plate, all in one. When you can do nothing else you can pray. If you can do many things besides, it will still be your wisdom to say, 'Let us pray!' But I think I hear you object, that our Lord had been praying, and yet his griefs were not removed. He had prayed himself into a bloody sweat with prayer, and yet he was left unprotected, to fall into his enemies' hands. This is true, and yet it is not all the truth; for he had been strengthened, and power for deliverance was at his disposal. He had only to press his suit to be rescued at once. The Greek word here is not the same word which would set forth ordinary prayer: the Revised Version puts it, 'Thinkest thou that I cannot *beseech* my Father?' We make a great mistake if we throw all prayer into one category, and think that every form of true prayer is alike. We may pray and plead, and even do this with extreme earnestness, and yet we may not use that mode of beseeching which would surely bring the blessing. Hitherto our Lord had prayed, and prayed intensely, too; but there was yet a higher form of prayer to which he might have mounted if it had been proper so to do. He could so have besought that the Father must have answered; but he would not. O brethren, you have prayed a great deal, perhaps, about your trouble, but there is a reserve force of beseeching in you yet: by the aid of the Spirit of God you may pray after a higher and more prevailing rate. This is a far better weapon than a sword. I was speaking to a brother yesterday about a prayer which my Lord had remarkably answered in my own case, and I could not help saying to him, 'But I cannot always pray in that fashion. Not only can I not so pray, but I would not dare to do so even if I could.' Moved by the Spirit of God, we sometimes pray with a power of faith which can never fail at the mercy-seat; but without such an impulse we must not push our own wills to the front. There are many occasions upon which, if one had all the faith which could move mountains, he would most wisely show it by saying nothing beyond, 'Nevertheless not as I will, but as thou wilt.' Had our Lord chosen to do so, he had still in reserve a prayer-power which would have effectually saved him from his enemies. He did not think it right so to use it; but he could have done so had he pleased.

Notice, that our Lord, *felt that he could even then pray.* Matters had not gone too far for prayer. When can they do so? The word 'now' practically occurs twice in our version, for we get it first as 'now', and then as 'presently'. It occurs only once in the original; but as its exact position in the verse cannot easily be decided, our translators, with a singular wisdom, have placed it in both the former and the latter part of the sentence. Our Saviour certainly meant – 'I am come now to extremities; the people are far away whose favour formerly protected me from the Pharisees; and I am about to be seized by armed men; but even now I can pray to my Father.'

Prayer is an ever open door. There is no predicament in which we cannot pray. If we follow the Lamb whithersoever he goeth, we can now pray effectually unto our Father, even as he could have done. Do I hear you say, 'The fatal hour is near'? You may now pray. 'But the danger is imminent!' You may now pray. If, like Jonah, you are now at the bottom of the mountains, and the weeds are wrapped about your head, you may even now pray. Prayer is a weapon that is usable in every position in the hour of conflict. The Greeks had long spears, and these were of grand service to the phalanx so long as the rank was not broken; but the Romans used a short sword, and that was a far more effectual weapon at close quarters. Prayer is both the long spear and the short sword. Yes, brother, between the jaws of the lion you may even now pray. We glory in our blessed Master, that he knew in fullness of faith that if he would bring forth his full power of prayer he could set all heaven on the wing. As soon as his beseeching prayer had reached the Father's ear, immediately, like flames of fire, angels would flash death upon his adversaries.

Our Lord's resort was not to the carnal weapon, but to the mighty engine of supplication. Behold, my brethren, where our grand resort must always be. Look not to the arm of flesh, but to the Lord our God. Church of God, look not piteously to the State, but fly to the mercy-seat. Church of God, look not to the ministry, but resort to the throne of grace. Church of God, depend not upon learned or moneyed men, but beseech God in supplicating faith. Prayer is the tower of David builded for an armoury. Prayer is our battle-axe and weapons of war. We say to our antagonist: 'Thinkest thou that I cannot now pray to my Father.' Let this suffice to display our Saviour's grand resource in the night of his direst distress.

II. Secondly, let me invite your attention to OUR LORD'S UNDIMINISHED POWER IN HEAVEN at the time when he seemed to have no power on earth. He says, when about to be bound and taken away to Caiaphas, 'I can presently call down twelve legions of angels from the skies.' He had influence in heaven with the Father, the great Lord of angels. He could have of the Father all that the Father possessed. Heaven would be emptied if needful to satisfy the wish of the Beloved Son. The man Christ Jesus who is about to be hung upon the cross has such power with the Father that he has but to ask and to have. The Father would answer him at once: 'He shall presently send me twelve legions of angels.' There would be no delay, no hesitation. The Father was ready to help him, waiting to deliver him. All heaven was concerned about him. All the angelic bands were waiting on the wing, and Jesus had but to express the desire, and instantaneously the garden of Gethsemane would have been as populous with shining ones as the New Jerusalem itself.

Our Lord speaks of angels that his Father would give him, or send him. We may interpret it that the Father would at once put at his disposal the glorious inhabitants of heaven. Think of seraphs at the disposal of the Man of Sorrows! He is despised and rejected of men, and yet angels that excel in strength are at his beck and call. Swift of wing, and quick of hand, and wise of thought, they are charmed to be the messengers of the Son of man, the servitors of Jesus. Think of this, beloved, when you bow before the thorn-crowned head, and when you gaze upon the nailed hands and feet. Remember that angels and principalities and powers, and all the ranks of pure spirits by whatsoever name they are named, were all at the beck of Jesus when he was newly risen from his agony, and was about to be led away bound, to the High Priest. He is our Lord and God, even at his lowest and weakest.

Jesus speaks of 'twelve legions'. I suppose he mentions the number twelve as a legion for each one of the eleven disciples and for himself. They were only twelve, and yet the innumerable hosts of heaven would make forced marches for their rescue. A legion in the Roman army was six thousand men at the very lowest. Twelve times six thousand angels would come in answer to a wish from Jesus. Nay, he says, 'more' than twelve legions. There can be no limit to the available resources of the Christ of God. Thousands of thousands would fill the air if Jesus willed it. The band that Judas led would be an insignificant squad to be swallowed up at once if the Saviour would but summon his allies. Behold, dear brethren, the glory of our betrayed and arrested Lord. If he was such then, what is he now, when all power is given him of his Father! Bear in your minds the clear idea that Jesus in his humiliation was nevertheless Lord of all things, and especially of the unseen world, and of the armies which people it. The more clearly you perceive this, the more will you admire the all-conquering, all-abjuring love which took him to the death of the cross.

Tarry here just a minute to recollect that the angels also are, according to your measure and degree, at your call. You have but to pray to God, and angels shall bear you up in their hands lest you dash your foot against a stone. We do not think enough of these heavenly beings; yet are they all ministering spirits sent forth to minister to those that are heirs of salvation. Like Elijah's servant, if your eyes were opened you would see the mountain full of horses of fire and chariots of fire round about the servants of God. Let us learn from our Master to reckon upon forces invisible. Let us not trust in that which is seen of the eye, and heard of the ear, but let us have respect to spiritual agencies which evade the senses, but are known to faith. Angels play a far greater part in the affairs of providence than we know of. God can raise us up friends on earth, and if he does not do so he can find us abler friends in heaven. There is no need to pluck out the sword with which to cut off men's ears; for infinitely better agencies will work for us. Have faith in God, and all things shall work for your good. The angels of God think it an honour and a delight to protect the least of his children.

III. But I cannot linger, although I feel a great temptation to do so. My text is full of teaching, but a main point is the third one – OUR LORD'S PERFECT WILLINGNESS IN SUFFERING. I hope I have already brought that before you. Our Lord would be betrayed into the hands of sinners, but he would go with them willingly. He had not shunned the garden though Judas knew the place. No part of our Lord's sufferings came upon him by the necessity of his nature. Neither as God nor as sinless man was he bound to suffer.

There was no necessity that Christ should endure any of the inflictions laid upon him, except the necessity of his fulfilling the Scriptures, and performing the work of mercy which he came to do. He must die because he became the great sacrifice for sin; but apart from that, no necessity of death was on him. They scourged him; but they could not have lifted the thong if he had not permitted it. He thirsted on the cruel tree; but all the springs of water in the world he makes and fills, and therefore he needed not to have thirsted if he had not chosen to submit thereto. When he died, he did not die through the failure of his natural strength; he died because he had surrendered himself to death as our great Propitiation. Even in his expiring moment our Lord cried with a loud voice, to show that his life was in him still. He 'gave up the ghost', freely parting with a life which he might have retained. He voluntarily surrendered his spirit to God. It was not snatched from him by a force superior to his own will: he willingly bore our sins, and willingly died as our Substitute. Let us love and bless the willing Sufferer.

Indeed, our Lord was not merely submissive to the divine will, but, if I may use words in a paradoxical manner, I would say that he was actively submissive. A single prayer would have brought our Lord deliverance from his enemies; but he exercised force upon himself, and held in his natural impulse to beseech the Father. He held in abeyance that noblest of spiritual gifts, that choicest of all forms of power – the power of prayer. One would have thought that a good man might always exercise prayer to the full of his bent, and yet Jesus laid his hand upon his prayer-power as if it had been a sword, and he put it back into its sheath. 'He saved others, himself he could not save.' He prayed for others; but, in this instance, for himself he would not pray, as he might have done. He would do nothing, even though it were to pray a prayer which even in the slightest degree would oppose the will of the Father. He was so perfectly submissive, yea, so eager to accomplish our salvation, that he would not pray to avoid the cruelty of his enemies and the bitterness of death. He sees it is the Father's will, and therefore he will not have a wish in opposition to it. 'The cup which my Father hath given me, shall I not drink it?' Remember, that he needed not to commit any wrong thing to prevent his being taken and slain: a good thing, namely, a prayer, would do it; but he will not pray: he has undertaken the work of redemption, and he must and will go through with it. He has such a desire for your salvation and for mine, such a thirst to honour and glorify his Father in the work which he had engaged to do, that he will not even prevent his sufferings by a prayer.

Wonderful is that question, 'How then shall the scriptures be fulfilled?' It is as much as to say, 'Who else can drink that cup? Who else can tread the winepress of Almighty wrath? No, I must do it. I cannot lay this load upon any other shoulders.' Therefore, for the joy that was set before him he endured the cross, despising the shame. He was willing, ay, willing from beginning to end, to be our suffering Saviour. He was willing to be born at Bethlehem, to work at Nazareth, to be mocked at Jerusalem, and at last to die at Calvary. At any one point he could have drawn back. No constraint was upon him but that of a love stronger than death.

I want you, dear hearers, to draw the inference that Jesus is willing to save. A willing Sufferer must be a willing Saviour. If he willingly died, he must with equal willingness be ready to give to us the fruit of his death. If any of you would have Jesus, you may surely have him at once. He freely delivered himself up for us all. If he was so willing to become a sacrifice, how willing must he be that the glorious result of his sacrifice should be shared in by you, and by all who come to God by him! If there be unwillingness anywhere, you are unwilling. He rejoices to be gracious. I wish the charm of this truth would affect your heart as it does mine. I love him greatly, because I see that at any moment he might have drawn back from redeeming me, and yet he would not. A single prayer would have set him free; but he would not pray it, for he loved us so!

> This was compassion like a God,
>   That when the Saviour knew
> The price of pardon was his blood,
>   He pity ne'er withdrew.

Do not grieve him by thinking that he is unwilling to forgive, that he is unwilling to receive a sinner such as you. Has he not said, 'Him that cometh to me I will in no wise cast out'? You will delight him if you come to him, whoever you may be. If you will but draw near to him by simple trust, he will see in you the purchase of his agony; and all the merit of his death shall flow out freely to you. Come and welcome, sinner, come.

IV. Now I must lead you, with great brevity, to notice OUR LORD'S GREAT RESPECT FOR HOLY SCRIPTURE. He can have twelve legions of angels, but 'how then shall the scriptures be fulfilled, that thus it must be?'

Notice, that our Lord believed in *the divinity of Scripture*. He says, 'How then shall the scriptures be fulfilled?' But if the Scriptures are only the writings of men, there is no necessity that they should be fulfilled. If they are merely the fallible utterances of good men, I see no particular necessity that they should be fulfilled. Our Lord Jesus Christ insisted upon it that the Scriptures must be fulfilled, and the reason was that they are not the word of man, but the word of God. The Scriptures were evidently the Word of God to our Lord Jesus Christ. He never trifles with them, nor differs from them, nor predicts that they will vanish away. It is he that saith, 'Think not that I am come to destroy the law, or the prophets: I am not come to destroy, but to fulfil. For verily I say unto you, Till heaven and earth pass, one jot or one tittle shall in no wise pass from the law, till all be fulfilled.'

He believed in the divine origin of the Scriptures and also in *their infallibility*. 'How then shall the scriptures be fulfilled, that thus it must be?' He does not hint that the Scriptures might be a little mistaken. He does not argue, 'I will bring the twelve legions of angels down to deliver myself, and it is no matter to me that then the Scriptures will be made void.' Oh, no! the Scriptures must be true, and they must be fulfilled, and therefore he must be betrayed into the hands of men. He settles it as a matter of necessity that Scripture must infallibly be verified, even to its jots and tittles.

See, brethren, *the priceless worth* of Scripture in the estimation of our Lord. In effect he says, 'I will die rather than any Scripture shall be unfulfilled. I will go to the cross rather than any one word of God should not be carried out.' The prophet Zechariah has written, 'Awake, O sword, against my shepherd, and against the man that is my fellow, saith the Lord of hosts: smite the shepherd, and the sheep shall be scattered abroad.' The fulfilment of that prophecy fell due that night, and the Son of God was prepared to be smitten as the Shepherd of the sheep, rather than the word of the Father should fall to the ground. Skin for skin, yea, all that a man hath will he give for his life; but Jesus would give his life for the Scriptures. Brethren, it were worth while for the whole church to die rather than any truth of Scripture should be given up. Let all our thousands be consumed upon the altar as one great holocaust sooner than the Scriptures should be dishonoured. The word of the Lord must live and prevail whether we die or not. Our Lord teaches us to prize it beyond liberty or life.

The force of our Lord's language goes further yet. Let me repeat the words and then enlarge upon them. 'How then shall the scriptures be fulfilled, that thus it must be?' Holy Scripture is the transcript of the secret decree of God. We do not believe in fate, a blind, hard thing; but we believe in predestination, the settled purpose of a wise and loving Father. The Book of Fate is cruel reading, but the book of divine Fore-ordination is full of charming sentences, and those lines out of it which are written in the Scriptures we joyfully choose to have fulfilled. It is the will of our Father who is in heaven which settles the things which must be;

and because of this we cheerfully yield ourselves up to predestination. Once being assured that God has appointed it, we have no struggles, nay, we will not even breathe a wish to have the matter otherwise. Let the will of the Father be the supreme law. It ought to be so. We find a depth of comfort in saying, 'It is the Lord, let him do what seemeth him good.' Now, the prophecies of Scripture were to the Lord Christ the revelation of the predestination of God that so it must be, and he cheerfully, joyfully, even without a prayer against it, gives himself up at once to that which must be, because God has appointed it. If any of you do not believe in the predestination of God, you will, probably, in some hour of depression, ascribe your sorrows to a cruel fate. The human mind, somehow or other, is driven at last to this decision, that some things are beyond the control of man and of his will, and that these are fixed by necessity. How much better to see that God has fixed them! There is the wheel revolving surely and unalterably; would it not comfort you to believe that it is full of eyes, and that it is moving according to the settled purpose of the Lord? That man who says, 'It is my Father's will' is the happy man. Predestination is as sure and as certain as fate; but there is at the back of it a living and loving personality, ordering all things. To this we cheerfully yield ourselves.

Beloved, let us value Scripture as much as Christ did; I was going to say, let us value it even more: for if our Lord valued unfulfilled Scripture – which was but a shell till he became its kernel – how much more should we value it, to whom the Scriptures are fulfilled in a large degree, because the Christ has suffered and has done even as it was written of him by the prophets of God!

Time flies so quickly that I must pass on. You perceive that I have a pregnant text; it is full of living instruction to those who desire to learn. God help us to receive with joy all its holy teaching!

V. But I must come to the last point. We will consider Our LORD'S LESSONS TO EACH ONE OF US in this text.

The first lesson is this: Desire no other forces for God's work than God himself ordains to use. Do not desire that the Government should come to your rescue to support your church. Do not desire that the charms of eloquence should be given to ministers, that they may therewith command listening ears, and so maintain the faith by the wisdom of words. Do not ask that learning and rank and prestige may come upon the side of Christianity, and so religion may become respectable and influential. Means that God has not chosen to use should not be looked upon by us with covetous eyes. Has he not said, 'Not by might, nor by power, but by my Spirit, saith the Lord of hosts'? Jesus has all those squadrons of angels at his disposal; do you not wish that he would use them? What a glorious vision is before us as we see their serried ranks and mark their glittering splendour! But Jesus bids them stand still and see the salvation of God wrought out without their inter-position. To them he has not put in subjection the new world. They must not meddle with the redemption of men. The conflict for truth is to be a spiritual battle between man and the serpent: nothing but spiritual force is to be employed, and that not by angels, but by men. Man must overcome sin by spiritual means only. Put up the sword, Peter! Jesus does not want its keen edge. Keep your swords in your sheaths, ye seraphim! Jesus does not want even your blades of celestial temper. His weakness has done more than human or angelic strength. His suffering and death have done the deed which all the hierarchy of angels could never have accomplished. The truth is to win the fight. The Spirit is to subdue the powers of evil. Brethren, do not ask anybody else to interfere. Let us have this fight out on the ground which God has chosen. Let us know that God is omnipotent in the realm of mind, and that by his truth and Spirit he will overcome. He holds back all forces other than those of argument, and suasion, and enlighten-ment by his Spirit: do not let us even wish to put our hand to any force other than he ordains to use.

And, next, take care that when other forces are within reach, you do not use them for the promotion of the heavenly kingdom. When you are in argument for the truth, do not grow angry; for this would be to fight the Lord's battles with the devil's weapons. Do not wish to oppress a person whose views are erroneous or even blasphemous. The use of bribes for the propagation of opinions is mean, and the refusal of charities to those who differ from us in sentiment is detestable. Let no threat escape your lip, nor bribe pollute your hand. It is not thus that the battles of truth are to be fought. If you ever feel inclined to shut a man's mouth by wishing him banishment, or sickness, or any sort of ill, be grieved with yourself that so unchristly a thought should have entered your head. Desire only good for the most perverse of men. Fighting for Christ would be wounding him sorely. The French king heard of the cruelties perpetrated upon our Lord, and he exclaimed, 'Oh, if I had been there with a troop of my guards, I should have cut the villains in pieces!' Yes, but Jesus did not want the King of France nor his guards: he came not to destroy men's lives, but to save them. The Lord Jesus desires you, my brethren, to fight for him by your faith, by your holy life, by your confidence in truth, by your reliance upon the Spirit of God; but whenever your hand begins to itch for the sword-hilt, then may you hear him say, 'Put up thy sword into its sheath.' He will conquer by love, and by love alone. If at this present moment I could take this church and endow it with all the wealth of the Establishment, and gather into its midst all the wisdom and talent and eloquence which now adorns society, and if I could do this by one single prayer, I should long hesitate to offer the petition. These might prove idols, and provoke the living God to jealousy. Infinitely better for us to be poor and weak and devoid of that which is highly esteemed among men, and then to be baptized into the Holy Ghost, than to become strong and be left of our God. We shall war this warfare with no unsanctified weapons, with no instrument other than God appoints. Speaking the truth in the power of the Spirit of God, we are not afraid of the result. Surely this is what Christ means: 'I could pray to my Father and receive at once a bodyguard of angels, but I will do nothing of the kind, for by other means than these must my kingdom come.'

And the next lesson is: Never attempt to escape suffering at the expense of truth: 'How then shall the scriptures be fulfilled?' says Christ: 'I can escape being taken, and bound, and made a felon of; but then how are the Scriptures to be fulfilled?' Would you like to be throughout life screened from all affliction? I think I hear a great many say, 'I should.' Would you? Would you be always free from sickness, poverty, care, bereavement, slander, persecution? How, then, could that word be true, 'I have chosen thee in the furnace of affliction'! What would that text mean, 'What son is he

whom the Father chasteneth not'? Jesus said, 'Except a man take
up his cross and follow me, he cannot be my disciple.' Are you to
be an exception to the rule? Oh, do not kick against suffering, for
in so doing you may be fighting against God. When Peter drew his
sword he was unconsciously fighting to prevent our redemption.
When we struggle against tribulation or persecution we may be
warring against untold benefit. Do you desire to ride through the
world like princes? Do not desire such a dangerous fate; for how
then could the Scriptures be fulfilled, that the disciple is not above
his Lord? Bow your spirit before the majesty of Scripture, and
patiently endure all things for the elect's sake.

Again, never tremble when force is on the wrong side. You see
they are coming, Pharisees and priests and the *posse comitatus*
sent by the authorities to arrest the Saviour; but he is not afraid.
Why should he be? He could command twelve legions of angels to
beat off the foe. The man who knows he has a reserve behind him
may walk into an ambush without fear. The multitude think that
there stands before them a mere man, a feeble man, strangely red
as with bloody sweat. Ah! they know neither him nor his Father.
Let him give a whistle, and from behind the olives of the grove,
and from the walls of the garden, and from every stone of the
Mount of Olives would spring up warriors mightier than those of
Caesar, valiant ones, before whom armies would be consumed.
One of these mighties of God slew of Sennacherib's army one
hundred and eighty-five thousand men in a single night; another
smote all the first-born of Egypt. Think, then, what more than
twelve legions of them could accomplish! Brethren, all these holy,
heavenly beings are on our side. 'Oh, but there are so many against
us!' Yes I know there are; but more are they that are for us. All the
myriads of heaven are our allies. See ye not the legions waiting for
the summons? Who wants to give the word of command till our
great Commander-in-Chief decides that the hour is come? Let us
patiently wait till he shall descend from heaven with a shout, with
the voice of the archangel, and the trump of God; then will the
reserves pour forth from heaven's gate, and all the holy angels shall
swell the pomp of the great appearing. Till that moment, wait! In
your patience possess ye your souls! The Lord Jesus waited; his
angels waited; his Father waited. They are all still waiting. Heaven's

longsuffering still runs like a silver thread through the centuries. Jesus will come with his angels in all the glory of the Father; but dream not that he must come tomorrow or else be charged with being slack concerning his promise. Desire that he may come in your lifetime, and look out for him; but if he tarrieth be not dismayed. If he tarry for another century do not be weary; if another thousand years should intervene between us and the bright millennial day, yet stand ye fast each man in his place, fearing nothing, but setting up your banners in the name of the Lord. 'The Lord of hosts is with us, the God of Jacob is our refuge.' We have no lack of strength, it is only that God wills that it be not put forth and that our weakness for the present should be the instrument of his most majestic conquests. Lord, we are content to trust in thee and wait patiently for thee; but leave us not, we beseech thee. Amen.